To Marcia
from Michel

REWRITING THE GOOD FIGHT
CRITICAL ESSAYS ON THE LITERATURE
OF THE SPANISH CIVIL WAR

REWRITING THE GOOD FIGHT
CRITICAL ESSAYS ON THE LITERATURE
OF THE SPANISH CIVIL WAR

Edited by:

Frieda S. Brown
Malcolm Alan Compitello
Victor M. Howard
Robert A. Martin

Michigan State University Press
East Lansing, Michigan
1989

Michigan State University Press
East Lansing, Michigan 48823-5202

Printed in the United States of America

Library of Congress Cataloging-in-Publication Data

Rewriting the good fight: critical essays on the literature of the Spanish
    Civil War / edited by Frieda S. Brown. . . [et al.].
        p.   cm.
    Based on papers presented at the 25th Annual Conference in Modern
Literature held at Michigan State University in Nov. 1987.
    Includes bibliographies and index.
    ISBN 0-87013-269-5
    1. Spain—History—Civil War, 1936–1939—Literature and the
war—Congresses. 2. Literature, Modern—20th century—History and
criticism—Congresses. 3. Spanish literature—20th century—History and
criticism—Congresses. 4. Politics and literature—Congresses.
5. Authors—Political and social views—Congresses. I. Brown, Frieda S. II.
Conference in Modern Literature (25th : 1987 : Michigan State University)
PN56.S67R48 1989
860'.9'358—dc19   88-43431
                                                                              CIP

For

ROBERT NAGEL
ROBERT TAYLOR
SAUL WELLMAN

who fought the good fight

TABLE OF CONTENTS

PART II: THE INTERNATIONAL RESPONSE

PREFACE

The studies presented here are revised and, in many cases, expanded versions of papers delivered at the 25th Annual Conference in Modern Literature held at Michigan State University in November 1987. The theme of the conference, "International Literature of the Spanish Civil War," was selected by the conference organizers and present editors to commemorate the events that wracked Spain from 1936 to 1939, and left an indelible mark not only on Spain but on the international community as well. In observing the anniversary of the Spanish Civil War, Michigan State University joined many academic and governmental bodies both here and abroad in recalling that significant moment in history which constituted the first armed struggle against fascism.

The echo of that moment resounds even today in the literature born of the war. As artists took sides, within and outside of Spain, the works they produced spoke eloquently of their responses and reactions and helped create a vivid and moving picture of the conflict. Yet it may require occasions such as this anniversary to shake the writing about the war from the dust of collective memory and return it to the forefront of critical attention where we may reexamine and revaluate its meaning and integrity. The aim of this volume is, in part, to provide just such a revaluation.

In Spain, of course, the almost forty years of Francoist dictatorship that followed the war fostered a socio-political and cultural ambience inevitably linked in the Spanish mind to the

Civil War. As a consequence, the war remained—and continues to be—an important ingredient in the creative endeavors of a new generation of Spanish artists.

It is the hope of the editors that this collection of essays, while it makes no claim to being a comprehensive view of the literature the war produced, may nonetheless serve as a statement of continuing critical interest in that literature and as a stimulating "state of the art" of studies on the subject. The scholars included here collectively analyze a variety of genres and artists ranging from Hemingway to Benet, from Sylvia Townsend Warner to Suárez-Galbán, from René Char to Carlos Saura. Employing varied critical approaches, they probe the works of well-known authors or introduce us to new or neglected writers. Each essay offers a critical response to the literature of the Civil War. On one level, then, it is probably fair to say that artist and critic alike rewrite the "good fight."

As befits a volume treating a subject in which text and context are so intricately bound, two "historical" essays bracket the critical analyses of literary works. Juan Benet's contribution on "Military Strategy in the Spanish Civil War," which was recently published in Spain, forms a fitting introduction to this book. What more appropriate synthesis of the relationship between history and literature could we find than this enlightening study of history as seen through the eyes of one of Spain's most distinguished novelists? We thank Mr. Benet for allowing us to include his essay here. The Honorable Luis López Guerra's "The Legacy of the Spanish Civil War Today"—the keynote address delivered at the conference—concludes this volume. Justice Guerra examines the ways in which the war continues to affect Spain. His commentary represents a sensitive and informed appreciation of the historical antecedents of contemporary Spanish society by a member of the generation of intellectuals who have now assumed the reins of the Spanish government.

Julie Loehr, Assistant to the Director of Michigan State University Press, has provided invaluable assistance in the preparation of this volume. We are grateful for her constructive suggestions, her patience, and her unfailing good humor.

This selection of studies represents only a small number of the essays presented at the conference. We therefore take this opportunity to thank our many other colleagues who contributed to the success of those meetings. Our thanks go also to Mark Van Wormer who so effectively arranged the venue of the conference, and to Alison Ridley and Eufemia Sánchez for their generous help in so many areas. We particularly wish to acknowledge the enthusiastic and constructive participation of Juan Benet, Martha Gellhorn, and Justice Luis López Guerra. To Robert Nagel, Robert Taylor, and Saul Wellman, the three veterans of the Spanish Civil War who graciously opened the conference by sharing their experiences and knowledge with colleagues, students and the community at large, and who continue to inspire us by the example of their courage and commitment, this book is gratefully and affectionately dedicated.

MILITARY STRATEGY IN THE
SPANISH CIVIL WAR

MILITARY STRATEGY IN THE SPANISH CIVIL WAR

Juan Benet

I

Toward the end of a little-known study on the military lessons of the Spanish Civil War, the French general Duval affirms that with regard to "a civil war . . . the further one gets from its beginning, [the more it] tends to become unintelligible."[1] General Duval had, in all probability, been sent to the rebel camp by General Weygand to study the characteristics of modern warfare and the efficacy of new tactics, especially with reference to the use of armor and air power. While these weapons were considered by many to be the most revolutionary and decisive available, their employment was more feared than fostered by some military high commands, among them the French. At the end of his study, General Duval felt obliged to recognize that one could extract few lessons from the war in Spain that would refute the strategic and tactical doctrines imparted in European military academies and war colleges, and it was not without a certain satisfaction that he submitted a report to his superiors, in which he put in their proper place the two military forces that would, two years later in the fields of Flanders, reduce the most powerful army in the world to nothing.

It might be said that the report Duval submitted was exactly what the French high command wanted, since it had already decided not to introduce any significant variation into its system of static defense, which had been derived from the lessons of World War I. Duval could only have felt his position validated when General Weygand—the technician "par excellence" who, in May 1940, inherited the ominous legacy of General Gamelin—wrote in the prologue to Duval's book:

> We find that in this war air power has been used to attack enemy troops on their own terrain without having to attack and destroy the opposition's bombers. With regard to assault vehicles, without the support of the infantry, they have all too often been found to be at the mercy of incendiary bombs or immobilized and employed as armored cannons, remaining exposed to the enemy's artillery fire and defenseless.[2]

During the first phase of the war, which Duval observed, the Nationalists entrusted air power and armor almost exclusively to the Italian and German forces aiding the rebels. Both Weygand and Duval had to view, with understandable relief, how what were reputed to be the most offensive of weapons—whose use in World War I gave inconclusive results as to their importance—were employed by their potential enemies in a traditional and defensive manner, inappropriate certainly in an aggressor force with the advantages it enjoyed. Yet, the dream of both generals was to last only a short time—two years, in fact—and if at some moment that dream took on the characteristics of a nightmare, it could never have been as horrible as would be the reality that awaited them.

A man alleged to be as unskilled in military affairs as was Julio Alvarez del Vayo, the civilian minister of state of the Spanish Republic, stated before the debacle suffered by the French armies in 1940 an opinion very similar to General Weygand's:

> These observations—he said—are sufficient to show that the tank does not constitute the "fourth arm" capable of deciding the result of a battle, as has been claimed.[3]

Alvarez del Vayo's mode of thought in 1940—filled with the

memories of a more protracted and bitter war than Duval witnessed—would have pleased General Weygand:

> The war in Spain discredited the new Italian and German theories of Douhetism and Blitzkrieg or lightning war and discovered that they were horror stories spread to frighten the timid. On the fields of battle in Spain those forms of warfare were a complete failure.[4]

Such was not to be the case in Europe two years later. The implacable application of Douhet's doctrine broke the Dutch resistance in ten days. Separated by some seven months—the period of time that the "drôle de guerre" was to last—the Polish and French campaigns would constitute the most irreproachable demonstration of the postulates of the blitzkrieg. In one of the few theoretical studies on the war in Spain, published after the fall of France and scattered with apologetic nuances in favor of the war strategy employed by the Nationalists, we still read "The armored vehicles do not go where one wants them to go, only where they are capable of going and in Spain they are capable of going in very few places."[5]

After the campaign in Flanders and the French capitulation, the general belief was that the employment of air power and armor were closely guarded secrets of the Italians and Germans and that their deployment in the initial campaigns of World War II caught the Allied general staffs completely off guard. Nothing, of course, could be further from the truth. Giulio Douhet had already published *The Dominance of Air Power* in 1921, in which he predicted the possibility of completely undoing the defensive capacity of any major power by bombing its nerve centers—including the civilian population. The doctrines of blitzkrieg and the utilization of armor as an autonomous fighting arm, capable of rapid penetration and independent of the infantry, had already been so often debated by a good number of specialists (Fuller, Liddell Hart, Manstein, Guderian, Tukhachevski, etc.) that such a latecomer to the debate as the then Colonel Charles de Gaulle felt obliged to take up the subject in a book of his own, *L'Armée du métier* (1935), designed to shake the French general staff out of its Maginot line mentality. Alvarez del Vayo, as enthusiastic as he was unanalytical, was on the verge of arriving at more correct conclusions as to the importance of the employment of armor; he had only to look beyond the obvious toward the definitive explanation of what its use portended. In describing the attack that the first Republican armored vehicles launched against the Nationalist flank in Seseña on 29 October 1936—a small offensive extensively aired on radio the night before, which, according to those who conceived it, Largo Caballero and the so-called "Victory Cabinet," was destined to change the course of the war—Alvarez del Vayo says the following:

> The tanks were followed by an attack line formed of infantry. When those troops found themselves at the critical point at some three hundred meters from the enemy lines, the tanks had already passed the first rebel positions. At that moment, intense machine-gun fire from those positions commenced, and the Republican infantry . . . suffered heavy losses and was definitively immobilized. . . . The tanks that had penetrated the enemy's lines with almost no losses discovered that the Republican infantry was not following them and therefore turned around . . . but on that return trip some of the tanks were put out of commission. . . . The results of this first tank attack of major proportions were, therefore, negative.[6]

Compare these circumstances—and the regrettable decision of the Republican tanks to return to their own lines—with the situation of Guderian's and Reinhardt's armored divisions on 16 May 1940, to the west of Sedan and the Meuse River, as described in the operations diary of the Second Panzer Division:

> With the exception of a few liaison officers 25 or 30 miles behind the 1st and 2nd Panzer Divisions, one could hardly see a German soldier. Munitions and gas were provided along a thin and unprotected supply line. The tanks' gas tanks were filled from gasoline cans and service stations captured from the French.[7]

It is certainly shocking to try to imagine Guderian's and Reinhardt's German tankers, launched fifty kilometers in the direction of San Quintín, at the moment they stopped their vehicles and looked back to see if von Kleist's infantry was following them.

Whatever the case, the negative outcome Alvarez del Vayo points to was doubly so. In the first place, it represented the first offensive failure of the Republic in its military attempts to take the pressure off the Madrid front. Second, and more importantly, it created a precedent. From that point forward, armor was never again used in the autonomous fashion conceived by the theoreticians of the blitzkreig. After the attack on Seseña, armored vehicles would only be used as a support force, as taught by military academies on the basis of the lessons received from the tentative use of armor by General Cambrai in the battle of the Somme. Even if all historians and specialists have recognized the superiority of the Russian armored vehicles, with which the Republic's Army of the People was equipped, over the German prototypes employed against them—and it must be remembered that in the Spanish Civil War they never opposed each other directly on the battlefield—the piecemeal manner in which the Republic deployed its armor always placed it at the mercy of the enemy's antitank artillery, especially the famous 8.8 mm guns.

II

In a recently published article, Stanley G. Payne draws attention to the fact that historians studying the Spanish Civil War have tended to pay little attention to its military aspects. As Payne says, "The number of monographic studies dedicated strictly to military aspects represents only a fraction of those dedicated to political ones, to the internationalization of the war and even to its literary impact."[8] Yet this scholar, whose research deals principally with political problems in contemporary Spain, is guilty—perhaps involuntarily—of the same margination. His short article, which studies the war as a "military struggle," hardly takes on the major enigmas about the military history of the war that need study. He limits himself to pointing out a few logistical details and, once again, focuses on the numerous national and international political movements that fed the conflict.

To my way of thinking, to find a solution—albeit an incomplete one—to the enigmas that the military history of the war holds out, it is not enough to study the relative strength of the two armies or to dispatch the Republican war strategy as merely defensive and incapable of wresting the initiative from the rebel forces. Undoubtedly, Payne recognizes that "Franco was a poor strategist," and he adds that "he did not even prosecute the war with exclusively military criteria but was looking for political advantages to be gained—just like the communists—and refused to leave any Republican initiative unanswered." Payne even attributes to Juan Vigón "the most important strategic innovation in the Nationalist war effort, the decision in 1937 to abandon the offensive in central Spain and eradicate the opposition on the northern front." But this decision, it must be remembered, was in no way exempt from important political considerations; it would help Franco impose his control over both military operations and the geographic stronghold of Mola, his most important rival. The south and its "viceroy," Queipo, a man of limited ambition in spite of his arrogant threats, were another matter completely.

Starting from Vigón's wise decision, one can affirm that Nationalist strategy never changed its final objective—the capture of Madrid—but that in 1937 it was limited to postponing that attack until after a "trip to the north." This trip, Madrid-north-Madrid, turned out to be a fiasco and, instead of a simple return trip, the route became a complicated and broken itinerary: Madrid-north-Brunete-north-Belchite-north-Teruel-Maestrazgo-Ebro-Catalonia and, finally, Madrid. That is to say, that the Nationalists' first objective became their last; and the only thing correct about the Nationalists' strategic planning was the presumption that the day Madrid fell the war would end.

Such radical changes in so simple a strategic plan can only be attributed, in the first place, to the Republican resistance. It was capable of mounting a defense through the use of a series of delaying offensives which, if they did not work the way the Republicans had planned, at least served to delay the attack on Madrid; the second cause for the change was, perhaps, the Nationalist high command's unstated decision to prosecute the war slowly; and finally, the manifest failure of the Nationalist high command to push forward with its primary strategy, to execute its plan of attack, and to put in practice the principles of modern warfare when, in 1937, it had at its disposal the means—personnel, logistics, advisors, and experts—to do so.

III

That both the Republic's Ministry of Defense, directed successively by Largo Caballero, Prieto, and Negrín, and the high command of the People's Army (always in a state of reorganization) were somewhat out of touch with modern tactics, as expounded by the more daring European theoreticians, is explicable without recourse to sociological analyses or psychological delicacies given the Republican armed forces' provisional, militia-like, and amateur beginning. What cannot be explained as easily is how the military professionals who rose up against the legally constituted Republican government could have been as deaf to the new military doctrines as were their adversaries. I know of not one rigorous study of modern warfare published before 1936 by a Spanish specialist, and the most cultured of Spanish experts, the one who had read not only the classics but Liddell Hart ("a modern, bold and strange writer, sure of his ideas . . . ") limits himself to citing—admittedly in a publication not aimed at experts[9] —the doubtful possibilities of the "indirect strategy."

Such theoretical outdatedness could not help but be reflected in the way those famous Nationalist generals and colonels deployed their forces and made use of their resources during the Civil War. Of course, it must be recognized that the few dozen antiquated armored vehicles and airplanes that the Nationalists possessed were merely for show. They were insufficient to allow them to form the basis for a new military strategy. In Spain, armor had never been used as a weapon, and air power had only served to provide supplies, to photograph Moroccan positions in the Rif, or to toss a hand bomb out of the cockpit. On the other hand, the Spanish military's European colleagues did not have any decisive data on which to base the employment of armor or air power. If the new military theoreticians were capable of alerting or upsetting their respective governments with regard to the potential of these weapons, it was due to their intuition, their audacity to deduce from inconclusive data, and their sparks of brilliance as to how those arms could be effectively used.

The difference between Spanish and European officers was one of professional preparation. European officers, after the fragile Treaty of Versailles and the political instability caused by the Russian Revolution and the weakness of the republics born of the disintegration of the empires of central Europe, had to confront their professional obligations with a view toward a possible future test of their preparedness on the same continental scope as in numerous prior conflicts. On the other hand, once the Moroccan campaign was complete, the possibility of a war with another European country never entered into the planning scheme of the Spanish military. For the most part, those Spanish soldiers with any professional ambition, from Primo de Rivera's coup on, were too occupied with internal political concerns to be very worried about a European war. What use could armor or air power have if with a pair of regiments one could always achieve the objective, be it the toppling of the government in Madrid or gaining control of a military garrison somewhere in Spain?

The Spanish Civil War, when viewed as a military conflict, did not begin in July 1936 but in November of the same year, when the advanced elements of the Army of Africa were at the gates of Madrid, poised for its capture. Until that date, one could not really speak of a war, that is, of a confrontation between two more or less homogeneous armies, but rather of a series of skirmishes, assaults, street battles, and marches that a regular army undertook against a hostile, armed people, mobilized and organized in its own manner. The war began with the assault on Madrid and ended two days after its capture; Franco himself predicted it would fall like a ripe fruit, one whose ripening would take more than a thousand days. Until that November of 1936, artillery had scarcely been employed, and if air power had made an appearance, it was due to its being used to transport the Army of Africa across the Straits of Gibraltar, supposedly dominated by the Republican fleet.

Although it sounds paradoxical, I would dare to affirm that the rebel military high command was as ill-prepared for the war as were their Loyalist adversaries. Historians all maintain that the war was won by the best organized, most competent, and, in a word, more professional army; but it is my opinion that the Spanish army was prepared for combat, not for war. This none too subtle distinction, to my mind, has never been proposed as one of the decisive factors accounting for the prolongation of a conflict that should have lasted a few days, weeks, or at the most, several months.

Beginning with the system of alliances imposed by Bismarck around 1872, territorial war had been the working hypothesis for every European government. Based on these alliances, one at least knew on which allies one could count and who would be one's adversaries. Because of the alliance system, European wars would always be carried out in accordance with strictly elaborated and well-defined plans that invariably began with a general mobilization, an extremely delicate and costly affair that, once initiated, could rarely be stopped. Inexorably, such a mobilization concluded in the expected conflict for, as General Sir Edward Spears, witness to the French mobilization of 1914, has said, "whoever turned back or mobilized slowly was in danger of leaving his country at the mercy of those who carried out their mobilization more rapidly."[10]

A mobilization of such proportions could not leave details undone and, once it was planned, was not open to changes. "Improvisation is unacceptable in an operation that mobilizes some three million men and 4,300 trains."[11] The mobilization process had to be undertaken according to Schlieffen's doctrine—accepted by all the European general staffs—and planned so that all objectives, both long-range and immediate, were centered on one obstacle: the enemy. In a national war, therefore, everything would initially be done in a very orderly fashion, until the first attack, whose results, in principle, would establish the validity of the pre-established plan or point out the necessity of modifying it. But a war would never be carried out without a plan, not even in the most critical moments.

In contrast to their European colleagues, the Spanish military in 1936 had no contingency plans for a war. The truth be told, they had no reason to have such plans. From 1898 on, Spain, more than a neutral country, was a country without enemies, a privilege afforded by its political decline, unless one were to conceive of the Moroccan rebels or the august, somnolent, and indifferent neighbor Portugal as enemies. Having no enemy on its border, having no plans of territorial conquest, lacking an exterior threat to its security, why should the Spanish army have had contingency plans for a war? Nevertheless, for the army of a modern society, a battle plan is as necessary as discipline. If there was no outside threat, was it not legitimate to imagine one inside Spain where so many prerevolutionary phenomena suggested the existence of a plot more underhanded and surer than any foreign ambition? But the enemy inside Spain is "uncivil"; it refuses to be treated like an army nor can it be combatted with a plan developed in accordance with prevailing military doctrines.

"A civil war," states General Duval, "takes shape in a manner quite inverse to the playing out of a war against a foreign enemy. The latter begins with major battles, many times decisive ones, that lead to the establishment of a main theater of battle. . . . A civil war, on the contrary, begins with forces scattered around numerous centers of struggle. In the strict sense there are no theaters of operation. Cities are the primary objective."[12] In effect, the principal objective—perhaps the only one—for those who rose against the government in July 1936 was gaining control of the Spanish state, an objective which had to be achieved using the technique popularized by Malaparte, starting with the examples of the 18 Brumaire, the Russian Revolution, and the march on Rome. The state resides in the cities, most especially in the capital—let us say 50 percent for example—and in the rest of the country's big cities in proportion to their population and their civil and military infrastructures.

The uprising of 1936 had no other objective than to occupy Spain's big cities. Failing in the majority of them, with the exception of Seville and Saragossa, the coup was of necessity forced to become a military campaign that, with the greatest possible speed, had to capture what the coup itself had been unable to take. After the surrender of the Montaña Barracks, Madrid not only continued to be the center of the part of Spain loyal to the Republic but also the closest geographical and rail hub for a good number of the insurgent forces who, in the first days of the conflict, succeeded in consolidating their positions and establishing a state of war in various provinces. Thus, Madrid, after the first weeks of skirmishes and street battles, was the center of the attention of the two large rebel forces: Mola in the center and north and Franco in the south. These forces positioned themselves to march on Madrid, one through the mountain passes of the Central System, the other over the undefended plains of Extremadura and La Mancha. The advance of Mola's forces was stopped in those mountains; the army under Franco's command arrived at the gates of Madrid after a march of some three months' duration. Both spearheads of the rebel army, connected by the mountains joining Avila and Toledo, were poised for the final assault on the capital that first week in November, an assault that awakened much expectation and many diverse sentiments the world over.

During those three months, no plan of battle had been elaborated by the rebel high command, or at least, to my knowledge, there is no record anywhere of any such plan. Of course, for the rebels, with their minds occupied with many other things, war could only have been a remote possibility that would evaporate once their forces took their assigned objectives. With the exception of the taking of San Sebastián and

Irún—an important blow that cut the Republic's frontier with France and bottled up the Loyalist opposition in the north—and a few other events more dependent on local initiatives than on any intervention by the general staff, the rebel high command came up with no strategic plan during those first three months except for the takeover of the Spanish state, an event that would end the conflict with triumph and thus fulfill its desires and satisfy its aspirations.

As is well known, the assault on Madrid began 7 November 1936; less well known to the nonspecialist is the fact that the assault was suspended *sine die* on the twenty-third of the same month, after sixteen days of furious combat along the Manzanares River. This decision resulted from a meeting that morning among Generals Franco—who had already assumed the position of chief of state in the Nationalist zone—Mola, Saliquet, and Varela, and their respective chiefs of staff, in a command post in Leganés. The tactical reasons supporting such a decision were obvious: an attacking force of six columns, assumed to be around 18,000 men, was demonstrated to be incapable of taking a city that had aligned some 35,000 men in arms for its defense, according to the calculations of an historian who could, with difficulty, hide his sympathies for the attackers.[13] It is therefore not unreasonable to affirm that on 23 November the coup ended and the war began, a war for which nobody, even at this late date—four months after the beginning of the hostilities—was technically prepared.

On 28 November, Franco concluded a secret agreement with Mussolini's emissary Cantalupo, through which Mussolini agreed to provide help to the rebels for the duration of the war. That same day, a certain General von Faupel, Nazi Germany's first "chargé d'affaires," made his first appearance at rebel headquarters. Von Faupel had at least two known merits, namely, the ability to speak Spanish—learned in South America—and the fact that during the Great War he had commanded a regiment in which a certain Sergeant Hitler had served. Five days after the meeting in Leganés, it was obvious to Nationalist high command that international aid was necessary to achieve a victory which, for the moment, had evaporated, and that to do so, the rebel forces would have to follow a path its high command had not yet taken the trouble to chart.

IV

Achieving victory through war: that was the situation at the end of 1936. That situation lends itself perfectly to the description of the Great War provided by Michael Howard:

> At the conclusion of the first year of the war it was obvious that the Napoleonic concepts inculcated in professional soldiers for one hundred years, the "Niederwerfungsstrategie" as the Germans called it, were no longer valid. As strategic examples, the wars of the seventeenth and eighteenth centuries in which the strategy employed was not aimed at destroying the enemy army but at using up his economic resources—the "Ermattungsstrategie"—were more pertinent.[14]

The more sycophantic biographies of Franco have often upheld that his decision not to conquer Madrid was based on humanitarian reasons, a line of argument that is belied by the fact that such humanitarian pity did not stop him from submitting Madrid to the longest and cruelest siege ever suffered by a major city in modern times, with the exception of Leningrad. Using such a foolish line of argument, some have also affirmed that the Nationalist failures in the Jarama and Guadalajara operations were perfectly in line with Franco's intentions, "'because now I can mount the campaign in the north that is so important to our goals. . . .' And he immediately picked up the phone and started to give orders."[15] When one is confronted with such a story, one does not know which to admire more, the resignation of the protagonist on receiving the news of these failures—a resignation worthy of Philip II—or the brilliant improvisation that allows him to alter his plans instantly and to conceive new strategic objectives. In other words, either Franco was so vain that he could not admit a setback and convert it to his advantage, or his leadership was so technically impoverished that he had to have recourse, because of a lack of planning, to inspiration. Even though his conduct gave the lie to his words after each failed attempt, Franco never tired of repeating that the conquest of Madrid did not constitute the primary objective of his planning. That objective was total victory which would only fall, like a ripe fruit, when the time was propitious.

However, on turning his eyes from the conquest of Madrid to the north, he suffered from the same lack of planning that until then had characterized the march on Madrid. And yet, at that date, he knew perfectly well what his resources were, as well as those of his adversary. The front had remained stable for some six months, and no new circumstances had been added to the precarious bellicose equilibrium achieved the previous fall. It does not appear that there was any excuse for the insolvency of a general staff that, after seven months of tranquility, had not known how to trace out a plan to liqui-date the pocket of resistance in the north in a short period of time, especially when it had all the geographical and logistical advantages and a troop superiority of at least two to one. In short, it was simply a matter of capturing some 40,000 square kilometers which were isolated, under siege, blockaded, sup-plied by the few ships that dared to challenge the blockade, and defended by some 100,000 men organized in 110 batallions;[16] that is to say, less than a company per kilometer of front, which means that Llano de Encomienda's Army of the North could count on one-tenth of the forces per kilometer of front that the Republic had lined up to defend the perimeter of the Manzanares in November 1936, or twenty times less than the French command had to defend its Alsatian border in August 1916.

The Nationalist liquidation of the Republican resistance in the north took a year, from October 1936 to October 1937. It was carried out using a simple "steamroller" technique, begin-ning at one end, Vizcaya, and ending at the other, Gijón. At no time was a more elaborate tactical maneuver attempted. One could—and should—compare such indolence in planning with the warlike conduct demonstrated two years later by a true aggressor: in September 1940, Hitler ordered the German high command to sketch a plan for an offensive against the Soviet Union. On 18 December of that same year, the high command released the famous Directive No. 21, Plan Barbarossa. The directive's supplementary documentation established the plan for the mobilization of some three million men, down to regimental level, for an attack along a 1,000-kilometer front by the three armies of von Leeb, von Bock, and von Rundstedt, which included some 141 divisions. In less than three months, the high command developed a plan that, without any changes until the battles of Smolensk, Viazma, and the Bog, was followed faithfully in the summer of that year and ended in a series of impressive victories. According to General Franz Halder, who was responsible for the preparation of this plan, the greatest difficulty faced by the Germans in their execution of the plan was its authors' lack of information about the military potential of the Russians.

This was not the case for Franco and Mola at the end of 1936. They knew the resources, down to the last screw, of the Republican forces in the north, whose defeat in a few weeks time, even with limited but well-concentrated means, would have been only a small "kriegspiel" for a well-prepared general staff.

The Nationalists' ineptitude in carrying out their campaign in the north permitted the Republic to rearm and counterattack. While these tactics were unsuccessful, the counterattacks were of sufficient force to stabilize the Madrid front and delay the fall of Bilbao. From the summer of 1937 on, the Republic's war strategy was similar to that of the unfortunate card player who, little by little, rebuilds his winnings only to lose again when the stakes are raised in the next hand; at least it was the Republic, and not the aggressor, that was calling the shots and determining the course of action. The slowness and lack of planning that characterized the first phase of the campaign in the north allowed the Republicans to mount counterattacks at Belchite and Brunete; the same lack of aggressiveness in the second phase of the campaign allowed the Republicans to launch the Teruel attack, where the war was definitively lost for them.

The indolence with which the Nationalist offensive on Valencia was carried out, against a Republic that was already divided in two, gave their adversaries the initiative to cross the Ebro and to begin the last great battle of the war, one that for all intents and purposes was unnecessary. One of the great exegetes of the rebel strategy would openly recognize this fact:

> Twice, with our army in the middle of an offensive (?), the enemy imposed a change of direction on us. But [because of their] lack of sufficient resources . . . we managed to contain the enemy, exhaust his strength and take advantage of the victories thus gained. They were victories whose directions our adversary laid out, thus pointing out for us the final orientation [of the battle].[17]

Victory, of course, justifies everything, even a way of thinking so incongruous as to admit the enemy forced a change of plans right in the midst of an offensive action. Nevertheless, that admission is clearly a painful confession of guilt that the direction of Nationalist actions was being dictated by a weaker enemy. Evaluated correctly, such a judgment is more incriminating than revealing and, in and of itself, serves to condemn those who conducted a long and bloody war using such methods.

Every plan of battle, one writer has affirmed, should be abandoned after the first day of combat. Tactics, the second son of military science, impose themselves on strategy, the first born. Yet a plan of battle is indispensable, even when one knows it must be abandoned and will not lead to victory. The lack of campaign and battle plans on the part of the rebel army was one of the most important reasons the war lasted three years; and if, after the failed attempt to take Madrid, Franco had known how to eliminate the resistance in the north in a few weeks' time, he would have had no difficulty ending the war in 1937. But he was not so disposed. The same exegetes mentioned above relate a very significant anecdote about this matter. On 25 July 1937, General Ungría, who had escaped from the Republican zone on a French cruiser, had a meeting with the Generalissimo. During that meeting, Ungría lamented not having been able to do anything for the Nationalist cause and expressed his uneasiness for not having been of use in a war that, in his estimation, was already won. "Let's not get ahead of ourselves," Franco responded, "the war is not won. The enemy is strong . . . and the war will last two years more."[18] Historians rave about Franco's prophetic ability to divine correctly, within only twenty-five days, the day the war would end. But such a divination surely could be turned against the one who made the prediction and lays bare a hidden intention which Franco took care not to confide to anyone. Only uncertainty—and Franco was surely not uncertain—could justify the prolongation of a military action of the nature of the Civil War at the price of incalculable loss of life and property.

V

For lack of strategic plans, even those drawn in the most general of ways, the rebel army under Franco's command always opted for what one may call "butcher's tactics," that is, attacking the enemy head-on, a procedure no expert on military tactics has ever failed to mention without contempt. It was, in short, a procedure emanating from brute strength, one which avoided any studied approach to the war. Throughout the entire Civil War one finds no maneuvers conceived on a grand scale in the movements of the rebel army, no flank attacks, no indirect approaches, unless everything that was not a frontal attack on Madrid is understood as such. The initial lack of strategic planning lasted throughout the entire conflict, which was prosecuted in accord with tactical orders, and, starting with the elimination of the northern pocket, in the form of frontal counterattacks after the Republic was no longer able to go on the offensive. According to the same sources cited above, during the first days of the battle of the Ebro, Franco—without abandoning his peculiar smile—upon observing the extent of the Republican penetration to the south of the river, commented, "This situation makes me wish that they would penetrate as far as possible so that we could then cut off the pocket produced by their penetration and engage the Republican army there, wear it out, finish it off once and for all."[19] And that is exactly what he did, repeating once again the "butcher's tactics."

Of course, one can say that the purpose of the Republican attack was no different; its commanders were familiar with that method of waging war: conceive a battle of great proportions—with some 300,000 men mobilized between the two sides—in rugged terrain which, after the initial penetration, would have to become a slow and constant battle of attrition if the enemy attacked head-on. Such was the battle of the Ebro, which, on a Spanish scale, was very similar to the offensive launched by Hitler in the Ardennes in the winter of 1944, with the objective of gaining time to develop his famous secret weapons. With its attack at the Ebro, the Republic sought nothing but to gain time. It was a battle which, in the light of the rapidly deteriorating European political situation, would have enabled the Republic to last until the seemingly imminent international conflict, but which it lost in Munich on 22 September rather than on the field of battle at Gandesa. This does not alter the fact that Franco's response was the most ill-conceived possible, the one that was most in line with Republican intentions, and a response that in the end led to a battle of some four months' duration and some 80,000 casualties. Nothing more eloquently characterizes Franco's way of conceiving the battle than the testimony of Manuel Tagüeña. Tagüeña was commander-in-chief of the XVth Corps of the Republican army, responsible for covering the Fayón sector, and his was the last Republican unit to recross the Ebro at the end of November. He was, therefore, the witness best qualified to judge the entire campaign.

> We were very well aware of the mentality of the enemy high command, [which allowed them] to sacrifice thousands of their men for reasons of prestige, so as to be able to recuperate the ground they lost, although their counteroffensives were never justified by strictly military reasons. . . . Once we crossed the river and conquered the bridgehead we were tied to our positions. The simplest thing for our adversaries would

have been to leave us there and to focus their attention in the direction of Lérida and Barcelona. . . . The road to the occupation of Catalonia was open . . . having done that, they could have achieved victory much earlier.[20]

In effect, according to accounts given by those who fought on both sides, the penetration to the south of the Ebro begun on 25 July was effectively contained by 1 August, with the three corps of the Republican army that had crossed the river pinned down in defensive positions, the possibility of retreat by recrossing the river difficult, and the Segre line almost completely dismantled—all of which makes Tagüeña's assertions little less than irrefutable. Once the battle had ended and there was not a single Republican soldier left on the south side of the Ebro, General Dávila, on 11 December 1938, sent General Instruction No. 50 to the Nationalist Army of the North, directing it "to isolate and destroy the mass of the enemy army entrenched along the Segre; to fix the enemy along the entire front and especially between our bridgeheads at Tremp and Serós; to break their lines at both points and counterattack through the breaches opened up during those operations." This was exactly what Tagüeña had feared three months before—and it was carried out by a Nationalist army four-fifths of which (the armies of Urgel, Aragón, Navarre, and the Italian CTV) had been no more than spectators in the terrible battle of attrition that the Nationalists could have resolved in a few days if, instead of crossing the Segre in the first part of December, they had done so in August.

Referring to the causes that provoked the Great War, A. J. P. Taylor points out that

one feels the temptation to assert that the European ruling classes provoked a great war when they realized that, if they did not do so, power would slip from their hands. But to make such an assertion is to give those ruling classes too much credit by attributing to them more intelligence and ability than they really possessed. The old "gang" had little idea of what they were doing and they went in a haphazard manner from problem to problem.[21]

Were these not words conceived in reference to continental events, one would say that they were directed to the Spanish ruling class and most especially to its military "gang."

On 23 November 1936, in the meeting at Leganés, Franco understood that he had before him a war for which the army he commanded was not prepared and—although his vanity led him to believe the opposite—for whose undertaking he did not bother to make the necessary plans. Around 25 April 1937, in an atmosphere of confidence that the final victory would be theirs, Franco confessed to General Ungría that the war would last two more years. This evaluation surely was in line with his political aspirations; for as long as the war lasted, his recently assumed position as head of the Nationalist government would not be questioned nor would he have to worry about the formation of the new Spanish state that had been so ambiguously defined. Finally, on 1 August 1938, on the Gandesa front, when he had before him an open road to an irrefutable victory, he opted to take the longest and most torturous of all possible paths, one that would prolong the conflict eight months at the cost of another 80,000 senseless casualties. Either this prolongation was the result of a complete lack of strategic vision—a fitting finishing touch to a war carried out entirely in that manner—or the extension was due to an excess of political acuteness that would have allowed him to divine the benefits to be derived from an unnecessary prolongation.

History has closed around this enigma. No document exists that can unravel it. General Duval was correct when he asserted that civil war tends to become unintelligible. The Hegelian march of the spirit and reason through history is only demonstrable when it is reason—a written and obvious one—that moves the muscles of the runner. When they are moved by silent impulses—like avarice, incompetence, ambition, and the lack of courage—that march becomes unintelligible and, therefore, investigable. It is worth saying, belatedly and uselessly investigable.

Translated by Malcolm Alan Compitello

NOTES

1. General Duval, *Enseñanzas de la guerra en España* (San Sebastián, 1938), 229.

2. Duval, *Enseñanzas*, 9.

3. J. Alvarez del Vayo, *La guerra empezó en España* (Mexico City, 1940), 209.

4. Alvarez del Vayo, *La guerra empezó en España*, 197.

5. Carlos Taboada Sangro, *La técnica de la batalla en España* (Madrid, 1941), 73.

6. Alvarez del Vayo, *La guerra empezó en España*, 209.

7. Alistair Horne, *To Lose a Battle* (London, 1969), 456.

8. Stanley G. Payne, "La guerra civil española como lucha militar," *Cuenta y Razón*, 1985.

9. Carlos Martínez de Campos, *La guerra terrestre* (Madrid, 1935).

10. Sir Edward Spears, *En liaison* (Paris, 1964), 49.

11. A. J. P. Taylor, *La guerra planeada* (Barcelona, 1970), 16.

12. Duval, *Enseñanzas*, 115.

13. J. M. Martínez Bande, *La marcha sobre Madrid* (Madrid, 1968). 201ff.

14. Michael Howard, *La guerra en la historia europea* (Mexico City, 1983), 201.

15. Luis de Galinsoga y general Franco Salgado, *Centinela de Occidente* (Barcelona, 1956), 228.

16. Ramón Salas Larrazabal, *Historia del Ejército Popular de la República* (Madrid, 1973), 939.

17. Carlos Martínez de Campos, *Dos batallas de la guerra de liberación de España* (Madrid, 1962), 28.

18. Galinsoga y Franco Salgado, *Centinela*, 274.

19. Quoted in Galinsoga y Franco Salgado, *Centinela*, 306.

20. Manuel Tagüeña, *Testimonio de dos guerras* (Mexico City, 1973), 230.

21. Taylor, *La guerra planeada*, 42.

PART I

THE SPANISH RESPONSE

JUAN BENET AND THE CIVIL WAR:
HISTORY MADE OF FICTION

David K. Herzberger

To "scumble," according to the dictionary, is to soften the contours or blend the colors that define difference in painting. In a broader sense, it is a way of overextending the folds of one thing into those of another without eliminating the discreteness of each. Scumbling is perhaps most evident in modern painting, where colors often bleed into one another to produce a new visual image, or in metaphor, where the juxtaposition of words creates consonance in dissonance and enjoins the reader to perceive a new semantic pertinence. In narrative, the most adept scumbling occurs along the lines of the real and the make-believe, or more specifically for my purposes here, along the lines of history and fiction. It is generally held, of course, that history reports on events that have happened in real life, while fiction relates imaginary events invented by the author. This is such an obvious difference between history and fiction, and such a dramatic one as well, that it may appear impossible to reconcile the two disciplines beyond superficial similarities. It is especially difficult in the twentieth century. Instead of relying on many of the traditions that have linked fiction and historiography in the past (e.g., trust in the soundness of objectivity, the belief in a beginning, middle, and end to narrated events, the one-to-one reference between word and object, etc.), twentieth-century novelists have in large part turned their craft against the traditional norms of history. This can be seen, for example, in the now common techniques of temporal fragmentation, linguistic opacity, multiple and contradictory points of view, and the like. It would appear, then, that if we took the contours of the well-written history today and laid them beside what it is that we consider to be a well-written novel, the two would not overlap and complement one another but would seem to be dissimilar and even antithetical. Faulkner, we would say, is not Shelby Foote, and Juan Benet, we might add, is not Hugh Thomas.

Twentieth-century historians have largely sought to define their discipline as a branch of science and have drawn upon technical and mathematical models of data analysis in order to generate objective and verifiable results. As a consequence, historians have resisted placing their work in the same frame with fiction, and critical thinking on the matter by literary theorists and historiographers has most often sustained the divergence.[1] In the past decade and a half, however, the writings of two theorists/philosophers, Hayden White and Paul Ricoeur, have shown how narrative discourse, the instrument of invention and expression shared by historians and novelists, "scumbles" the meaning of their separate endeavors. The arguments of White and Ricoeur are developed in several essays and books and will serve as an entry into my discussion of Benet and the role of history in his novels. It would of course be unjust to Ricoeur and White to reduce the complexities of their thinking to a few short paragraphs. Their carefully reasoned positions are heavily endowed with philosophical, literary, and historical theories that preclude easy synthesis or categorization. It will be helpful, however, to explore briefly the outline of their theories, for the intimacy of historical and fictional narration that both have posited reveals how a writer such as Benet is able to enhance our understanding of the Spanish Civil War even when what he writes in his novels is plainly fictitious.

The first and foremost point addressed by White and Ricoeur has to do with the nature of narration. In broad terms, narrative consists of a series of events that have been configured by language in order to convey meaning. In both historical and fictional narration, the author chooses what is relevant for inclusion in the desired configuration, as well as what elements are appropriately excluded, either because they are considered tangential to the material at hand or because their inclusion runs counter to the story as the narrator wishes to tell it. In the case of history, as White points out, the narrative seems to convey a desire to have real events framed in coherence and integrity as a way for the reader to comprehend them fully. Furthermore, it is precisely because historical events contain within them a narrative structure (i.e., life is sequenced in time) that historians are justified in using stories as legitimate representations of events and, conversely, in viewing these representations as valid explanations of historical events. In fiction, however, the same qualities of completeness and congruity may be perceived as ingenuous or inappropriate. This is especially the case in the twentieth century, when fiction is often termed anti-narrative and consciously eschews straightforward narration in favor of a more peripatetic one. In either case, however, the configuration of events turns upon the notion of referentiality: the perception that one narrative strategy or the other more accurately illustrates life as we are able to know it. In large part, therefore, preoccupation with mimetic adequacy motivates both forms of narrative strategy. As Ricoeur astutely notes, "The argument for verisimilitude has merely been displaced. Formerly, it was social complexity that called for abandoning the classical paradigm; today, it is the presumed incoherence of reality that requires abandoning every paradigm" (*Time*, 2:14). It becomes clear, therefore, that while integrity and closure in historiography seek to convey what is essential and reveal the deep meaning of the events narrated, a like argument can be made for the openness and opacity of contemporary fictional narratives. The paradigm of incompleteness in fictional discourse is found in the world (i.e., the narrative paradigm is mimetically adequate to life); hence the revealed meaning stems from the perceived coincidence between reality and narrative form. This idea is particularly relevant to the fiction of Juan Benet, even in those instances when Benet appears to undercut all means of rational knowing.

Historical and fictional narratives also share another crucial element of configuration: temporality as their ultimate referent. Both fiction and history are symbolic discourses to the extent that they mediate human perception of the workings of life. Furthermore, both configure their narratives in order to flesh out what is pertinent and revealing about existence. And what emerges as most pertinent, what is revealed by each, are the aporias of human time. As White notes, speaking of Ricoeur, "If histories resemble novels this may be because both are speaking . . . 'symbolically' about the ultimate referent [time]" (*Content*, 175). The issue of time in historiography is crucial for Ricoeur because he insists that historical narrative imitates human actions, which are driven through time by the overt intention to achieve meaning. Ricoeur argues that human lives aspire to coherence (meaning), which allows the historian to discern the beginnings, middles, and ends inherent in their actions. Historical discourse thus follows a pattern originally laid out by events and now incorporated into the traditions of historiography itself.

The consequences of Ricoeur's position are extreme, of course, because they preclude a historiography modeled on experimental and anti-narrativist discourse. Historiography rejects this kind of writing, primarily because it refuses to submit to the authority of coherence and integrity that Ricoeur finds in the intentionality of all human actions. Certainly, it is not the case that the historian thinks less complex thoughts than the novelist, or that history itself is perceived as exempt from the enigmatic. It is rather that the historian will admit ambiguity and indeterminacy only at the level of content (i.e., all of the facts are not known), as if form were a matter apart, a container that holds the more important content of discourse. Hayden White is less restrictive in this regard, but he views the problem only from the side of history. He asserts that the plots of history may depend as forcefully upon the strategies of narration as upon the "found" plots within events themselves, but he does not resolve the more complicated issue of the commingling of historical and fictional purposes in a single work.

Both White and Ricoeur stop short of explaining how novelists such as Faulkner, who writes a history of Yoknapatawpha, or Benet, who narrates 150 years of life in Región, afford insights into history even as they restructure the temporal coherence of human intentionality. There is no easy answer, of course, but a possible solution is intimated in Ricoeur's view of the tragic nature of time (*Time*, 1:38). The human quest for meaning is carried out with a supreme awareness of the corrosive power of time, and the quest is meaningful (and distinctively human) precisely because of this awareness. The pathos of being "in time" is in fact nothing less than being "in history," which, as White points out, "cannot be absorbed by human thought except in the form of an enigma" (*Content*, 181). Furthermore, "If this enigma cannot be resolved by pure reason and scientific explanation, it can be grasped in all its complexity and multilayeredness in symbolic thought and given a real, if only provisional, comprehensibility in those true allegories of temporality that we call narrative histories" (181). Such a view of time is closely relevant to the novels of Juan Benet, whose recurrent concern for the aporias of time and the enigmas of temporal flow insinuate the proximity of his works to the foundations of historical narrative.

It is not my purpose here to show that Juan Benet is a historical novelist. The definition of the historical novel has been diluted beyond its usefulness, and the term now tells us very little. I am interested more specifically in the lines of coincidence between fiction and history in the novels of Benet and what insights his fiction may offer into the contingencies of the Civil War. By coincidence between fiction and history in Benet I do not mean proximity in a referential sense (for example, I am not concerned whether the so-called "facts" of Benet's fiction are referentially correct when he refers to the Republican Command or if his description of Nationalist strategy in Teruel is true to life). Coincidence occurs instead on a moral, metaphysical, and above all, a formal level, all of which are determined by the nature of Benet's narrative. The truth that may be found in Benet's writing is not a matter of simple logic (i.e., logic tells us that something is true or that it is not), but rather truth must be seen in relation to Benet's view of what narrative discourse (both historical and fictional) is capable of doing. Benet has written extensively about the nature of fiction and narration, but he has also intimated on occasion a view of history that is not unlike his understanding of fiction.[2] And in important ways, his concept of history and fiction can be linked to the notion of narrative proposed by White and Ricoeur.

In *La inspiración y el estilo,* one of his early books on writing, Benet subordinates what might be termed the historian's history to the wider notion of history that explicitly includes the novel:

> The meaning of the word history can be as broad as one wishes, as long as it includes everything written with the purpose of awakening our interest in a specific set of facts; in our own time it would also have to include almost the whole field of the novel and the majority of those short stories that are still called "historias."[3]

Benet does not lay out explicitly what distinguishes the historian from the novelist, but he hints at the latter's more profound intellectual quest. For Benet, the historian would narrate a story according to the traditional premises of followability. The novelist, on a different plane, seeks the more ambitious goal of scrutinizing "a reality that is hidden behind events, behind words, and behind reason" (*Inspiración,* 166). The three components of Benet's scheme here, events, words, and reason, are permeated by the overriding element of narration (as in Ricoeur and White) and beyond narration, by the structures of human time: "the narrator, before and above all, draws upon the axis of time to establish the regimen of his discourse."[4] The notion of time and narration is further integrated into what is the fundamental pursuit of Benet's discourse: exploration of the "zone of shadows" (*En ciernes,* 32 passim). Reason is not admitted in this shadowy zone, where enigma becomes the deep meaning that is explored and where the exploration itself (i.e., discourse as ontological) is paramount: "And what greater importance [is there] than the attempt to limit and to resolve, when possible, the innumerable enigmas of nature, of society, of man, and of history—all of these being functions that correspond fully to science—what greater importance than the desire to present [enigmas], to preserve them, to conserve them in their unfathomable obscurity, to demonstrate their gnoseological insufficiency and insolubility" (*En ciernes*, 48-49). History and fiction are thus at once allied and opposed for Benet. The latter obtains if history is viewed as a scientific endeavor, the former if history probes what it is unable to perceive and if it enlists the polysemy of language (the "thaumaturgy of style," as Benet puts it [*Inspiración*, 168]) to move beyond language. That Benet envisions the potential commingling of history and fiction can be deduced from the broad view of history outlined above and from the way he props fiction and history against life in order to reveal the elusiveness of all narrative endeavors. He has sought to eliminate from his fiction "the demon of exactness" (*En ciernes*, 48), an idea akin to the enigmas of Ricoeur, and he prescribes a similar task for the historian: "only ambiguity has the capacity to make history."[5] In both fiction and history, then, to present the enigmatic means to narrate it, which is to stylize it, to configure and emplot it, and thus to know it in a way that we can know the mysteries of life as a whole within the frame of all narrative discourse.

The question persists, however, what is it that is historical about Benet's novels, and what do they convey about history?[6] On the simplest level, that of direct reference, Benet tells a tale of the Civil War. As in real life, the Republican forces stand against the Nationalists. In addition, the novels allude to Franco, to the General Command and other fronts of the war, to foreign troops, weapons and battlefield strategy, and to the final Nationalist victory. All of these elements are evoked in varying degrees of detail and with an air of authenticity about them that may well lead the reader to conclude that, indeed, he or she has garnered important information and achieved clarifying insights into the complexities of the Civil War. Still, these are novels; they are *about* the Civil War, but they are only fictions. Furthermore, the narrative of these works bears scant resemblance to the coherent structures of historiography as outlined by Ricoeur. Benet spurns a clearly delineated beginning, middle,

and end to his discourse, while human intentionality, the decisive impetus for all historical acts, often appears suffocated by
the natural and supernatural tangles of the environment. The
chaotic reality of Región, the intense contingencies of existence there, and the nihilism of time seem to suggest that the
only legitimate reading of Benet's fiction must proceed from
allegory rather than symbol. Yet, in the end precisely the opposite occurs. Despite the obstacles to history, we sense that we
discover more about the war and penetrate more deeply into
it from Benet's fiction than from his brief "history" published
in 1976, ¿Qué fue la guerra civil?, or from many of the other
official "histories" of the war written by a number of important
historians.

The reason for our sense of historical discovery turns primarily upon Benet's view of time in fiction and upon the
configuration that gives his novels their specific composition.
Benet's strategies for emplotting his work are complex, diverse,
and even chaotic at times; but for my purpose here, these strategies may be divided into two groups: those that narrate the
events of the Civil War and those that do not. The two groups
are clearly and purposefully demarcated in Benet's fiction
and create a narrative tension engendered by their opposing
schemes of configuration and reference. The juxtaposition of
the two is crucial on a formal level, of course, because it brings
all of Benet's narrative to the edge of metaphor. The literal sense
of his discourse is shattered by the apparent incompatibility of
its component parts, and a deeper (in this case, historical) reality
emerges from the tension between meanings preserved by the
literal sense and the new meanings derived from the perceived
dissimilitude among the parts. The metaphorical undercurrent
lends a fresh authenticity to Benet's historical strategies, as do
all good metaphors, and moves his narrative closer to the realm
of truth, both in the sense of probing reality with new semantic
pertinences and in the larger frame of universal and abstract
meaning.

For many obvious and not so obvious reasons, Benet's novels
are hard to make sense of. Indeed, readers view his narrative as
permanently unsettling and difficult to penetrate. Critics have

studied this difficulty at length, and there is no need to repeat such an analysis here. There is another side to Benet's fiction, however, the side of historical narrative that focuses on the war, which stands largely removed from this nonhistorical, peripatetic narrative. This historical category can be subdivided into two strains of narration: those first- and second-person voices that evoke the war through memory (e.g., Sebastián and Marré of *Volverás a Región*, the first-person narrator of *Una meditación*, the cousin of *Saúl ante Samuel*), with all the uncertainty that Benet attaches to the process of memory, and the voice of the third-person narrator who builds the events of the war into a configuration that in many ways parallels the integrity of historiography. Time, place, and description are configured in these segments into a series of instances that invite the simple triumph of narrative order. Of course, the triumph remains always incomplete in Benet's writing because his third-person narrator remains always Benetian. What is affirmed is later called into question, the professed inability to know all that lies beneath the surface of the war is constant, and the intimation of the enigmatic permeates the texture of the narrative throughout. The result is a recurrent commingling of anti-narrativist and narrativist traditions in Benet's novels that creates the oxymoronic correlative between assertion and denial, the real and the imaginary, which shapes Benet's view of fiction and history as a whole.

Benet's first-person narrators most often give their historical accounts the generic feeling of a memoir. They are to be mistrusted, not because they set out to lie or to evade the truth, but because the nature of their evocation relies upon memory. For Benet, even though memory remains essential to the discernment of meaning, it is largely aporetic. This is so for a number of reasons, but above all because memory shows a clear concern for beginnings rather than endings.[7] His first-person narrators are most often immersed in the past, thus the structural flow of their discourse is toward an antecedent or beginning rather than toward linear progression and an end. Memory, of course, serves as catalyst and agent for the narrator who seeks to recover all that has escaped him. The first-person narrator thus believes (implicitly, at least) that time is able to disperse nothing without the possibility that the mind will reconstruct it as a vital component of the present. This holds true for Marré's recollections of the Civil War in *Volverás a Región*, for the "yo" of *Una meditación*, and for the cousin of *Saúl ante Samuel*, who hope to define and understand history by conjuring up and exploring events that were anterior to them.

As he does with many elements of his narrative, however, Benet establishes a personal framing of history only to shatter it. Memory becomes a correlative of an open structure of beginnings that are incapable of sustaining continuity and moving toward completed endings. As the narrator asserts in *Una meditación:*

> For memory, there is never continuity: a band of hidden time is devoured by the body and converted into a series of dispersed fragments by the workings of the spirit. . . . Thus is produced a fragmented and disordered story that leaps through time and space, that accumulates facts, images, and impressions. . . . (31-32)

Such a view runs counter to the narrative control that Benet exercises over third-person historical discourse and points to the ineluctably aporetic nature of experience as it is reconstituted through time. Memory thus ruptures the narrative link with history because it refuses to admit the integrity of traditional modes of storytelling.

The third-person narrator in Benet's fiction, however, relates the story of the Civil War as if immediately present to its ongoingness. He emplots and tightly controls the telling of events and produces the illusion of pure reference. It is of course an illusion, but when set against the fragmented and wandering discourse of the nonhistorical narrative, or the ramblings of first- and second-person narration, the illusion appears to stand all the more firmly on the level of the real. The third-person narrator generally affirms the traditional premises of cause and effect when telling about the Civil War (i.e., he adheres to the structure of "one because of the other," which Aristotle distinguishes from "one after the other"), and provides the sense of a regulated order. Benet's third-person narration largely conforms to the traditions of how the real ought to be talked about, and it limits the possibility of awkward questions asked by the reader. It also deters the break-up of the illusion of fact and plays to the myth, as Frank Kermode has suggested in another context, "that felicitous assertion equals accurate reference."[8] Few writers, it could justly be noted, are the equal of Benet in making the "felicitous assertion."

Benet further sustains the myth of the real by allowing the narrator to doubt his own assertions without undermining the presentation of their accuracy. For example, in *Herrumbrosas lanzas I*, the narrator makes the following observation about Captain Arderíus, one of the principal figures in the Republican chain of command:

> The indistinctive cap pulled down too far over his right ear—was it one more sign of his fellowship with popular attitudes, so distinct from military ones, or did it reflect the way of putting on his hat he had learned on the *rive gauche*? (17)

While affirming neither the Captain's commitment to the masses nor his contrived imitation of stylish liberalism, the narrative suggests that the truth lies somewhere in between. Arderíus is later shown to be duplicitous (he is a Nationalist spy), though the motivation for his treason and the depth of his commitments are never clearly established. What is important about Arderíus from the standpoint of narrative strategy, however, is that the manner of his presentation parallels the way in which Benet presents history as a whole. That is to say, when a third-person narrator in Benet's fiction offers more than a single explanation for some event of the Civil War, when he conjectures about one thing or another, it is not that he seeks refuge in ambivalence, or that he eschews the possibility of meaning. On the contrary, he is laying out the boundaries within which potential meanings are located. Benet teases the reader with the ambiguity of facts, which is a way, of course, of showing how the position from which one perceives reality determines what is seen and how the way of telling determines the meaning and importance of what is told. For this reason, Benet demands that interpretation (by both narrator and reader) stand as the basis for all understanding. However, while the narrative and its rendering of history is open to interpretation, it remains closed to unbounded speculation because by his conjecture, by his telling of one side *and* the other, rather than one side *or* the other, the narrator adumbrates the scheme within which potential meanings lie.

The openness of Benet's narrative of the Civil War is thus not an "open" openness, as we might find in the radically anti-narrativist texts that Raymond Federman has called surfiction.[9] Benet's narrative is not, as Federman puts it concerning surfiction, "illogical, irrational, unrealistic, nonsequitur, and incoherent" (13). What perhaps best describes the narrative strategy of Benet's novels is the idea of a "framed" openness: one that leaves gaps and open spaces but always within the broader confines of meaning delineated by the third-person narrator. Benet achieves diversity of meaning in a variety of ways but most frequently opts for the technique of multiple explanations. In *Herrumbrosas lanzas I*, for example, the narrator observes the following concerning the political alignments of a small group of Republicans:

> As the political tendencies and affiliations of the people slowly came into focus—and rather than from old conflicts, they were produced in the majority of cases as a consequence of the necessary association with a party of every individual who was prepared to participate in the conflict . . . either from the reluctant abandonment of a neutrality maintained only with great difficulty in such compromising times, or as maintainable as the lesser of two evils in the face of the growth of a group or ideology viewed with displeasure, or to save with membership one's indecisive skin, or also because of a sincere conversion, a frequent transmutation in an atmosphere ozonized by so many doctrinal discharges of one kind or another. (138)

Clearly, Benet wishes to advance more than a single reason for the political allegiances of the Republic, but he does not seek to privilege one reason over any other. The result is a stylistically fluid passage that disperses meaning in a number of directions, but one which flows always within the broader limits of the history Benet sets out to convey. In this instance, Benet underscores the inconstancy of political motivation, which is often misconstrued by those who portray it solely as a product of commitment and passion.

In terms of historiography, the refusal to categorize through the adoption of straightforward affirmation shapes Benet's view of his task. As the narrator of *Herrumbrosas lanzas III* notes concerning these matters: "Truly, the final verdict on such a disputed event is not found, nor will it be found, in a particular place, because for every moment history has many explanations" (123). The historian who seeks to lay out the truth by speaking only to the so-called "facts" speaks naively and diminishes history. Benet understands that control through conjecture permits him to shape interpretation and defer meaning so as to offer the more attractive notion of polysemy. While the historian places truth and meaning on the same plane of expression, Benet is more apt to differentiate between the two so that the latter remains ever open to change, and thus to exegesis. His representation of a reality always in flux, bereft of conclusive sense, demands a rigorous formal paradigm capable of sustaining a virtuality that does not upset the undercurrent of referentiality. The swings away from history in his narrative (e.g., the portrayal of Numa, elements of the fantastic, memory, etc.) and the concomitant shifts in style and technique thus serve to enhance the followability of history in his novels and the believability of their insights. Equally important, they serve to sustain the tension of his discourse as an ongoing metaphor.

Formalist and structuralist theories of the twentieth century have shown that all discourse is metadiscourse. Language is about itself as well as about what it mediates, hence narrative always reveals to a greater or lesser extent the strategies of its composition. Benet's historical narrative is most often aware of what it aspires to do and draws upon traditional historical devices to show that it functions as history within a work of fiction. In broad terms, historical discourse is always guaranteed by metatextual announcements, by references to sources of information, and by assurances of the authenticity of witnesses. Benet's narrative is buttressed by these devices throughout. For example, in the third volume of *Herrumbrosas lanzas*, the narrator interpolates a report of data on men and armaments of the Republican army in Región (136-38). It is a strategy that in this instance puts the reader in direct contact with "facts" as if in a chronicle, and it moves the immediacy of the Republican position to the fore without the taint of narrative bias. Benet achieves the same sense of non-narrative objectivity with the battle maps inserted at various stages of the novel. The nearness in time to the events of history and the documented proof of the men and their battles serve to enhance the illusion of what is real at the level of reference.

Benet uses a similar strategy when he includes two other sets of data concerning the Civil War: the letters of Eugenio Mazón in volumes I and III of *Herrumbrosas lanzas*, and a series of footnotes that tell what happens to important individuals after the war or how a particular political problem is later resolved. The letters are important devices in these instances because they reveal the viewpoint of the present tense of the war. They are of course narrated documents and thus stand once removed from the events they describe. But they are significant to the strategy of the historian because they reveal the thoughts of a witness, traditionally relied upon to offer a first-hand (though biased) view of "real" happenings. The footnotes also enhance the authenticity of the narrative: they suggest scholarly investigation and add to the discourse an aura of seriousness of purpose. They lend as well the sense of an ending to events that are left incomplete in the main body of the text and reveal the traditional historiographic desire for wholeness and closure.

One of the most important strategies that Benet uses to narrate history, and to narrate about history, has to do with the nature of storytelling. Benet's commentaries on storytelling are highly intentional. They show how facts are malleable and how the requirements of the reader shape the way that facts are laid out. The most revealing example of self-conscious storytelling, though there are many others in Benet's novels, is found in *Herrumbrosas lanzas II* and involves the gladiator combat of Eugenio Mazón in the mid-1800s. The narrator of the tale, Ventura León, is an eyewitness to the combat in which Mazón vanquishes the champion in Pamplona and wins renown as a man of great skill and courage. Ventura León later relates the events to the public of Región with a keen sense of emplotment and the effect that his narrative will produce. He is an "eyewitness" of the action and thus bears the authority of experiencing the reality that he relates. As Benet clearly demonstrates, however, his story turns less upon the innocence of unadulterated fact than upon the exigencies of the well-told tale. In other words, history as human intentionality yields to narrative configuration, which is determined not by the "found" structures within the event itself but by the requirements of dramatic narration. For example, the "eyewitness" is forced to replace a metaphor ("[Eugenio] freed himself like a cat" [95]) when it displeases the listening public. More importantly, however, as the public learns the "historia," but wishes to hear it repeated again and again, the narrator begins to embellish the facts: he includes details that he had previously deleted and soon begins to expand the paradigm of the story with background information about Mazón's life. Eventually the demands of the public compel León to invent a whole mode of being for Mazón. He refines the story each time that it is told until the story itself co-opts and supersedes the reality from which it was originally engendered. As León (i.e., the historian) realizes, "A good story creates more emotion than the best spectacle" (99).

That such a story about telling stories is interpolated into the midst of Benet's historical narration intimates more than a plot of compelling interest. It is a simulacrum on a small scale of how configuration overrides what is given as fact and points to the way in which the storyteller projects himself and the reader imaginatively into history in order to understand beyond the surface level of event. This is precisely what Hayden White has claimed for the historian, who necessarily creates "verbal fictions" (*Tropics*, 82) and whose histories are the modern version of yesterday's myths. However, this in no way denies the truth-value of such narrative. On the contrary, the narrative pushes truth to a level beyond the specific form and content of the events at hand because it refers both *to* the events and *away* from the events as they are configured and reconfigured by narrative. This kind of split-referencing of the narrative, which is particularly acute in metaphor but inheres in the sense-making process of all narrative discourse, is deeply pertinent to life. It is, in fact, a metaphor of being. As Ricoeur puts it, split referentiality "constitutes the primordial reference to the extent that it suggests, reveals, and unconceals the deep structures of reality to which we are related as mortals who are born into this world and who *dwell* in it for a while."[10] It is in this way that Benet's narrative reveals the truth of the Civil War, and it is why his fiction must be seen as a close and complementary ally of history.

University of Connecticut

NOTES

1. For a fine overview of the current state of theory and its relation to history and fiction, see Leonard Schulze and Walter Wetzels, eds., *Literature and History* (Lanham, Md.: University Press of America, 1983); Hayden White, *The Content of the Form* (Baltimore and London: The Johns Hopkins University Press, 1987), *Tropics of Discourse* (Baltimore and London: The Johns Hopkins University Press, 1978), and especially his *Metahistory: The Historical Imagination in Nineteenth-Century Europe* (Baltimore and London: The Johns Hopkins University Press, 1973); Paul Ricoeur, *Time and Narrative* (Chicago: University of Chicago Press, 1984-1985), 3 vols. Further references to these works will appear in the text.

2. For an overview of Benet's ideas on fiction and narration, see, for example, Malcolm Alan Compitello, "The Paradoxes of Praxis: Juan Benet and Modern Poetics," in *Critical Approaches to the Writings of Juan Benet* (hereafter *CAJB*), ed. Roberto Manteiga, David K. Herzberger, and Malcolm Alan Compitello (Hanover, N.H., and London: University Press of New England, 1984); David K. Herzberger, *The Novelistic World of Juan Benet* (Clear Creek, Ind.: The American Hispanist, 1976); Janet Pérez, "The Rhetoric of Ambiguity, in *CAJB*, 18-26; Vicente Cabrera, *Juan Benet* (Boston: Twayne, 1983).

3. Juan Benet, *La inspiración y el estilo* (Barcelona: Seix Barral, 1973), 166. All quotations are from this edition. The translations from this and other works in Spanish are mine.

4. Juan Benet, *En ciernes* (Madrid: Taurus, 1976), 16.

5. Juan Benet, *El ángel del Señor abandona a Tobías* (Barcelona: La Gaya Ciencia, 1976), 56.

6. I am referring primarily to *Volverás a Región* (Barcelona: Destino, 1967), *Saúl ante Samuel* (Barcelona: La Gaya Ciencia, 1980), and the three volumes of *Herrumbrosas lanzas* (Madrid: Alfaguara, 1983, 1984, 1986), though the Civil War is present to some degree in nearly all of Benet's fiction.

7. For a discussion of time in Benet's novels, with particular emphasis on Bergson and Faulkner, see Randolph Pope, "Benet, Faulkner, and Bergson's Memory," in *CAJB*, 111-19. For a more general view of time, see Roberto Manteiga, "Time, Space, and Narration in Juan Benet's Short Stories," in *CAJB*, 120-36; and Herzberger, *Novelistic World*.

8. Frank Kermode, *The Genesis of Secrecy* (Cambridge and London: Harvard University Press, 1979), 117.

9. Raymond Federman, *Surfiction, Fiction Now . . . and Tomorrow* (Chicago: The Swallow Press, 1975).

10. Paul Ricoeur, "The Metaphorical Process as Cognition, Imagination, and Feeling," in *On Metaphor*, ed. Sheldon Sacks (Chicago: University of Chicago Press, 1978), 151.

HEROES, MYTHS, AND MONSTERS:
SUÁREZ-GALBÁN'S
BALADA de la GUERRA HERMOSA

Fidel López-Criado

The events that took place in Spain between 1936 and 1939 constitute one of the most significant and traumatic chapters in modern Spanish history. However, much of what has been written about those events in history books has been obliquely filtered through the biased prism of political creeds or convenient historical perspectives. Ideological apologists from the right see the Spanish Civil War as a crusade to rescue law, order, and traditional social values from the clutches of international Judeo-Masonic communism which conspired to drag the ancestral glory of Spain into the dark abyss of atheism and anarchy.[1] Apologists from the left see the war as another episode in the continued struggle of the proletarian masses to free themselves from their ancestral enemies: church, monarchy, and wealthy oligarchy.[2] Lost in the rhetoric of aphoristic proselytism, both the right and the left have sought a causal anchor for the conflict beyond the temporal and geographical confines of the war itself. In fact, it would seem that the war was incidental, either a symptom of emerging fascism or the consequence of communism, a prologue or an epilogue to something else of greater importance.[3]

The sublimation, idealization, or distortion of historical events is not new, and it is certainly not exclusive to historians;

the Spanish novel of the so-called "postwar" suffers the same ills. Whether it is through the testimonial approach of García Serrano, Gironella, or Agustí, or the various forms of social realism of Cela, Laforet, Quiroga, Sánchez-Ferlosio, Goytisolo, and many others whose world view is shaped by the experience of events unleashed in 1936, the portrayal of the war is always reduced to a referential experience which almost never appears as the corpus of narrative concerns.[4] It may be present in the narrative background as unexplained dementia, a crippled child, a blood-stained Jarama, ancestral hate, or societal ills of all sorts; but it is always elusive, deflected by the shield of allusion or sublimated as archetypal and universal. The traumatic immediacy of war, censorship, and literary concerns may account for the particular phobic treatment of the war; but as with other forms of artistic endeavors, what is important is not the cause but the consequence of literary expression—in other words, what matters is not the author's perception of his or her lived experience but the interplay of the fictional reality of the text and the contextual reality of the reader. This, more than any other single thing, explains why children and grandchildren of ex-combatants still meet to discuss a particular series of events in which they did not participate, but which has engendered all the heroes, myths, and monsters that roam the dark corridors of a half-century of literary production. They represent the collective fears, hopes, and delusions of more than one lost generation of Spaniards for whom the war still rages unresolved, and in no case is this more aptly exemplified than in the plight of the exile.[5]

No matter how we may interpret the present circumstances of our beloved Spain, the fact remains that the essential differences that brought about the war have not been fully reconciled, inside or outside Spain. The accommodating socialism that guides Spain and stands shoulder to shoulder with a pragmatic monarchy, reborn in the agonizing throes of Francoism, bears little resemblance to its forebears of the Popular Front. The Republic has not returned to Spain, and the children of the Loyalists continue in exile, victims of a past that denies them access to their future as Spaniards. The prime directive of many a consular representative of our socialist Spain seems to be to discourage—or at least not to encourage—the return: "You are better off where you are. Send money, but stay away." Nevertheless, in spite of these and other impediments, some of the second-generation victims of the war decide to go back home, and when they do, they must go through the brutal rite of initiation peculiar to exiles: they must fight the war again and win it psychologically. This is the case with Eugenio Suárez-Galbán, author of *Balada de la guerra hermosa*, which won the Premio Sésamo of 1982.[6]

Suárez-Galbán is a child of exile who grew up in New York City, rejected by a society which would not accept him and in which he was not sure he belonged. In 1975, at the age of thirty-seven, he returned to Spain, and, in the agony of the "Caudillo," he set out to relive the psychological inheritance of 1936, which was to yield *Balada de la guerra hermosa*. In many ways, the novel is an exorcism of inherited fears, hatreds, and suspicions; but more than anything else, it is a literal reconstruction of the past, a search for the "hilo suelto," or loose thread, of history that can enable him to connect with the present. The answer for him lies in the accurate reenactment of the war experience, but this proves an arduous task; the journey back into the past of Spain simultaneously leads him to his future, and the only guide along the way is a deceitful one: History.

The anecdotal component of the novel is a seemingly simple one to follow: the story of three friends trapped in the whirlwind of war and its consequences. However, the narrative structure is anything but simple. The reader is born into a Nietzschean universe in which reality is not anchored by any basic truths and continuously shifts with the perspective of each character who, at random points throughout the novel, assumes the role of narrator and continues the story in either the first, second, or third person. This is, in many ways, a world attempting to fill the void of novelistic creation, a nascent consciousness attempting to define itself and its circumstantial reality without any reliable points of reference. The ensuing distortion is the first step into the dark hallway of history, a first step in a journey of self-discovery.

The novel begins with a confluence of narrative voices which simultaneously announce and deny the presence of the mythical figure of "el Corredera," the runner:

> People along the coast are sure of it: it's the runner. Around Punta Sardina and Roca Prieta, in view of Santa María de Guía, they've seen him and so swear.
>
> They say he has never denied it. He just laughs. But he does not deny it. Juan García himself.
>
> They also say it's got to do with witchcraft. Witchcraft from Cuba, from that black that was seen one dawn on the docks of Las Palmas. Nobody ever found out where he came from. . . . Nothing. Never. He appeared with the sun. . . . He was coming back in search of his roots. . . . He asked for Salvador Guerra, Mencey. The answer was that he was nowhere to be found, that he had fled to the mainland. Then the black's face turned white with laughter: he was there in the Canaries, on Grand Canary itself. What happened was that he was not called Salvador Guerra anymore. He was called Juan García, the runner! (11)

Amidst the chaos, two distinctive voices bid for control of this emerging universe: that of Mencey's female lover and that of his male friend—both of whom remain nameless throughout the novel to heighten their archetypal significance as female and male principles, the anima and animus of a narrative consciousness in the process of becoming. She has not seen Mencey since 1936, when the war first intruded on their lives, and she needs or wishes him back in the figure of "el Corredera." On the other hand, he has not seen Mencey since they both deserted Queipo's troops and fled to France, and he does not believe that Mencey has returned at all. Her reality is grounded in intuition and folklore; his is fashioned with the stuff of history. She trusts the people and hearsay, and witchcraft is simply a prism of reality for her. On the contrary, for him, there is only one reliable reality: the lived experience of self. Since we will never meet Mencey or hear him speak for himself, we are left to choose which version of Mencey is real, and we will even come to doubt if Mencey is real at all. This broken mirror of history, with its many fragments of reality, will pierce the reader's mind as these two narrative voices bid for belief.

The male voice contends that "el Corredera" is a mythical creation, and that is why he is said to appear only at night: "so that the same lies that have always been told about him can continue" (12). He is the dreamed reality of the Guardia Civil as well as of the people, for that reality justifies the repression by the first and the hopes of redemption of the second. However, the female voice argues that she will not allow herself to be deceived by the external appearance of reality: "But not me. I know the truth. I know what they say and what they don't. I know how the papers change things, how the kids imitate him in their games, how the women dream of having his child, or being his lover. I know it all" (12). Hers is an intuitive reality not subject to the ulterior motives and machinations of historical reality. The male voice rebukes her:

> And what about what happened in Seville, do you know that, too?
> Yes.
> And about that certain woman from Madrid?
> Yes.
> And about the kids, do you know that, too?
> And what of it? I know everything.
> How do you know so much? You haven't seen him in years, since before the war, and everything I told you happened after.
> We women know things you men never even imagined. (12)

He points to the illusory nature of reality. "Dreams, I tell you, dreams, they're nothing but dreams" (12). He, not she, is to be believed: "I, on the other hand, I really do know. It's true not everything the papers report is accurate. But the same goes for what the people say. Because the people hear and say what they want. I, on the other hand, was with him in Cuba, and during the war. What can they tell me about him?" (12). Are we to believe the official reality of the press or the unofficial reality of the people? Is Mencey the brave and idealistic "Corredera," or is he the frightened fugitive who will never return home?

Mencey's name is Salvador Guerra, and in it we see the embodiment of the narrative schism: the liberating savior of the female and the war-battered victim of the male. The male narrator sees both the war and their role in it as a grotesque farce. He and Mencey are forcibly conscripted by the rebels and flown to Africa "like potatoes in a sack" (13), where they are received by the pathetically comical Moorish troops:

> and I don't know what the fuck they had told those damn Moors, but every time somebody came to attention, bam, they all came to attention, like the dumb shits they were. They had nothing to do with anything, at least we, who had something Spanish in us, had some stake in the thing, but them, they didn't have the slightest idea what was going on (13).

The war seems as irrational as it is brutal: "Your nerves, the heat—Andalusia in August is like a sweatbath—the lack of water, the horrible food, not having a woman, why one day they grabbed a little communist soldier, a boy, and they left his little ass red, and not only the Moors, let me tell you" (16). But the worst part is a sense of unreality: "The worst is not knowing what was going on in the war" (16). The unimaginable blends with the mundane. "War is like dreams, where anything can happen, no matter how crazy it may seem to you" (20). Mencey's manly stoicism allows him to endure the horrors of war: "you got by on guts alone" (18); but his lack of political consciousness or partisanship in the conflict, more than Queipo's sadistic "clean-up operations" and the horrors of the battlefield, drives Mencey and the male narrator to desertion.

The female's vision of the war is radically different. To her, the war is inconsequential in and of itself, except for the fact that it has taken away her beloved. It is a personified rival, the embodiment of all other potential rivals: "I think about it, Mencey, I think about it, and I know that it was not like that, that it couldn't have been like that, like he's going to tell me, and I would be able to repeat to him that we women know things. we have our ways of knowing things, that men would never understand" (19). For her, Mencey is not the selfish brute of the male narrator but a sensitive and compassionate individual, almost effeminate: "You're kind of strange, odd, Mencey, you have such a reputation for being a ladies' man, but, the truth be told, you are more like a woman, you are more like us. I don't know how to explain it, it's something I feel, that I just know" (19). The male narrator thought he had shocked her with his tales of deception during the war: "I bet you can't believe it, right?" (22); but she can gauge the depth of suffering and pain precisely because she is a woman: "They didn't have to tell me, Mencey. I'm a woman and I can figure everything out" (25). Man grows callous to pain and learns to survive by compromising or suffocating his principles, as the male narrator states to her: "You get used to it, a man gets used to everything" (34). However, woman's feminine frailty is the source of real courage and idealism; she does not compromise:

> Not a woman, Mencey. That's what men believe, that we are born to give birth and suffer. But they are fooling themselves. We give birth shouting and suffering with our teeth clenched. We support the weight of a man on top of us, everything except allowing ourselves to become resigned to it. (34)

It is the feminine principle that affords hope and continuity, and she shapes the reality of the future with sheer willpower: "You'll return, and then I'll again see my smile in your eyes" (36). Her self-assertion is the assertion of reality.

Caught in the titanic tug-of-war between the opposing realities of the male and female narrators, the reader struggles to weigh and measure arguments, hoping to grab the "real" Mencey just beyond the next page, but to no avail. The male voice continues to recount their experiences in the war. Rape, murder, theft, cowardice, hunger, fear, and hate—all have shone in the darkness of war as clear illustrations of man's inhumanity to man. To accede to the reality of this narrator is to acknowledge the mythology of political ideals: there were no heroes, just monsters; there were no basic truths or romantic principles, just the conjugation of raw animal instincts. Within reality, Mencey's desertion is the direct result of his apathy and detachment from idealism. His primary concern would be self-preservation at all costs.

The male narrator's cynical view of the war justifies Mencey. The Communist workers of Portugal and France who save his life are simply ideological fools, "party men," and the Marseilles prostitutes who provide a living for him are simply opportune. The narrator shows his insensitivity and disbelief in human kindness as he describes the death of one of the prostitutes at the hands of a sadistic client: "It wasn't the slap in the face as much as the fall that messed her up: her skull cracked when she hit the wall, even though a little blood trickled out of her mouth where he had hit her. She was at the end, her leg was twitching like a mule" (46). All concern is for himself: "Imagine the picture, a Spaniard, with false papers, with a dead whore half-naked to boot, just picture it" (46). However, the reader cannot condemn Mencey for being no better than anyone else. His efforts to survive are heroic, if not exemplary; but just before we can conclude that, in a dog-eat-dog world, it is a wise dog who thinks first and last of himself, we are confronted with the unexpected perspective of another female narrative voice.

The first female narrator conjures up the perspective of another woman who has known Mencey: "That woman from Madrid . . . don't say anymore. I know it all. I wasn't with you, Mencey, that woman from Madrid told me everything" (46). The second female is an extension of the first, and it is through her that we are drawn into Mencey's experience of the French refugee camps, the forced conscription of Republican soldiers in the war against the Germans, and Mencey's subsequent horrors in an S.S. concentration camp. The male narrator speaks in the first-person voice to illustrate how subjective or projected reality is more reliable, since it is emitted rather than received. Thus, what this third-person narrative voice would offer the reader is the intermediate position: not the received reality of the "I" nor the emitted reality of the "You" but the transformational context of the experience itself. The woman from Madrid affords us contact with Mencey directly, for she will speak with his voice in the first person; but it is clear that she will tilt the scale in favor of the female narrator, as she is much more than a "medium": "They threw him in a dark cell, a kind of pen for animals" (50), she continues:

> From the truck to the cattle car. He didn't fit, it was already overloaded. Pushing and shoving and everything else, until they could close the doors, and him all the time thinking, like I imagine he must have been thinking, since he is from the Canaries: What the hell am I doing here? In a cattle car full of Jews and mongoloids . . . (50-51).

Her imaginings are part of the feminine principle, the woman's subjective reality, and they serve to counter the rugged manliness of Mencey with his sensitivity and vulnerability at the hands of the S.S.

The narrative sequences occur in this fashion. The female narrator quotes the woman from Madrid who quotes Mencey who supposedly provides us with immediate reality and the source of "truth." However, the reader can properly suspect that we are encountering a "Russian doll" syndrome, for not even Mencey seems to be in control of the experience of his immediate reality: "I know he did not live that, I can't believe that he lived that. And me, if I really did go through it, I keep asking myself how in the hell did one country gather together such a collection of S.O.B.s" (54). This is a turning point in the reader's perceptions of the written text: Mencey can no longer be the ultimate dimension of reality, and, therefore, all interpretations are valid. Moreover, as we are introduced to the introspective and idealistic Mencey, we suspect that they may all be shades of the same unreality.

The Mencey of the concentration camps evolves into a committed patriot who is willing to lay down his life for the Republican cause. The male narrator, who has meanwhile become an "extraperlista," or war profiteer, denies the potential reality of this compassionate Mencey by suggesting that he has become insane and effeminate:

> I found him changed. And with everything that had happened to him, it wasn't a small change. He was screwed up, it was like he wasn't there. And one day he goes and tells me that he had gone crazy in that concentration camp. . . . No, men aren't like that. (87)

As he attempts to discredit the woman from Madrid, his ultimate vindicator is history. Mencey's idealism was the posture of a fool or madman: "Has history proved me right or not?" (87). The Mencey of the Spanish resistance is a "historical" unreality, and the male narrator provides the following Calderonian admonition to the female narrator: "They say he went crazy. I think he was crazy before what happened in the concentration camps. I already told you. They say he went completely crazy, that he wanted to go back to Madrid. . . . To begin again, to continue to dream. But dreams, I tell you, are only dreams" (94). At the beginning of the novel, the male narrator had accused the female narrator of having dreamed Mencey: "Dreams, I tell you, dreams, they're nothing but dreams" (12), and this new reiteration of the potential existence of a dreamed reality brings the novel to a full cycle and the same original uncertainty. However, the narrative voice structure is not circular but spiral. A full circle would have joined the male and female principles of reality, reconciling them in a final, neat vision of reality as a composite of two basic extremes. The novel would end in an anticlimactic cliché.

As much as the reader hungers for a definitive closure, the novel is disturbingly open-ended. No reality predominates; instead, there is the disconcerting dialogue between the male and female narrators:

> I hear steps.
> They're mine.
> Are you leaving?
> Yes, I have to.
> Wait awhile. Don't leave me alone. Don't go until he [Mencey] gets here . . . wait a while longer, he will be here soon . . . who's knocking on the door? Is it you? I knew it! I always knew it! (94-95)

Did Mencey really return? Or is Mencey the war of 1936, the shared, reciprocal hallucinations of more than the one million dead Spaniards that haunt our lives? The male narrator had proclaimed that Mencey's dementia was exemplified by his desire to go back to Madrid, where it all ended, and begin anew. Is that the common dementia of all children in exile? The end of the narrative is followed by a postscript composed of three "official documents": the death certificate of the female narrator, naming syphylitic dementia as the cause of death; the black's drunken denial of necromancy or acquaintance with Mencey; and the male narrator's disavowal of any connection with Mencey, "el Corredera" or Juan García. Officially, the novel is either false, unreal, or the product of collective dementia; but the Guardia Civil lieutenant does acknowledge that (1) coercion was involved in the case of the black, and that (2) a skirmish has taken place between several Guardias and someone suspected of being Juan García, alias "the runner." Perhaps the female narrator was right. The war rages on.

Rollins College

NOTES

1. See Agustín Del Río Cisneros, ed., *Mensajes del jefe del estado* (Madrid: Dirección General de Cultura, Ministerio de Información y Turismo, 1971), and Carlos Fernández, *Antología de 40 años (1936-1975)* (Coruña: Ediciós do Castro, 1983), where the most representative figures of the right speak unabashedly of fascist ideals, fears, and aspirations.

2. Like the fascists, the political left can best be approached through memoirs and other first-person narrative accounts of the war years. Of particular importance are Ignacio Hidalgo de Cisneros, *La República y la guerra de España* (Paris: Société d'Editions de la Librairie du Globe, 1964), and Leon Trotsky, *The Spanish Revolution, 1931-1939* (New York: Pathfinder Press, 1973), as they exemplify the conservative and the radical extremes of the Republican coalition. Of lesser value because of their assumed pseudo-scientific approach to their recounting of the war experience, but clearly within the bounds of traditional historical interpretation, are the following accounts: Felix Morrow, *Revolution and Counter-Revolution in Spain* (New York: Pathfinder, 1976); Stanley G. Payne, *Historia del fascismo español* (Paris: Ruedo Ibérico, 1965); Rafael Gómez Parra, *La guerrilla antifranquista, 1945-1949* (Madrid: Editorial Revolución, 1983); and E. Portuondo, *La Segunda República* (Madrid: Editorial Revolución, 1981).

3. In the best cases, when the historian's treatment is distanced from the war by time or professional discipline, his account is still filtered through modern geo-political attitudes which force the Spanish conflict into the backdrop of the Second World War and subsequent East-West considerations. Fernando Díaz Plaja, *El siglo XX, la guerra de España, 1936-1939* (Madrid: Editorial Faro, 1962) typifies this kind of historical perspective within Spain, while Raymond Carr and Juan Pablo Fusi, *Spain: Dictatorship to Democracy*, 2nd ed. (London: George Allen and Unwin, 1983) represent the same approach outside of Spain.

4. See Rodolfo Cardona, *Novelistas españoles de posguerra* (Madrid: Taurus, 1976); Santos Sanz-Villanueva, *Historia de la novela social española, 1942-1975* (Madrid: Alhambra, 1980), and Ignacio Soldevila Durante, *La novela española desde 1936* (Madrid: Alhambra, 1982).

5. Although the term "exile" is generally understood within a political frame of reference only, many of the Spaniards who are presently scattered throughout the world left Spain after 1939 under the aegis of "emigrant," a more subtle and appropriate term used to describe in many instances the same flight from oppression. I consider the difference between these terms to be more formalistic than real, but I will use the term "exile" solely in a political sense.

6. Eugenio Suárez-Galbán, *Balada de la guerra hermosa* (Madrid: Fundamentos, 1983). All references to the text are from this edition; the page number is indicated in parentheses after the quotation. All translations are mine.

THE BIBLICAL PERSPECTIVE ON CIVIL WAR IN BENET'S *SAÚL ANTE SAMUEL*

Nelson R. Orringer

In his book of essays, *La inspiración y el estilo,* Juan Benet offers a skeptic's view of the biblical perspective in general.[1] He affirms that a single intention, style, and source of inspiration inform the Old Testament: nothing lies outside divine creation; hence, nothing is left over for the field of human freedom. God's original creation, narrated in Genesis, implies within itself every quest for human perfection, every task undertaken by man's spirit. The Hebrew writer must perform no research nor must he engage in any novelistic invention. Endowed with unquestioning faith, he must celebrate the power and glory of God with the very words conveyed to him for that purpose by Jehovah himself. To change the wording of the Old Testament by substituting vagueness for imprecision is to cross the subtle line between history and fiction, between faith and doubt, limitation and freedom (38-40).

In other words, the free poet strikes Benet as the man of "few previous convictions and little love of the rules, though patently inclined to set down all he receives by simply letting it pass through the filter of his aesthetic awareness" (50). In Benet's novels, in fact, absolutisam gives way to probabilism, faith to skepticism, boundness to freedom. However, these preferences do not signify the exclusion of biblical elements from Benet's prose. Quite the contrary, the ancient narremes can certainly fit into what Benet calls the aesthetic awareness of a free, unbound poet. As an admirer of Faulkner, Benet may well have known the American novelist's statement, "To me, the Old Testament is some of the finest, most robust and most amusing folklore I know."[2]

Where the Bible finds its way into Benet's fiction, it provides a dogmatic point of reference for the skepticism and relativism of an open-ended text. Hence, in his 1980 novel, *Saúl ante Samuel,* he welds biblical allusions into a two-edged sword, reflecting multiple perspectives on the Spanish Civil War. He draws chiefly from the Old but also from the New Testament, at times modifying biblical narrative to his own purposes. By placing ancient characters in new situations, he conveys a Heraclitean metaphysics of reality as strife; an ethics of evil as the *sine qua non* of good; and an aesthetics of the sinister as a component of the beautiful.[3] Little wonder that Randolph Pope, alluding to this novel, has pointed out "the crucial impor-tance of . . . biblical references as a guide to the reading of a text or as a submerged paradigm"! (113). Until now, though, only the obvious Cain-Abel motif has received concentrated critical attention in David K. Herzberger's excellent article, "The Theme of Warring Brothers in 'Saúl ante Samuel'" (*CAJB,* 100-119). But the title of the novel, its plot, structure, and ideological frame-work seem to point not so much to Gen. 4 as to 1 Sam. 15 as the main allegorical framework for the novel. Here I shall show how all elements of the novel employ this passage as an ideal referent, highlighting the Civil War as interpreted by Benet.

In the classical period of Hebrew prophecy, soothsayers, mere foretellers of the future, were outlawed (1 Sam. 28:3).[4] Prophets, consecrated from birth to God's service, acted as His messengers to the people of Israel and their rulers. In this spirit, the prophet Samuel broke with King Saul for his disobedience to God. The Lord had commanded Saul to destroy without quarter the sinful city of Amalek, all its inhabitants, and all their possessions. Instead, swayed by the populace, or so Saul maintained, he had spared the finest cattle, intended for sacrifice to God, and had not put Agag, the Amalekite king, to the sword. Samuel, therefore, prophesied that the Lord would dethrone the disobedient Saul and cause his crown to pass to his neighbor, the younger David. Saul recognized the error of his ways, yet asked Samuel to honor him by accompanying him in public worship. Samuel did so, then personally slew King Agag (1 Sam. 15:2-33).

In Benet's *Saúl ante Samuel*, the figure of Saúl corresponds to an unnamed Nationalist leader, resigned like the Israelite king to his own impiety, yet at the same time filled with himself, as a "non-believer blown up with his own pompousness" (132). He desires, like his biblical counterpart, to cut a dazzling figure in public. His grandmother, who has prophetic powers not unrelated to Samuel's, predicts that his sway over the family has passed and that the time has come for his younger half-brother Martín to assume control (18). Resentful of Saúl's overweening pride, Martín is less a David-figure than a Cain for the falsely "pious Abel" (132; cf. Heb. 11:4). Out of a desire for vengeance, Martín engages in what the grandmother calls "incestuous adultery" with his sister-in-law, Saúl's wife. The grandmother foresees that, like Lot's wife, Martín will one day change into a pillar of salt, not for the sin of looking backward but for the bitterness of having cuckolded his own brother and having made love to his own sister, as it were (132). With the outbreak of civil war, Saúl has fallen prisoner to the Republicans. His father, filled like the aged Jacob with patriarchal concern for the loss of his lineage (28; cf. Gen. 42:36), urges Martín to join the Republicans, feign loyalty to them, and do all in his power to save Saúl. However, Martín's inertia in performing this familial duty runs parallel to the ineptness of the Republican forces in wresting the district of Región away from the Nationalists, as Herzberger has perceived (*CAJB*, 104-5).

The Spanish Civil War, waged by both sides in the cause of good against evil, like Saúl's campaign against Amalek, conceals petty, personal motives that cause the conflict to degenerate into sporadic, undisciplined skirmishes: the right merely fights to retain its material possessions; the left, to avenge itself on its former masters. Consequently, the war becomes a mere game without transcendent consequences. With no participant truly responsible for his own acts, the war takes on an impersonal cast. As the implied narrator puts it, "The war is also an ego" (63). Or as the imprisoned Saúl tells his captor Martín, "The only cause is the war in itself . . . independently of supposed differences provoking it" (312). Hence, Saúl plays a Heraclitean variation on the rhetorical question of Job (7:1), "Is there not a time of service to man upon earth?"[5] Since all main actions of the novel are referred to the Civil War, and since the war is *causa sui*, the subjects of the sentences in *Saúl ante Samuel* often go unspecified. The reader must himself supply most of the agents in this polysemic text. Where he understands a Republican action, he could just as easily comprehend a Nationalist one in a war that never winds down because it never really gets started.

Individual irresponsibility for war actions lends an equivocal character to prophecy. A. W. Schlegel and José Ortega y Gasset write that history is prophecy in reverse.[6] Yet, in a nation at war, incapable of making history, prophetic wisdom can only amount to suspicious penetration into humdrum, present-day events with the conviction that they can only be repeated. In a clear reference to Martín's grandmother, with her gift for prophecy, the narrator affirms, "Prophetic wisdom is made of much suspicion and few guesses, with complete confidence in monotony, likeness, and inertia, and with reliance on the unforeseen only to meet a trance head-on" (44). The implied contrast between the grandmother and the prophet Samuel establishes the Hebrew seer's situation as the unattainable, ideal limit for hers. Yet this comparison also allows insights into Benet's vision of the Spanish Civil War. Whatever Samuel predicts comes to pass afterwards, but the substance of the grandmother's prophecies applies to simultaneous action in a novel where nothing happens of historical consequence. Hence, the novelist often superimposes the grandmother's prophetic words over actual war scenes, giving them a pseudo-apocalyptic cast. For example, during a Republican offensive against the Nationalists, a military truck belonging to the Republican convoy becomes lodged in a public water conduit. The narrative suddenly stops, and the grandmother's prophetic voice resounds: "I guarantee you that none of you will be able to dodge defeat.

Yes, you'll all be beaten, somehow forever" (117). In a nugatory, cat-and-mouse game, after two identical, unsuccessful Republican offensives to capture the mountain passes of Región (320), the Nationalists put the Republicans to flight without attempting to seize them, as if to follow their example. Therefore, the war as such never seems to come to an end (396). Nonetheless, even had the Republicans won, the result would have been the same: the district of Región would still have felt threatened by whatever outsiders held the mountains (101).

Irresponsible playing at war, which makes prophecy ludicrous when not superfluous, has its immediate causes in the psychology of the combatants and its deeper explanations beyond the battlefields. Spain as a whole, as portrayed by Benet, was engaging in self-delusion, while the few Spaniards endowed with self-awareness were practicing duplicity. This situation has rigorous parallels in the Israelites' campaign against the Amalekites. The Hebrew populace went into battle with the idea of ridding the world of sinners, yet unwittingly sinned by saving some of the spoils for sacrifice. Their king Saul knew that they were sinning but sanctioned their wrongdoing for his own self-aggrandizement. The prophet Samuel, painfully aware of Saul's duplicity, branded his feigned piety superstition, more forgivable to God than disobedience (1 Sam. 15:22-23). In drawing our analogies with *Saúl ante Samuel,* let us focus first on the Spanish populace and afterwards on their two-faced leaders. "Never did a people fight so in vain," laments the narrator, "never did any other get so inebriated on such a deceitful elixir; that is why modern history will never again produce so religious a war, so Cathar, so uncivic" (329). The key to this opinion lies in the adjective "cátara," comparing Spaniards to the Cathars, medieval Christian heretics with a Manichean view of good and evil. Indeed, the entire novel is best definable as "that oil-painting with a Biblical theme taking place on a feudal landscape" (352). The landscape has produced a race of Cainites, "true homunculi, . . . marked forever like the Enochs, the Irads, the Lamechs [Cain's son, grandson, and great great-grandson, respectively: Gen. 4:17], with the curse of the first of them etched in fire on the brow of anxiety" (173).

Spaniards, divided into landlords and tenant laborers, all displayed fratricidal tendencies. The older generation of proprietors, embodied by Saúl's father, unable to preserve its fortunes through its own efforts, fearful of losing what it owned, opposed reform and disguised its fear as consecration of its property titles. Any threat to its holdings became for it a mortal sin. Yet, Martín's cousin Simón observed that those proprietors were themselves sinning against the second commandment of worshipping no gods before Jehovah: they adored Mammon. Meanwhile, their employees and their enemies, to redeem their fault, sinned against other commandments, like the fourth (consecrating the sabbath) and the fifth (honoring parents). Violence and disobedience came out of excessive pride of ownership, which tried to safeguard its excesses behind the shield of the divinity (252-53).

What of the younger generation, from which sprung the leaders of the left and the right in the Spanish Civil War? In Simón's judgment, both his cousins, the Nationalist Saúl and the Republican Martín, acted with duplicity stemming from scorn for their father's fear and greed (230). Duplicity is a major theme of Saúl ante Samuel, especially occupying the central panel of the triptych that forms the novel. Indeed, the entire work is a masterpiece of double-talk, focused on the character of Martín. In the first part, mainly dominated by the perspective of the prophetic grandmother, Martín is viewed as being as treacherous as a not entirely evil Judas Iscariot, feigning to save his brother but betraying him perhaps for the good of Christendom (106-8).[7] In the second part, where the point of view of Simón prevails, with his repressed homosexual love for Martín, this character acquires a Satanic grace, like that of an inverted Christ figure.[8] In the third and final part, where the implied narrator most often takes the floor, Martín's presumed betrayal of Saúl is presented as a tacit service performed on behalf of both Saúl himself and Saúl's father.[9] All three parts of the novel adapt biblical allusions to the duplicitous purpose, so to speak, of painting the youthful leaders of the Civil War with un-Manichean nuances, so that they appear as neither absolutely good nor absolutely evil. The structure of Saúl ante

Samuel, unlike the biblical text on which it is mainly based, calls for the suspension of ethical absolutism with respect to the main characters. Only in this way can there emerge an unbiased vision of the Civil War on the individual plane.

What lies at the base of the duplicity in the main characters and in the self-deception of Spaniards in the Civil War? Evidently, a yearning for unbirth, as Freud predicated of all mankind. Martín cannot bring to completion the Republican campaign he has initiated, because, as his grandmother suggests, his enterprise belongs to "a legendary past" like the biblical narratives that form the ideal limits of Benet's novel. Freud combined with Heidegger's concept of *Geworfenheit,* our state of being flung into the world, generates the notion of "a blind drive for return which man preserved when he was flung here" (132).[10] Martín, the Republican leader, feels this nihilistic yearning; yet so does his half-brother, the Nationalist head, Saúl. Martín's presumed revolutionary goals strike him as counterproductive.

> The only revolution is death, my boy, and every program for the betterment of society is radically conservative. The most brilliant idea won't be ahead of its time, but against its time, going backwards toward extinction; and its program will be nothing but suicide. (317)

Having failed in his program to reform society, having done nothing to prevent Saúl's death, having lost the Civil War, Martín fulfills his grandmother's prophecy of fleeing Región. His cousin Simón, equally a nihilist, who seeks his own duplicitous return to the womb through lovemaking, harbors the fear that Martín will not return. He reads his fear in letters of lamentation and elegies like that which Ezekiel (2:9) read on the scroll of his divine vision (301).

The craving for nothingness is not privy to the youths in the novel. Older characters like Saúl's father and grandmother experience it as well. The father clings to his heritage of the past with an attitude of "Jehoachin driven from the temple," promising himself a return to his flock one day (35).[11] He retains the memory of early infancy because society wants to keep within him a sense of weakness, the need for a protecting hand (35). His mother-in-law, the prophetess, could have exercised a power comparable to the prophet Samuel's in society. Instead, accepting the rebellious condition of her neighborhood, rather than attempting to educate it, she has chosen to immerse herself increasingly in her mystic isolation so as to enter a state of nirvana, "for the purpose of forming a single body with the silent, faraway numen which by governing all things was able to compel obedience to its rules through the path of predestination" (24).

In conclusion, just as Valle-Inclán's *esperpentos* constitute deformations of European epics, so *Saúl ante Samuel* forms an ironic and elaborate stylization of a biblical allegory. The prophet figure does not keep her reverent distance from divinity the way that Samuel does but, in a way characteristic of Spanish quietism, attempts fusion with it. She has little to prophesy in a land, unlike biblical Israel, without a transcendent history. The subject of Spanish history is not a people and its king disobedient to a wrathful God, but an impersonal principle of strife, established by a playful, capricious god—called at one point of the novel "a spoiled child" (300)—and dominating a self-deceived populace with duplicitous, nihilistic leaders. Just as the Israelites' war against the Amalekites betrays materialistic motives on the part of the victors, so the Spanish Civil War conceals petty egotism. However, whereas Saul and his army go after the spoils, the combatting Spaniards either seek to retain what little they possess, or, if they possess nothing, simply pursue the enemy out of a sentiment of revenge. Neither in the war against Amalek nor in the Spanish Civil War, as depicted by Benet, do the fighters fulfill their religious obligation to obliterate the foe. The biblical Saul loses his throne as a result, whereas in post-Civil War Spain, an armed peace continues the status quo of the war mentality, with no one receiving genuine prizes or punishments, "since everything was mere fiction" (300).

Because personal identity plays so little a role in this novel, the work lends itself to multiple interpretations, and the present exegesis of Benet's biblical viewpoint of the Civil War is certainly not the definitive one. Let the narrator of the novel speak for the author and for me as his critic: "The changeless fullness . . . of an artwork, while stimulating the exegete's labor, embodies and embraces all its interpretations, none of which will cancel out the cycle of attraction that it exercises on the researcher's instinct of any period" (265).

University of Connecticut

NOTES

1. Juan Benet, "Inspiración, probabilidad, fascinación," in *La Inspiración y el estilo* (Madrid: Revista de Occidente, 1966), 40. Further references to this work will appear in the text. All translations from this and other works in Spanish are mine.

2. Quoted by Randolph Pope, "Benet, Faulkner, and Bergson's Memory," in *Critical Approaches to the Writings of Juan Benet*, ed. Roberto C. Manteiga, David K. Herzberger, and Malcolm Alan Compitello (Hanover, N.H., and London: University Press of New England, 1984), 147 n.7 (hereafter *CAJB*). Further references to this and other studies in *CAJB* will appear in the text.

3. Since I am mainly concerned here with the ideology of *Saúl ante Samuel* (Barcelona: La Gaya Ciencia, 1980), I do not explore the sinister as the dark side of beauty in the novel. Among the many possible examples, take, for instance, Benet's modification of the *locus amoenus* commonplace: "black land, carpeted all year by thick grass, fresh and sickening, with blades bowing to caress the thirsty stones and sand of the macadam and only overshadowed by the violent bushes and nettles" (172). Another excellent example is the "beautiful, lonely holm oak of over a hundred years old" where, however, the shepherds would hang "the bodies of the serpents they would kill" (192). Cf. Eugenio Trías' theories on the beautiful and the sinister, *Lo bello y lo siniestro* (Barcelona: Seix Barral, 1982), as a contemporaneous vision of aesthetics that could easily be applied to Benet's novelistic practice in *Saúl ante Samuel*, published only two years earlier. Further references to this novel will appear in the text.

4. *Sagrada Biblia*, tr. Eloíno Nácar Fuster y Alberto Colunga, 12th ed. (Madrid: Biblioteca de Autores Españolas, 1962).

5. The Book of Job, it should be recalled, receives considerable attention in *La inspiración y el estilo*, 35-38.

6. As Ortega puts it, "When Schlegel said that the historian is a prophet in reverse, he conveyed a thought as deep as it is true" (José Ortega y Gasset, *El tema de nuestro tiempo* [1923], in *Obras Completas*, 5th ed. [Madrid: Revista de Occidente, 1962], 3 [1917-1918]: 153).

7. Cf. Jorge Luis Borges' Judas Iscariot, the unappreciated martyr who made human redemption possible. In the story "Tres versiones de Judas," in *Ficciones*, 8th ed. (Buenos Aires: Emecé, 1956), 172-74, the betrayer of Christ is represented as making a personal sacrifice commensurate with that of Christ. Judas is singled out among the apostles as the only one cognizant of Christ's divinity and awesome purpose for living. Just as the *Logos* humbled Itself by assuming human flesh, so Judas humbled himself by becoming a betrayer, condemned to hell. Borges' fictional theologian Runeberg therefore regards Judas as an ascetic of the spirit, who pre-meditated his faults. He acted with humility, believed himself unworthy of being good, and sought hell because the glory of the Lord was sufficient for him.

  In *Saúl ante Samuel*, the antinomy Christ-Judas symbolizes the only datum of Benet's novelistic world—the principle of reality as strife. Judas becomes a necessary instrument of Christ, resolved to bring not peace but war into the world; hence, Martín's grandmother distinguishes Judas from among all the apostles for his capability of perceiving Christ's universal mission. Judas strikes Benet's prophetess as "the most illustrious man, willing to sacrifice anything," for he remains in the shadows without earning the gratitude of redeemed mankind (106-7). To my mind, Benet's debt to Borges is unquestionable. Both are literary skeptics vis-à-vis biblical narrative, regarded by both as fixed and dogmatic; but the debt is only relative, because Benet better integrates the doctrines on Judas into his narrative without resorting, as Borges does, to the fiction of a book review.

8. Simón attributes to Martín a "virgin birth," although his mother had been visited not by the Holy Spirit but by "a force that wandered by night." Like the matriarch Leah, distressed that Jacob does not love her even after she has borne him children (Gen. 29:32-35), Martín's mother is horrified by the idea of his having been born a creature of her body, not of her spirit. Like the matriarch Rachel, who gave her maidservant Bilhah to Jacob and claimed Bilhah's child as if her own (Gen. 30:3), Martín's mother preferred the fiction of the child's legitimacy to her husband's hate (170-71). Martín's appetite of "original vengeance" supersedes his heritage of Original Sin (351). Hence, like a reinherited Esau, coming to reclaim his birthright

(cf. Gen. 27:31), the bastard son Martín, on whom his family depends to save his half-brother, is compared by Simón to "the hairy man who showed off that he was fully entitled to the firstborn's birthright" (217).

9. In view of Saúl's lofty self-image (327) and his father's idea of him as a war hero (324), perhaps Martín serves the interests of both in not rescuing Saúl lest the truth come out about his valuelessness to his Republican enemy (323).

10. By no means do I affirm that Freud is the only possible literary source of Benet's often fictionalized "impulse for return." Unamuno, influenced by Henri-Frédéric Amiel, spoke of a desire for "desnacimiento" ("unbirth"), of a dream of return to infancy, in *La agonía del cristianismo*, and he transmitted that dream to the fiction *San Manuel Bueno, mártir*. See my study of that novel, "Saintliness and Its Unstudied Sources in *San Manuel Bueno, mártir*," in *Studies in Honor of Sumner M. Greenfield*, ed. H. L. Boudreau and Luis T. González-del-Valle (Lincoln, Neb.: Society of Spanish and Spanish-American Studies, 1985), 177.

11. Note that with the Old Testament figure Jehoachin (2 Chron. 36:9; 2 Kings 24:8-17; Jer. 24:1; Ezek. 1:1, 2:5), Benet takes considerable liberties, just as he does with Job, whom he pictures reading "in the gutter of the roof-tile" the eternal lesson of failure (301). Evidently, these narremes do not appear in the Bible. Benet is exercising his freedom as an "unbound poet" to lend gravity to situations lacking it.

THE GREAT IBERIAN BULL RAGES ON:
THE CIVIL WAR AND POSTWAR REPRISALS AS NATIONAL SUICIDE IN JOSÉ LUIS OLAIZOLA AND VICENTE SOTO

William R. Risley

Borges' clever essay, "Kafka y sus precursores," shows how the nature of Kafka's work lets us look back through history and find his roots in writings of Zeno, Han Yu, Kierkegaard, Browning, and others, because "each writer *creates* his own precursors. His work modifies our conception of the past, just as it will modify the future."[1] Although the corpus of Spanish Civil War literature may be too vast and varied to permit accurate generalizations about it, the passage of nearly half a century since the end of the fighting has given time for reflection, study, and clearer understanding of how individuals' direct experiences of the war fit into the "big picture," the *national* experience and its lessons. By carefully researching and reconstructing experiences of the war and the postwar period, contemporary fiction has produced novels that are both intensely national in the circumstances and details of what they recount and genuinely universal as a meditation about intransigence, paranoia, and irrational hatred, major factors in Spain's continuing tendency to destroy much of what is best in itself. From our perspective of 1987, we can look back, as Borges did, and find the precursors of this important vein of Civil War novels in such works as Galdós' *Doña Perfecta* (1876),

Unamuno's *Abel Sánchez* (1917), and even Lorca's play, *La casa de Bernarda Alba* (1936). Two recent novels squarely in this vein are *La guerra del general Escobar*, by José Luis Olaizola, and *Tres pesetas de historia*, by Vicente Soto, both published in 1983.

Olaizola, a Madrid lawyer, has reconstructed the experience of Antonio Escobar Huertas, the Civil Guard soldier who rose from sergeant to general, put down the military uprising in Barcelona in July 1936, was chief of security for Catalonia during the May 1937 anarchist violence, and commanded the Army of Extremadura, crushing the Communist insurrection outside Madrid. Twice he recovered from apparently mortal wounds that had led doctors to declare him clinically dead. He was regarded by both his men and his military opponents as a brilliant soldier. Yet, because he was apolitical, because he chose to remain loyal to his sworn oath and fought on the losing side, he was tried by Franco's kangaroo courts and executed in 1940. He was the first person shot by a firing squad to be accorded full military honors at his execution, although his official record in the national military archives lists him only as a sergeant.

Part of the novel's exceptional power lies in its presentation of Escobar as an exemplary person whose irresistible profile gains the reader's sympathy completely. A man of great honor, he is modest, deeply ethical, deeply religious; having taken the Franciscan vow to poverty, he actively helps the poor. He is bright, clear-thinking, impeccably courteous, and conscientious. He takes pride in his penmanship, in the clarity and precision with which he writes, and in having read all the Spanish, Russian, French, and English literary classics owned by the library of the Civil Guard Academy of Getafe. An inspiring leader and astute psychologist, he is a total professional, a proud career officer from a distinguished military family who is devoted to preserving human life and dignity above all else. Optimistic and altruistic, he is an equally superb family man. He seems the very definition of virtue, in the classical sense of the term.

What gives the novel even greater power than Escobar's noble profile, however, is its special first-person narrating perspective, somewhat reminiscent of Cela's *La familia de Pascual*

Duarte (1942): the spiritual autobiography of a prisoner waiting to die. Escobar has rejected a sure escape from Spain, which the admiring Nationalist General Yagüe, "a gentleman who did everything in his power to save my life,"[2] offered and begged him to accept. Held incommunicado in Barcelona's Montjuich castle during his trial, he is scrupulously writing what most consoles and preoccupies him from his knowledge of the war and its harsh aftermath. This unburdening thus is not *the* truth about the war, which fellow prisoners had urged him to tell but which would be impossibly problematic. Rather, it is his own personal truth, as the novel's title, *La guerra del general Escobar*, suggests: *his* war, *his* right action according to the high principles of his conscience—and also his own deep anguish, always played down, in the midst of absurd circumstances. Escobar's veneration for those few who risked their lives to save many others from indiscriminate slaughter, his constant celebration of the preservation of lives, culminates in a memorable expression: "Personally, it gives me great comfort to see what can be accomplished by the honesty and courage of just one man" (98). This statement, of course, blatantly duplicates Olaizola's and the reader's own inevitable view of the protagonist himself. It is a powerful antithesis both to the Republican politicians' cowardly consent to brutal reprisals, on the one hand, and to Franco's demand for unconditional surrender, his nullification of legal protections for prisoners of war, and his dictation of swift and terribly severe sentences for the losers, on the other. In the face of the new regime's decree of its own infallible rightness and the sanctification of its legitimacy through victory, in the face of its view that all acts performed by its enemies are high treason and its claim that, because of men like Escobar, what should have been a simple restoration of order became instead a civil war, the prisoner boldly tells his military tribunal, "The truth is the truth even if it be upheld by only a minority. Even if that minority be just one person" (198). Escobar's rectitude confers symbolic value on his repeatedly mentioned solitude: his is the extreme aloneness of a man of honor and principle in an alien environment of falsification and perfidy.

The flow of Escobar's memory is marked by abrupt shifts between "then" (the war, past family life) and "now" (the overwhelming solitude and, despite his optimism and good humor, the deep sadness of his cell). The juxtaposed times and situations underscore his strong desire to live and his equally strong conviction that he will be executed. This contrastive technique parallels one of the novel's major successes, its fine depiction of the moral schizophrenia related to a chaotic, fratricidal war. Civil Guards do battle alongside anarchists and against their military comrades, their own family members, and their innermost feelings. At the outset of the war, Escobar's superior, General Aranguren, exclaims, "How hard it will be to fight against our comrades in arms!" When Escobar replies firmly, and in doctrinaire fashion, "No comrade of ours has the right to revolt against the legitimately constituted Government and to put us on the brink of civil war. Our obligation is to prevent it," Aranguren congratulates him on his conviction and wishes he himself had it. Escobar confesses to himself and the reader, "On the inside I was being eaten away by doubt." Aranguren then voices his incredulity: "But do you realize, Escobar, that we are actually fighting alongside of the *anarchists?*" (51). Similarly, Escobar himself ponders the absurdity of having had to serve a government whose ideas he could not share and to fight against his son and his brother. At one point, "I didn't know whether I wanted to save Spain or my son, José" (34). Nearly Kafkaesque is the prosecutor's distortion of events and facts during Escobar's trial, and his keen hindsight: he sustains that as of 19 July 1936, the general should have foreseen everything that was going to happen and therefore acted differently. "He simply cannot understand how I did not find out that Spain was irremissibly divided into two camps and the one that corresponded to me was the other" (25).

Escobar's integrity and dignity produce the directness and understatement that give his reflections the ring of irrefutable truth. His restraint achieves scenes of great intensity, such as his last meeting with his favorite son, whose life "was the most important thing in my own" (46). Olaizola is skilled at portraying communication between friends and loved ones, and he has a fine sense of the tiny details and incidents that bind a life. The result is a moving "human document," in the long-standing Spanish tradition, on the tragic waste of excellence. Its powerful message about injustice compels the reader to agree with the author's final wish about his fiction, expressed in a brief epilogue: "If only what is recounted here had been fiction, too" (216).[3]

The novel is not without a great many insights into the Civil War period. They consist of Escobar's impressions of major figures such as Azaña, Negrín, Rojo, Companys, Mola, Yagüe, etc., and of those well-known trends of the epoch that most deeply trouble him: the Republic's terrible internal strife, its politicians' lack of common sense and inability to heed good advice, the intractability of the radical left, the dreadful senseless violence. At times, they yield interesting images, such as the characterization of the May 1937 chaos in Barcelona, when barbers had machine guns, as "an operetta war" (147). Occasionally, the text sounds like the eternal *tema de España*, the lament for self-destructive Spain, as when it deplores "our sad, unfortunate internal strife" (147) or asks, "If you can't be friends when you disagree, what meaning does life have?" (123). Other times, it rises above the entire situation to sermonize on a universal level: "Can there be anything that justifies us men aligning ourselves against one another to inevitably destroy each other?" (115). The recent Spanish novel it most reminds me of, as a historical reconstruction, is Jesús Torbado's *En el día de hoy* (1976), a fictionalized anti-history based on the gimmicky notion that the Republican side won the Civil War. Like that work, Olaizola's won the Planeta Prize in a disputed verdict, and like that work, it uses for strong ironic effect its characters' supposed naiveté toward the future versus the reader's awareness of how events really turned out. Torbado had Julián Zugazagoitia, who in actual history was shot by Franco's order, appear in the novel urging clemency toward the losers: "If Franco had won the war and I had fallen into his hands, I'm sure I would not be shot."[4] Similarly, Olaizola has Escobar note—supposedly about his own political ingenuousness—that "We military men do not possess political vision, but we are more practical. Military men who get into politics are a disaster" (122).

My reason for playing down this overtly historical and ideological side of *La guerra del general Escobar* in the present paper, however, is to stress the importance of Olaizola's focus on Escobar and his portrayal of him as an ideal man and a victim who did not deserve his fate. The novel has been seen as having little literary value by the critic Abraham Martín-Maestro, who believes "it reads well but its merits end there, since the author develops in depth neither the main character nor the style, attentive only to the impact that such a story [as Escobar's] can have."[5] Like the critique by Sarrias cited above (note 3), this opinion fails to appreciate how tightly the novel's content and style are circumscribed within, and thus dependent on, the personality of its protagonist/narrator. Consequently, Martín-Maestro's view seems to diminish what may be the novel's main achievement, essentially a structural one, and carefully calculated. Presenting Escobar as exemplary has the effect of strongly condemning qualities and conduct antithetical to his: persons who are duplicitous, secretive, self-serving, opportunistic, dishonorable; in other words, General Franco, who is personally pulling the strings and ordering the executions ("and that is why the verdict reached is so harmful to the accused" [194]). It hardly seems coincidental that Escobar is virtually a summary of those traits publicly held in the highest esteem by the Franco regime (which General Rojo, a strong Catholic, accused of "having appropriated our religion" [83])—not to mention that Escobar's father was a hero of the Cuban war, his two brothers Civil Guard colonels, one son a Falangist, and his sister and daughter, devout nuns. Thus, while vindicating the memory of an admirable Spaniard, the novel also uses it to expose the hypocrisy of the regime's official moral stance. The culmination of this structure is a scene in which Escobar's daughter Emilia has an audience with Franco to appeal for her father's life: "Franco's eyes became moist, but he said that what was to become of me did not depend on him" (201). To a significant degree, the novel appears to be written directly against Franco: against the pusillanimous Caudillo of

the postwar reprisals who, instead of healing Spain by drawing
its divided people together, chose to punish his "enemies" as
severely as possible.

The self-exiled Vicente Soto resides in London and is an
established novelist and short-story writer who won the Nadal
Prize for *La zancada* (1966). In contrast to Olaizola's reconstruction of the victimization of one exceptional individual, some of
whose tribulations are representative, Soto has probed modern Spain's greatest upheaval as a collective experience, a vast
tragedy that left its mark—always an exceptional one—upon
every single Spaniard. Although his 1983 novel *Tres pesetas de
historia* is artistically more ambitious than Olaizola's, its impact
nevertheless derives as much from the sheer power of the raw
material itself as from the author's shaping of it.

Soto offers virtually a narrative equivalent of Goya's series
of prints, *The Disasters of War,* and of his large canvas, *The
Third of May 1808, at Madrid: The Shootings on Príncipe Pío
Mountain.* Viz, a Spanish expatriate, finds a cryptic letter and
three one-*peseta* bills of Civil War vintage and sets out to track
down the novel they may contain. Interviews in the small towns
and cities of southeastern Spain gradually uncover tales—each
more shocking than the last—of heroism and horror during the
postwar *franquista* retributions, "lost stories of people now lost
forever."[6] A former mayor of Castellar, the mother of nine children, who did everything possible to save her people from murder and starvation during the war, was jailed for eleven months
under sentence of death. The exhumation of the body of the
last mayor of Villacarrillo—highly symbolic of the novel's own
undertaking—inspires an account of the firing-squad executions
of over six hundred people there, many of them innocent, to
avenge three Nationalist dead. The witness who describes it was
fortunate: classified by a clerical error as a Socialist, he was *only*
imprisoned for four years and then exiled. The detailed experiences of a wife and a mother who accompanied their loved ones
until the end and heard them shot underscore how "Those were
things that could never even be imagined, you know, not even
imagined" (139). The wife was told by her husband to hug and

kiss one of his companions in death who had asked if she could, since he had no one to say goodbye to. She did so for him and for six others whose wives could not be there. The mother poured out her grief over the separation from her son in a powerful primitive ballad which generalizes her experience onto all of Spain. The climactic episode—reminiscent of Ronald Fraser's *In Hiding*[7]—is the odyssey of a man who by chance was not killed by the firing squad; he lay motionless in a mass grave for several hours and has since spent forty-one years closed up in the back room of his own house, afraid to go out into a world that thought him dead.

These hair-raising tales of firing-squad victims, gathered by the mature expatriate, alternate with the autobiography of the Valencian youth of Titín/Vicentín/Vicente, the young Viz (i.e., Soto) before and during the Civil War. It is dense *intrahistoria*, a social atmosphere rendered intensely personal through Vicente's memories: of the new Republic, of the funeral cortege for Blasco Ibáñez in Valencia, and of the audacious, magical new poetry of the Generation of 1927, incarnating a new orientation in art and politics. He recalls how "reality was fleeting, reality was uncertain. What was needed was to fix it in place by creating it anew" (110)—and how "Never has Spain known a poetry so youthful nor more daring . . . they unveiled an art in which reality was recovering its virginity. Submerged in this phenomenon there flowed, warm like blood (it *was* blood), a political and social orientation that was also new, also a true revolution" (110). He remembers feeling that the literary and artistic renovation, centered in imagery, constituted "a medium of communication among men completely unknown until then" (110). Its appearance coincided with the awakening of love and of his writer's vocation. But he also remembers Primo de Rivera's coup and the failed counter-uprising (the *sanjuanada*), the Casas Viejas repressions, the forced politicization of Spanish life despite the wave of popular enthusiasm for the Republic, and the escalating collective madness. He remembers having had to hide the harmless musician Rigoberto, uncle of his best friend, because fanatics wanted to kill him for being "religious" and a "rightist." Vivid in his memory is Rigoberto's great anguish at not being able to play his instruments for fear of being found by his persecutors and of bringing harm to his protectors. Finally, one day he buried himself under three blankets and played his saxophone to avoid going mad. The episode seems to sum up and to symbolize the fate of artists and their new revolution. Lastly, Vicente recalls his agonizing experience—in Madrid, as a soldier at the front—of "the essential inverisimilitude of war" (238). It can be conveyed only through paradoxes such as "this horrible, interminable explosion of the silence of war" (224).

This sort of "second novel," the autobiography, concludes with Vicente's excruciating, futile wait for his best friend Bernabé to return from the Ebro campaign. In fact, the last five of these eighteen chapters (which alternate with the nineteen that tell of the older Viz's travels) consist of only one sentence noting that there has been no letter from Bernabé. It is the story of a silence, an absence, a death never finalized. In reality, though, the two plot lines converge in an impassioned meditation on Spain's homicidal, suicidal violence about which Vicente/Viz, "a person who lost the war, had the obligation to write" (250). He feels that he has "lived" the deaths of so many others that he is bursting with *their* pain and solitude. "He loved the dead people, a great deal, and, naturally, he hated death. To death. . . . He felt he belonged to each dead person's family; he would remember the dead person and an immense solitude would invade him" (80). The Villacarrillo cemetery "deep, deep within its earth holds the bones of those who were executed: bones like roots. They reach down and take root in the very heart of Spain, where they become tangled and twisted together, exploring the history of a people" (96). From paradoxes and images, Viz passes to maxims to condemn *el toro ibérico* (115), the great Iberian bull of intolerance and murderous vengeance that carries hatred beyond the tomb and makes life nourish itself on death: "We must learn not to kill; we must have the virginity of not having killed and must preserve it as an untouchable taboo"; "one dead man is all dead men" (114-15). "Life cannot nourish itself on death"; to kill is to die, to partially kill oneself: "don't let your cadaver survive you" (248).

Near its end, the novel reflects on post-Franco Spain. The strength of Franco's coup, Soto believes, was in the thousands of young men who had nothing to do with him and who acted out of "the terrible force of fear" (239). It implanted exaggerated patriotism, *"patrioterismo,* a reactionary deformation of patriotism" (240). The *pueblo* is good, but vulnerable, because it is too willing to believe: it must be taught to analyze before believing. Soto feels contemporary Spain has by now left its fear and suicidal madness behind and needs not to be saved but to be left in peace, so it can *"truly* enter into the philosophy of the world, far more important than the Common Market" (248). These reflections—and possibly Soto's writing of this novel—are seemingly interrupted by Tejero's coup attempt. It stupifies the patriotic author, who thought Spain had finally extricated itself from its "pit of rancor and revenge" (261), but he takes consolation from King Juan Carlos' message defending the constitution and the democratic process.

Because much of the human testimony of this novel is overwhelming, Soto's style is generally simple and direct, even in its impressionistic recalling of the past and its moral probing; yet, it is not without poetry, subtlety, and considerable structuring. Central unifying images are straightforward but also multiple and highly suggestive. The real winter coldness represents not just all the collective suffering, fear, and death but also the calculating and intransigent Franco, alienation from oneself, and the chilling effect of stories about the executions. Stars, as tiny points of light, are battlefield gunfire, the firing squads' bursts, all the lives snuffed out, yet also an ironic gesture of hope for the Spain of the future, of reaching for the heavens: "The stars can be grasped with our hands" (263).

From Soto's total identification with, or absorption into, the subject matter of his book, and from his increasing obsession with its ongoing creation, a metafictional dimension emerges. The making of this "novel, whose protagonist was many people and also no one, a delicately absurd novel" as Viz foresees it in a dream (25), is called an "adventure" (27), a "movie of images" (97), an "unfinishable crossword puzzle, useless and indispensable" (256), and, in a traditional notion reminiscent of Unamuno's *Niebla*, "an endless skein becoming endlessly entangled" (113) like the bones of the war's victims taking root in the Spanish soil. During his interview with the former mayor of Castellar, Viz finds her to be "overwhelmingly human" (57), a phrase that characterizes Soto's novel perfectly. The line between fiction and reality—a reality consisting of so many events that seem unreal—becomes blurred; there is a continual "transfusion between human beings and fictional characters" (18). The people Viz meets are "beings of blood and flesh and bone who were fantastically authentic, intense like literary characters" (13). He comes to "learn by living it that reality is a feeble manifestation of art" (86). Through the interesting division—or fragmentation—of his personality, the narrator acts as historian, protagonist, and, ultimately, scapegoat. A vast and thoroughly symbolic sensation of confinement generated by the novel—hidden fugitives, suppressed artists, sentenced prisoners, corpses in the earth—parallels Viz's sense of carrying inside himself the whole national nightmare of intense fear, entrapment, and death: the entire Civil War, unended, until he purges himself by completing the novel, or "exorcises himself from it" (216). His catharsis leaves a work of great power, tenderness, and understanding.

At a time when Spanish fiction is displaying considerable variety, inventiveness, and complexity, here are two works that have carefully researched and reconstructed old-fashioned "human documents" and "cases of conscience," direct testimony about the moral drama of the most basic and universal human values. In doing so, they help insert the Spanish Civil War novel into the "theme of Spain" tradition that stretches from the *Poema del Cid*, through the picaresque, Cervantes, Quevedo, Cadalso, Larra, and the Generation of 1898, to the present, probing once more the eternal enigma that is Spain. And the enigma of human personality in tragic circumstances as well.

University of Wisconsin-Madison

William R. Risley

NOTES

1. Jorge Luis Borges, "Kafka y sus precursores," in *Otras inquisiciones* (1952), *Prosa completa* (Barcelona: Bruguera, 1980), 2:226-28. The quotation is on p. 228. All translations from this and other works in Spanish are mine.

2. José Luis Olaizola, *La guerra del general Escobar* (Barcelona: Planeta, 1983), 116. Further references to this work will appear in the text.

3. The reviewer Cristóbal Sarrias finds the novel "so aseptic that I cannot see how it can be considered even as a fictional document about our Civil War" ("*La guerra del general Escobar:* Una semblanza distante," *Reseña de Literatura, Arte y Espectáculos* 148 [1984]: 12). For him, the work is unrealistic because of Escobar's dispassionate, distanced, and inhibited character; his excessive attention to surface details and appearances; a lack of any strong inner feelings; and his strict adherence and total obedience to orders, regulations, and discipline. "A man who is going to die and who wishes to leave the testimony of his experiences and the reasons for his attitudes cannot be so cold, so insistent on traits belonging wholly to a disciplinary epidermis, so reiterative about the emotional problems that arise in him during a time of such intense drama" (12). He considers Escobar's recollection of falling in love with his future wife to have "the naiveté of a superficial *novela rosa*" (12). Sarrias believes that by presenting Escobar in this way, instead of showing him being ripped apart by an internal struggle, Olaizola "is hiding him from us completely, or perhaps they [the author's sources] have hidden him from Olaizola" (12). I attribute Sarrias' negative view of the novel largely to an inability to understand the military ideal of the tight-lipped, stoic officer, to appreciate Escobar's absolute and very deliberate personification of it, and to see how completely Olaizola has written the novel from inside Escobar's personality.

4. Jesús Torbado, *En el día de hoy* (Barcelona: Planeta, 1976), 182.

5. Abraham Martín-Maestro, "La novela española en 1982 y 1983," *Anales de la literatura española contemporánea* 9 (1984): 149-74. The quotation is on p. 152.

6. Vicente Soto, *Tres pesetas de historia* (Barcelona: Argos Vergara, 1983), 7. Further references to this work will appear in the text.

7. Ronald Fraser, *In Hiding: The Life of Manuel Cortes* (New York: Pantheon Books, 1972).

TEXTUAL AUTOBIOGRAPHY IN "HISTORIA de DETECTIVES" AND "EL FANTASMA del CINE ROXY"

William M. Sherzer

One of the techniques most essential to Juan Marsé's novelistic style is intertextuality. He constantly calls upon previous texts in the creation of new ones and at times even evokes future texts yet to be written. Such is the case in *La oscura historia de la prima Montse*, where the description of Hortensia, a young immigrant recalled from the previous novel, evokes the young orphan girls who engage in erotic games with the teenage protagonists of *Si te dicen que caí*, a novel written three years later. In "Historia de detectives," one finds the intertextual process in all its rigor, with an importance for the story that calls to mind Barbara Johnson's description of the concept of difference in a text:

> In other words, a text's difference is not its uniqueness, its special identity. It is the text's way of differing from itself. And this difference is perceived only in the act of rereading. It is the way in which the text's dignifying energy becomes unbound, to use Freud's term, through the process of repetition, which is the return not of sameness but of difference. Difference, in other words, is not what distinguishes one identity from another. It is not a difference between (or at least not between independent units), but a difference within. Far from constituting the text's unique identity, it is that which subverts

the very idea of identity, infinitely deferring the possibility of
adding up the sum of a text's parts or meanings and reaching
a totalized, integrated whole.[1]

Nowhere will one find a more fitting description of Juan Marsé's
"Historia de detectives," the opening story of his recent collection, *Teniente Bravo*.

The plot of this narrative moves gradually forward, toward
the culmination of a relatively simple hermeneutic, but the same
signifiers that create the plot and plot structure are used simultaneously to look backwards metafictionally so as to describe
the author and his personal view of his craft. Marsé has entered
his texts before (as a minor character in *Ultimas tardes con
Teresa*, for example), and may be closely identified with Paco
Bodegas, the first-person narrator of *La oscura historia de la
prima Montse*, but this is the first text in which the author
undertakes a systematically encoded description of his personal
relationship with his narrative technique.

A reading of this story presents the problem that Marsé's
penchant for intertextual narration constantly creates. An
uninitiated reader of Marsé will find himself before a conventional plot structure in which a group of young boys of
the immediate postwar period plays at detectives, sending one
of them to follow a woman whose husband is thought to be in
prison as a result of the war. After the appearance of a few
stereotyped characters from the historical moment, a distraught
second figure appears, purportedly the husband of the woman
we have already seen. A second boy follows him and will later
relate his findings to the group, as did the first young detective.
At the conclusion of the story, the supposed husband is found
hanging, a tragic suicide. There is no proof of the relationship
between the two characters, but the leader of the young detectives, Juanito Marés, seems to possess an unquestionable ability
to divine the truth. The problem created is that this is but the
surface narrative. For the reader who is familiar with Marsé's
previous texts, the language and characters created here serve
as a theoretical introduction to the techniques and style the
writer employs both in this story and in those that follow. At

the same time, this language and these characters reintroduce the author to the reader, both as author and as narrator, and clarify Marsé's prose development in what one might call his "second epoch," that which began in 1973 with the publication of *Si te dicen que caí.* It becomes clear to the reader, in this story and in the second narrative of the collection, "El fantasma del Cine Roxy," that with the exception of *La muchacha de las bragas de oro,* an interlude in which the author parodies the memoirs of Pedro Laín Entralgo, the literature produced by Marsé since 1973 is a product of and reconnection with the inventive mind and experiences of his youth.

The fact that the key character in "Historia de detectives" is named Juanito Marés constitutes an obvious clue that the author sees himself inside his narrative. But the obvious is only a point of departure for a much more complicated plot structure that continues to constitute a definition of the author in relation to his work. Marés is, in effect, the everyday Marsé, fully involved with the characters he creates; what literary criticism refers to as the author, as opposed to the implied author. The first-person narrator, Mingo Roca, tells us early on that Marés speaks with a "ventriloquist's voice"[2] and later describes the importance Marés represents for the group's collective imagination:

> When all is said and done, Juanito Marés was somewhat older than us, he had been raised here and was Catalán, also a bit of a contortionist and ventriloquist: more serious, he knew more languages, he was better prepared than we were. That's why he was the leader. (29)

Marés' ideas inform Roca's narration. Roca becomes, therefore, the implied author, the author as author of this particular narration.

This secondary identification of Roca as Marsé is not simply a deduction drawn from the narrative structure. Fictitious and real biographical information coincide to support the identification. A neighborhood merchant, speaking pejoratively of Roca, tells us that his father "is in jail because he's a robber and

because he's a red separatist" (17). Two pages later, Mingo
accepts, amplifies, and corrects the merchant's description:

> When he said that stuff about my father being in jail, I low-
> ered my head, took off my hat and stuck it inside my shirt;
> not because I was ashamed, but because of the anger he
> provoked in me by what he said. It's a very flexible hat, one
> of the good kind, a real Stetson, especially good for following
> blondes around on rainy days. I did it for my father, out of
> respect for the memory of that red republican separatist gun-
> man with the snap-brimmed hat over his eyes. (19)

One sees here a possible reference to Palau, one of the *maquis* of
Si te dicen que caí, who, enveloped in a raincoat and hat, follows
his son Mingo to the Hotel Ritz in order to rob a blonde call girl
who has just received some jewels from the boy, an apprentice
in a jewelry shop. Without discarding the validity of this reference, one must also add the direct connection to Juan Marsé
himself, whose father was in jail in the forties, having been
first a member of Esquerra Republicana and later of the PSUC.
The two references are neatly joined by the fact that Marsé also
began his career as a jeweler's apprentice.

Continuing to apply narrative terminology to the characters
of this text, we may see Jaime and David, the two remaining
boys, as internal readers of Mingo Roca's narration, an audience upon which the implied reader eavesdrops. Two more
narrative constructs develop, however, for David has followed
the husband and assumes the role of an internal narrator (what
Genette calls a metadiegetic narrator)[3] in order to inform Roca
of what he has recently witnessed. As a culminating action,
Juanito Marés, the one character who has not left the car that
serves as a base of operations, presents a complete and plausible
resolution of the mystery that has developed through the other
characters' narrations. His method is novelistic, a hermeneutic
developed in relation to the internal narration:

> He always said the same thing and acted in the same way,
> putting off as long as possible the resolution of the enig-
> ma. . . . He analyzed all the data, he confronted it all, he asked
> for certain clarifications on certain details which seemed

unimportant, and, finally, after rejecting our suggestions, imposed his criteria through deductions about cause and effect that always seemed plausible to us, giving the suspects' behavior a bitter motivation that we had not foreseen. (28)

The readers' lack of confidence is similar to that expressed by Sarnita's youthful public towards the end of *Si te dicen que caí*. Here, as in the earlier work, the speaker's authority is questioned:

> —Don't fire blindly, Coyote—I told him.
> Proof, chief—said David slapping him on the back—we don't have any proof. (34)

At the conclusion of the story, Marés prevails. His version of the events turns out to be the true one, and the narration concludes with Roca's evocation of his friend's magical ability to see and create the unsuspected truth:

> But above all I think about Juanito Marés huddled in that old rusted-out shell of a Lincoln Continental, alone, enveloped in the pure blue smoke of his aromatic herbal cigarettes, intoxicated with thoughts of crimes and dangerous widows, unfortunate loves and complicated crimes. (39)

Through this interrelation of characters, Marsé defines the tension that exists between his real self and his narrating self. Marés' rectification of and imposition upon the implied author is a manifestation of Marsé's inability to remove that real self who experienced the *barrio* life of the immediate postwar period from the narration he writes. What one finds here is a fiction invented in order to describe the real-life process through which that fiction and others that preceded it came about.

The series of particular autobiographical[4] elements of this story begins at the very outset of the narration, with the introduction of the two worlds that constantly clashed in Juan Marsé's adolescent life and continue to do so in his contemporary fiction: adventurous fantasy and drab reality. From the northern outskirts of the city, previously Manolo Reyes' perch early in *Ultimas tardes con Teresa*, the narrator evokes an imaginary vision of earringed, tattooed pirates in the port of Barcelona, only to contrast it with the real world of the author and the youths who served as prototypes for his later fictitious characters:

> But on those gray days, his gaze gets confounded with the mist and the scratchy smoke that infest the labyrinth of Horta and La Salud, and is never able to get beyond it. The city—remote and gray—is stagnant, like a muddy pool, like standing water. (7)

As a self-taught writer, Marsé's first attraction was the adventure novel. This was to clash with the real world of the poor youths he found daily in the streets of postwar Barcelona. Marsé the novelist reflects this division. The young boys of *Si te dicen que caí* invent fantastic adventures in order to escape from the poverty-stricken world described above. Everything in the present narration seems carefully styled to reflect this double reality. The four boys are seated in a Lincoln, but it has a shattered windshield and is situated in a deserted lot. The young Señora Yordi appears as if in their dreams, "with a gray beret and a light-colored raincoat, very pale, very beautiful and tearful" (8). Her description is typical of a film heroine and fits neatly into the evocation of *The Naked City* that follows immediately, but she is also reminiscent of Aurora Nin, the ephemeral and decrepit heroine of *Si te dicen que caí* who dies in a similar vacant lot alongside a broken-down Ford.

The actantial movement of this story, independent of autobiography or metafiction, begins when Roca leaves the car:

> I threw away the cigarette, pulled my hat down till it almost reached my nose, and got out of the car without being able to take my eyes off those long legs obscured by her stockings and the rain, as she crossed a sea of black mud. (9)

But Roca's movements are not narrated in an actantial mode. The chapter ends with the sentence, "On seeing her disappear around the corner, I turned up the collar of my jacket and picked up my pace" (11), but chapter two finds Roca back in the Lincoln, prepared to narrate what he has been doing for the past two hours. Roca's category of narrator/implied author, as opposed to actor, is in this way emphasized. This internal narrator who lights a cigarette and narrates is, at the same time, a creation of Marsé and a vision of Marsé as author.

Regarding this self-vision, Marsé creates an ironic twist that has appeared earlier in his fiction. In *Ultimas tardes con Teresa*, Marsé laughed goodheartedly at himself by naming a perverse, rear-pinching character Juan Marsé. In "Historia de detectives," when Roca describes Señora Yordi in poetic phrases typical of Marsé, Marés silences him immediately, stating dryly, "When I want details about her, I'll ask for them" (12). Once again, the author makes light of himself, as the adventure-minded author (Marés) censures the poetic tendencies of the implied author/narrator Roca. This passage is extremely representative of a basic tension in Marsé's prose. In a career that spans from 1957 to the present, Marsé manifests a definite consciousness of the evolutionary changes that have taken place in the style and format of contemporary Spanish prose. Although he has made singular contributions to that evolution, notably with *Si te dicen que caí*, he has always preoccupied himself with preventing technical innovation from obscuring anecdotal content.

Another possible self-definition might be seen in Señora Yordi's description of the young detectives: "they are only kids acting as if they were in the movies" (18). Marsé worked in a film studio early in his life, and later wrote the script for "Libertad condicional" and collaborated on the film version of *Ultimas tardes con Teresa*. Film, especially when evoked in a nostalgic vein—"El fantasma del Cine Roxy" is the best example—is a constant source for Marsé's melodramatic and romantic moments.

As the story line evolves, the signifiers continue to work in both directions: toward the development of a plot resolution and toward a constant evocation of characters and situations from previous works. When Marés guffaws at Roca's pretending to tie his shoe in an attempt to find a posture from which to see his prey more closely, the initiated reader understands that he is privy to an inside joke. Roca's action is a recreation of that of a perverse old vagabond, Mianet, in *Si te dicen que caí*, who used to look up young women's dresses through mirrors installed in his shoes. The Lincoln Continental calls to mind a Ford which serves various purposes, again in *Si te dicen que caí*. The Cine Roxy is practically a character in previous novels and will definitely become one in the second story of this collection. The imaginary sequence in which Roca saves Señora Yordi through mouth-to-mouth resuscitation is an adventure similar to those narrated by Java and Sarnita in the earlier novel. David and his "rocky marmalade cough" is a recreation of the tubercular Luisito Lage, one of the young boys of the 1973 novel. We have already seen that Mingo Roca is virtually the son of *Si te dicen que caí's* Palau. The Falangist who offers to help Señora Yordi, while taking advantage of her sexually, is a resurrection of *Flecha Negra*, the malevolent Falangist of the same novel. Marés' declaration that he knows the typical actor's mentality—"I know them and I can smell them from a distance, many of them have been in my house" (30)—reminds one of the situation of Paco Bodegas of *La oscura historia de la prima Montse*, whose mother lived with a series of men who were all involved in the world of film. And, returning to the essential connection with *Si te dicen que caí*, two all-important sign functions are formed that sum up the concept of intertextual flow as the basis for the organization of this story: Marés' shaved head that "smelled like powder" (36), and his transformation into a scorpion toward the end of the story. The scorpion is a figure that travels throughout *Si te dicen que caí*, appearing in all levels of society. Among other things, it represents the ultimate societal interrelation between the various characters and groupings of the world of the novel. The shaved head, though reminiscent of so many children in the early postwar period,[5] is directly connected to Sarnita of *Si te dicen que caí*, Marsé's favorite fictitious narrator.

One sees Marsé here using elements from earlier works, not simply because his author found success or satisfaction with those elements, but because Marés is Marsé, not the implied but the real author, making use of this particular text to portray the biography of his narrative technique. Two final examples from the text clarify this point even further. When Marés disdainfully says to his companions, "Is it clear, you damn illiterates from Murcia?" (30), he enunciates the difference that exists between Juan Marsé, the author, and the young men of Murcia who grew up around him and became the source of so many of his works. And when Marés redescribes, with important modifications, the character who meets Señora Yordi in the bar, he is totally in line with the novelistic technique of his creator, who has often revised texts in later editions, the most salient case being *Esta cara de la luna*. "El fantasma del Cine Roxy" is another, and the most recent example of this technique.

In conclusion, although there is a definite plot line to this story, its actantial dimensions are very sparse, and almost all knowledge of that plot is acquired through metadiegetic narration. The true direction of this story, while paying lip service to the concept of plot and hermeneutics, seems to be an autobiographical portrait of the author as text through the evocation of those elements, mostly from *Si te dicen que caí*, that have gone into the evolution of Marsé's style since the publication of that all-important novel.

In "El fantasma del Cine Roxy," one finds a practical application of the technique Marsé defines in "Historia de detectives." Here Marsé creates a nostalgic vision of the Republican soldier, in the person of Vargas, and connects that figure metonymically to the decline in direct resistance to the Franco regime. Certain elements from the first story are repeated. The former soldier/vagabond lives in the same Lincoln that housed the four young boys of the first story. More importantly, there is again a fantasy-reality division, represented by the writer (fantasy) and the director (reality) of the film for which the writer has prepared a script. The director is simply incapable of capturing the emotional connection to the past that, for the writer, erases the distinction between fantasy and reality. The Cine Roxy, for example, while unimportant for the director, is an essential site for the writer (Marsé) in his youth, as all readers of *Si te dicen que caí* well know.

The obsession with the theater and the films shown in the Roxy leads the writer to connect the character of Vargas to Shane, the solitary hero of the movie of the same name.

The connection is ironic, because while Shane maintains his heroic character throughout, and moves on to other possible adventures at the end of the film, Vargas gradually declines in stature and finally takes on the role of servant rather than that of savior. While the Vargas-Shane relationship is clear from a textual reading of "El fantasma del Cine Roxy," a secondary reading of this character results from an intertextual comparison with his predecessors: "El Taylor" of *Si te dicen que caí,* and Jan Julivert of *Un día volveré.* All three men are *pistoleros,* and in the evolution of this figure one might discern Marsé's pessimistic attitude towards anti-Franco resistance from 1942 to 1985 (the first vision of "El Taylor" and the last of Vargas).

The three characters are introduced similarly: through the eyes of young boys inside the text. "El Taylor" is known to the reader as an urban maquis but also to the youths as a romantic neighborhood hero. His nickname (his real name is Meneses) derives from his resemblance to Robert Taylor:

> The silent shadow that at that moment passed them was Margarita's boyfriend: he passed them by without seeing them, his pockmarked face white and hard as ice. Sarnita crouched down as if she had heard a mortar shell. "El Taylor" walked with his arms apart as if he had tumors in his armpits, not paying attention to anything, with his black hair all greased down, and he passed so close to them that they smelled the sweat in his armpits.[6]

Aside from this cinematographic image, the pistols of "El Taylor" also serve to define him. His arms are separated from his body, as if he had swollen glands in his armpits, when in reality what causes this are the pistols that he wears in twin shoulder holsters: thus the leathery smell. These weapons come into play during one of the most heroic moments of the text when "El Taylor," after killing one policeman, finds himself in a shoot-out with two others:

> "El Taylor" drops the box, changes his revolver to the other hand, takes his other one out of its holster and begins to fire with both of them at the same time running in a crouch toward the next column. He feels a burning sensation on his

> wrist, his gun drops from his hand and falls to the floor. He
> slips and falls on his hip at the same time the two cops jump
> on him, but they don't get up, and he begins to run through
> the tunnel that leads to the subway. (246)

Marsé's final words in this novel show his skepticism (looking backward, of course): "Men of iron, forged in so many battles, dreaming like children" (368); but one recognizes in these words, and throughout the novel, the heroic quality the author attaches to the urban maquis. "El Taylor" will come to a violent end, but only after fighting valiantly in the streets, and his final moments also remind the reader of the romantic aspect of his character:

> His eyelids were heavy, but he did not have time to close them.
> As if Margarita all of a sudden were at his side, he noted with
> surprise how the blood was leaving his body. When Jaime
> stood him up, he was already dead, and they left him there,
> with his face against the steering wheel just as if he were
> sleeping. (336-37)

Jan Julivert's character, similarly introduced through the eyes and adventures of neighborhood youths, is equally shrouded in mystery and adventure: "a man with his attributes, an ex-boxer and ex-gunman, was an invincible and fascinating combination."[7] While "El Taylor" was just one of the maquis in *Si te dicen que caí*, Julivert is the central character of *Un día volveré*. At the outset of the novel, he is about to be released from prison, after many years, and he is expected to resume his rebellious ways, at least in order to punish those who caused his incarceration. His character goes through a gradual degradation. Not only does he not take up his urban guerrilla battle where he left off, he places himself in a totally servile relationship to the people upon whom the reader would expect him to take vengeance. Amid suggestions that Julivert has a homosexual relationship with the very judge who sentenced him to prison, the novel concludes with the assassination of both men. But while the judge's death is a planned assassination, Julivert, unarmed, virtually forces Klein's killers to shoot him, pretending to reach for a nonexistent pistol.

The transition from "El Taylor" to Julivert is ironic. While "El Taylor" is only one of the myriad characters in the novel in which he appears, Julivert is the protagonist and by far the most important figure in *Un día volveré*. However, Julivert's greater importance for this work is accompanied by a total degradation of the man who was once at least equal to the heroics and bravery of "El Taylor." He has been vanquished, and though still a hero in the eyes of his nephew Nestor, he marches slowly towards the death he accepts.

Vargas is Marsé's latest commentary on the plight of the vanquished of the Spanish Civil War. Once again the reader encounters a gunman, and once again he is focused on through the eyes of young boys, who see him approach, and whose youthful innocence creates a sense of camera-like objectivity in the description of the protagonist:

> The dirty faces of three boys pushed against the glass (looking out from inside) amidst folders and books and colored pencils and the vagrant advancing, still in the distance, his face (a blurred reflection in the glass) on the other side of the avenue endless like a sea of mud.[8]

The cinematographic quality of Vargas' first appearance and the original evolution of his character from effacement to hero is contradicted by a preemptive plot summary that undermines any heroic potential created from the perspective of the children, internal readers of the text, as were David and Jaime in the first story of his collection:

> We have a young immigrant, pariah-deserter, or whatever you want to call him, who, in 1941, arrives half dead at the northern outskirts of Barcelona, and destiny makes of him the defender of a young Catalan widow and her little girl, standing up to some young Falangists and tough guys of the neighborhood and who winds up working for them the rest of his life.[9] (53)

This early statement of the entire plot, a trait that is found earlier in Marsé's prose, returns the reader to the concept of authorial omniscience that was highlighted through Juanito

Mares' power to rewrite Mingo Roca's narration in "Historia de detectives." The story loses its direct connection to the anecdote as seen in the eyes of the children and Susana, the bookseller, and takes on a second expression, stated from the vantage point of the author only. What the reader encounters in this second expression is the potential for heroism that Vargas possesses, but a potential that is viewed with definite pessimism, since, from the beginning, one is told simply that he will work for Susana and her daughter the rest of his life. The Shane figure is slowly undone. Although he acts with bravado more than once, Vargas never achieves a stature that the course of events seems to prepare him for. There is only an insinuation of romance, and the return of Susana's husband, Estevet, puts an end to its possible fruition. The reader's last glimpse of Vargas is one of a tired old man, a faithful helper to his employers, with no trace of his previous heroism:

> The last image of Vargas: an old lame and distracted old man who is cleaning the windows of the ROSA D'ABRIL bookstore with a cloth, and who has a shock when he sees some kids come by making a lot of noise with firecrackers, and who throw a cherry bomb at his feet. (106)

The reader has come a long way from the combative, heroic figure of "El Taylor." It is very interesting to compare the concept of submission that evolves through these three characters. "El Taylor" simply did not submit, but died in battle. Jan Julivert, for reasons purposely left unclear, submits to a character from the victorious side of the Civil War. Vargas submits to Estevet, who has also lost the war, thus making Vargas' final situation, in a sense, a submission to the second degree. Vargas represents the final degradation, a total pacification of the heroic figure of the maquis, of the active combatant in favor of freedom and democracy in Spain. Marsé's tragic message could not be clearer.

As in all of Marsé's work, each of the texts mentioned here exists as an independent entity. The adventures of Juanito Mares and his friends can be read simply as that adventure, and Vargas' forty-four years in the bookstore can be seen as the life story of a particular veteran of the Republican army.

But "Historia de detectives" is also a manual on how to read Marsé's prose; and when one applies that manual to the second story, the significance of its protagonist is far greater. Vargas, seen intertextually in the light of "El Taylor" and Jan Julivert, constitutes not just a particular character in a particular text, but a part of a larger evolution in Juan Marsé's continuing creative process, as well as the final element of a romantic but tragic portrayal of those who hoped to resist the rule of fascism in postwar Spain.

Brooklyn College

NOTES

1. Barbara Johnson, *The Critical Difference* (Baltimore: The Johns Hopkins University Press, 1980), 4.

2. Juan Marsé, "Historia de detectives," in *Teniente Bravo* (Barcelona: Seix Barral, 1987), 8. Further references to this work will appear in the text. All translations are mine.

3. Gerard Genette, *Narrative Discourse,* trans. Jane E. Lewin (Ithaca: Cornell University Press, 1983), 29.

4. I prefer autobiographical to metafictional in this case, because what the reader finds is actually a continuous text's (Marsé's intertextual production) autobiographical description of its own coming into being.

5. The shaved head is equally prevalent in the fiction written about that period. Cf., for example, Jesús Fernández Santos' *Cabeza rapada.*

6. Juan Marsé, *Si te dicen que caí,* ed. William M. Sherzer (Madrid: Cátedra, 1982), 97. Further references to this work will appear in the text.

7. Juan Marsé, *Un día volveré* (Barcelona: Plaza Janés, 1982), 13.

8. Juan Marsé, "El fantasma del Cine Roxy," in *Teniente Bravo,* 51. Further references to this work will appear in the text.

9. Curiously, in an earlier version, Marsé chose not to prestate Vargas' entire history, ending this paragraph with the word "neighborhood."

FOXÁ'S
MADRID, de CORTE a CHECA:
FASCISM AND ROMANCE

Antonio Varela

Anyone interested in exploring deeply into Spanish fascism's reason for being and its relation to the events and personalities associated with the Spanish Civil War will be enlightened by a reading of *Madrid, de corte a checa.*[1] This fairly well-known, but not seriously studied, novel first appeared in 1938, in the midst of the Spanish Civil War. Its author, Agustín de Foxá (1903-1959) was a member of Falange Española, the fascist movement founded by José Antonio Primo de Rivera. The novel contains a fascist theme, protagonist, and value system. It is the story of why one man chose to become a fascist. Its view of fascism is especially Spanish, and thus it provides valuable information, not only about an individual's personal fascistic impulse, but also about the nature that impulse was forced to take within a specific society and time.

It is *Madrid, de corte a checa*'s connection to social realities and specific historic events and personalities that makes it a more significant work for this study than the other two well-known Spanish novels that deal with nascent fascist spirits: *Eugenio o proclamación de la primavera* by Rafael García Serrano (1938) and *Leoncio Pancorbo* by José María Alfaro (1942).[2] The work of García Serrano is so intensely lyrical, and its characters so reduced to compulsion in their actions, as to be almost completely disembodied from specific social reality. Alfaro's more philosophical approach gives *Leoncio Pancorbo* a quality that recalls the Generation of 1898's tendency to create abstractions of social reality which are used as the basis of a search for ultimate human truths. This technique can lead to profound insights, but it also tends to distance itself from specifics. It is *Madrid, de corte a checa* that provides the reader with a specifically fascist delineation of the events, political parties, ideologies, and personalities that would carry Spain into its Civil War.

Madrid, de corte a checa is also paradigmatic of Spanish fascist discourse. This study, therefore, includes an attempt to further the important task of demonstrating the nexus between fascist attitudes and fascist textual form. In this vein, Anthony Geist discovers in his study of popular Spanish fascist poetry that "ideology functions as a subliminal presence determining the configuration and formal shape of a literary artifact. Sociopolitical structures determine aesthetic structures."[3]

The single most determinant factor in *Madrid, de corte a checa*'s discourse is its narrative mode. It is a Romance. Hayden White, following Northrop Frye's groundbreaking *Anatomy of Criticism*, has defined Romance's essence thus:

> The Romance is fundamentally a drama of self-identification symbolized by the hero's transcendence of the world of experience, his victory over it, and his final liberation from it—the sort of drama associated with the Grail legend or the story of the resurrection of Christ in Christian mythology. It is a drama of the triumph of good over evil, of virtue over vice, of light over darkness, and of the ultimate transcendence of man over the world in which he was imprisoned by the Fall.[4]

Much has happened to Romance from its inception to the present day, but the truth is that on its modal framework can be mounted the majority of Spain's fascist novels.[5] In this, *Madrid, de corte a checa* is paradigmatic. In it, against the backdrop of a Manichean struggle between forces embodying good and evil, is presented the search for self-identification of a hero who incarnates idealism and good. Self-identification, itself, is usually expressed by fascists as a union between the individual and the fascist sense of Nation.

Romance's great achievements in European literature tend to belong to precapitalist times. Since the advent of capitalism and the bourgeoisie, realism and psychology have eroded Romance's hold on serious fiction. *Madrid, de corte a checa* as a political novel of the twentieth century bears some of the trappings of realism and psychology in its presentation, but its basic view of the world is that of Romance. Fascism is essentially incompatible with either the realist or the psychological novel as they are normally understood. Realism seeks to understand its characters' lives by investigating their entrapment within a social scheme, and the psychological novel likes its characters victimized by impulses that are universal. Neither of these genres have much use for heroes. *Madrid, de corte a checa*, true to fascist belief, sees the social scheme and the individual as objects to be dominated by a fundamental fascist concept, *will* (both personal and national). The individual is to *create himself* according to fascist ideals, and society exists to be revolutionized and invigorated by him. A strong society will in turn give a dignified existence (understood in strictly fascist terms) to its people. Will, for the fascist, gives meaning to life. There is room here for Romance and heroes.

Madrid, de corte a checa, for all its politics, does borrow its basic structure from an author who was hardly inclined toward fascism. The novel is constructed like one of Benito Pérez Galdós' *Episodios Nacionales*. Indeed, Foxá, in the first edition, called his work an "Episodio Nacional" (5). Like an "episodio," it recounts, as history, events that occurred close to, or contemporary with, its author's life. It also consists of two interwoven plots; one can be described as the historical plot and the other as the fictional. Galdós' interweaving of plots could be quite subtle, as Hinterhauser has indicated.[6] Nothing on the finest Galdosian level occurs in Foxá's work.

What *Madrid, de corte a checa* does have is a need to define a fascist ideal and to contrast that ideal to what is not fascist. The ugly contrasts tend to occur within the historical plot, while the ideal is revealed within the fictional plot. The two plots carry different themes. The historical one concerns itself with national degeneration, while the fictional one concerns itself with a personal regeneration that is eventually to save the nation.

The titles of the three parts of the novel make plain what is outlined in the historical plot. The first part is called "Flores de lis"; it deals with the decline of the reign of Alfonso XIII. The second part is "Himno de Riego" (the title of the liberal anthem of the nineteenth century), and it presents the Republic that Franco would try to overthrow. The third part, "Hoz y martillo," deals with the first months of the Spanish Civil War when the Republic's government comes under the influence of Communists. The work's title thus moves us from the "corte" of the Bourbons to the "checa" (or CHEKA), the Soviet Union's secret police force against counterrevolutionaries and the predecessor of today's KGB. According to the novel's value system, Spain degenerates. The country goes from the ineffectuality of the monarchy to the Republic with its chaotic debates and slow way of proceeding, to the ultimate horror, the dehumanizing spirit of communism.

Interwoven through the tripartite historical framework of the novel is the fictional plot. It is the biography of José Félix Carrillo, a young man trying to find himself. José Félix, in the beginning and middle of the book, develops from a serious but callow youth, who is easily seduced by the decadent political and cultural life of Madrid, into a follower of José Antonio. The last third of the novel does not take the development of this character forward; rather, the story of José Félix lapses into a series of melodramatic adventures depicting the witch hunt of fascists by Republican forces. Eventually, José Félix escapes to France and from there reenters Spain to continue his struggle within the regular Nationalist army. Running counter to the historical situation is the theme of regeneration that is expressed by José Félix's rise to fascism. The fascist regeneration produces the hero who strives against all odds and eventually shows the way to salvation.

For clarity's sake, it would be best to discuss the significant content of each plot separately. The historical plot will be studied first, because it will help focus fascism in relation to political personalities, events, and attitudes with which the reader probably will be more familiar.

Fascism in *Madrid, de corte a checa* is a set of political values and partly a spiritual attitude. In a novel dedicated to showing the fascist way, all other political views are shown to be corrupting influences on the individual and the state, or ineffectual in solving problems. The value system of the work advocates the destruction of fascism's two great opponents, democracy and communism. Democracy is viewed as fragmenting the national fabric and destroying character, because it causes strong values to weaken through the process of perceiving and accepting other points of view. Communism is viewed as a vicious import (not born out of Spanish historical experience) that desires to turn the natural social order completely on its head, because it exalts a coldly materialistic view of life. Typically, fascism likes to view itself as neither of the left or right; it is the nation that is to be served, not a party or a philosophy.

Juan Ignacio Ferreras has made some observations about novels that exalt the Nationalist cause: these novels employ an easy moral dualism; they often demonstrate rancor toward their enemies or the defeated; they aim to justify rather than explain.[7] These traits can be applied directly to *Madrid, de corte a checa*. In its description of fascism's enemies, Foxá's discursive technique has a tendency to caricature and ridicule; this stratagem explains nothing, but it does justify the true believer's hatred of the enemy. The procedure can be noted in the following example drawn from the novel. Described is Manuel Azaña, president of the Spanish Republic.

> He was the symbol of the mediocre in their glorious hour of revenge. A mean and gray world of pedagogues and petty postal bureaucrats, of dumb little lawyers and interminable talkers who were triumphing. He was the wreaker of vengeance for the anonymous Garcias and Gonzalezes and their little pots of stew and their coldwater flats, overladen with kids and with envy, strolling with their fat wives in the West Park . . . he was the symbol of a colorless world that smelled of a cheap heater, of the *Heraldo de Madrid* and of a renter's contract. (104)

This description of Azaña, standing bare within the context of this study, does not give a real clue to how the reader is to take this character. Dickens, in *A Tale of Two Cities*, employs at times a similar style to describe characters that are not likeable but are nevertheless comprehensible, because the reader is permitted to understand their motives. In Dickens, there is a cause to go along with the effect. In *Madrid, de corte a checa*, there is no cause given for Azaña's actions except his personality, which is described through his way of speaking: "He spoke coldly, icily and profusely. His phrasing was literary and spiked with cynicism and irony, with false pride, because he wanted to 'dazzle,' to disconcert, to wound. . . . He was a poet of hate, a polemicist of vengeance" (104). Although this man and his followers seem to have some ax to grind, the reader is never told exactly what it is. More significantly, the reader is not invited to feel their cause. Why do these people have a desire for vengeance? The focus is not on answering that question, but, rather, in defining them as dangerously angry. Naturally, this technique justifies reprisals taken against them. The Manichean division of social questions, brought about by description without explanations, leads naturally to a hierarchy of morals and values. Those who oppose fascism are relegated to an inferior position because they are ignorant, lazy, or evil; and the more they oppose, the more inferior they are forced to become.

This vertical approach to the ordering of social forces conjures up the hierarchical concepts of monarchy, its attendant aristocracy, and the Church. These were precisely the institutions which could best express themselves through the narrative mode of Romance, a narrative mode neatly taken over by fascism. It should, therefore, not be surprising that in the novel the old monarchy and the Catholic church are the most favored groups within Spanish society's non-fascist elements. Historically, in fact, the Carlists, with their monarchical and Catholic fervor, were with the Falange, the most intensely dedicated Nationalists.

The monarchy, however, does receive criticism. Monarchists are depicted as living in a poetic and romantic past when the nation was united, and at times very powerful, and, hence, close to a fascist ideal; but in the circumstances of the present century, they are perceived as having no new ideas. Instead, they are prone to while the time away with their now meaningless ceremonies, which are viewed as little more than occasions for wearing fancy costumes. The worst aspects of archly rightist politics are gathered in the figure of the old-line monarchist, Miguel Solís, who represents all that is mindlessly traditional and spiritually moribund. The character is treated no better than Azaña. Still, significantly, José Félix is of aristocratic stock. His father is a monarchist, and although the older man at first cannot understand his son's attitudes, the son never loses reverence for his family. Monarchists and aristocrats are rendered in broader perspective than Azaña and his followers. Among the aristocracy, there are good and bad; there are those worth keeping and those not.

Solís' death is of special concern, because it also points out how powerful the force of Catholicism is in the work. José Félix's great love is Pilar. She is married to Solís. In one episode, Pilar, who is brutally treated by Solís, plans to run away with José Félix. At the last minute, she reneges because of her strong Catholic faith. She is permitted to unite with José Félix only after Solís' death. Thus, the sanctity of the Catholic view of marriage and family, already seen in José Félix's respectful attitude towards his father, is maintained. The traditional Catholic concept of family, of the protective and dominant father and the nurturing mother, links easily to Hernán Vidal's description of the fascist concept of family.

> The male head of the family embodies, on the family level, the principle of authority that the fascist leader exhibits on the national level. The father figure acquires the image of a warrior that needs the support, comfort and physical pleasures of his wife to renew his corporal and spiritual energy for the daily struggle. A wife must, therefore, sublimate herself. She must be simple, "feminine," and maternal, the perfect nurturer. She is exhorted to be proud of being the unifying force in the home out of which come the soldiers of the country.[8]

It would be too much to accept Catholicism as favoring only the creation of warriors, but the notion of family as reflecting the larger social bonds of leader and unified national family, of the active father as leader, the nurturing mother as unifying force, could be and was easily absorbed by fascism in Spain. These concepts certainly found their real application in such cornerstones of the Movimiento Nacional as "el caudillo" and the central tenet of strong centralist authority.

To the aristocracy and the Church can be linked the clear historical truth that Spain's greatest moments of military and imperial glory were linked to a crusading impulse that saw Spaniards drive the Moors back, defeat the Turks at Lepanto, and conquer the New World. How easy, then, for Franco to weld fascism and Catholicism to create the appropriately named "Cruzada." Payne points out that Franco created a shotgun marriage between fascism, the Church, monarchists, and conservatives in order to create his Movimiento Nacional. Franco so gutted fascism that it was no longer fascism.[9] This is true, but it is also true that all fascists responded deeply to the Reconquest and to the imperial might of Charles I with their blend of political power and religious fervor. Spanish fascists did not reject the Church fully. Foxá, Alfaro, and García Serrano either accepted Catholicism or did not object strongly to it. José Antonio himself took the very symbols of Spanish fascism, the yoke and arrows, from the Catholic kings and Charles I, as he declared in a speech at Valladolid. In his speech, he quotes from a letter sent in 1516 by the city of Valladolid to Charles I:

> Your Highness should come to take in his hand the yoke that your grandfather, the Catholic king, left us, with which so many fierce and proud men were dominated, and in the other hand, take the arrows with which that incomparable queen, your grandmother Isabella, pushed the Moors so far away from us. (29)

From the aristocracy and the Church as historical institutions with the capacity to still inspire patriotic fervor, *Madrid, de corte a checa* moves down the vertical ladder created by fascism's standards of patriotism to the conservative political parties representing those institutions. Democratic conservatives are depicted as ineffectually trying to convince others to accept their platform. Even worse, these people are not connected to the romantic impulse in politics. Gil Robles, head of the Catholic Democrats, for example, "knew how to make politics but not History, because he lacked that poetic emotion, that burning desire to communicate possessed by those who really know how to lead the people" (142). For the fascists, it is not a question of convincing but of dominating. Those who understand the fascist message carry it in their bodies and souls more than in their heads, as will be shown. It does need to be said, however, that with the conservatives, there is also a moment of acceptance. Calvo Sotelo, the Monarchist democratic leader slain by the Guardia Asalto, is highlighted as having the right ideas (only the democratic methods are wrong) and dying a brave death. Calvo Sotelo's character and death are handled carefully, one suspects, because the death was the specific reason used by the Nationalists for the rebellion of the generals that precipitated the Spanish Civil War. The conservative leader no doubt had to be lionized to justify such a reprisal.

No acceptance is given to other groups. The rhetorical technique used to present Azaña has already been discussed. Suffice it to say it is applied to all other political groups below the conservatives in the vertical political chain-of-being of Spanish fascism. "Hoz y martillo" ("Hammer and sickle"), the last part of *Madrid, de corte a checa*, consists of one Republican or Communist atrocity after another. Communism is neither analyzed nor explained; rather, atrocities committed by Communists are described in order to justify attitudes against them. *Madrid, de corte a checa* becomes little more than an adventure novel, albeit a briskly paced and vigorously written one. Alas, however, any intellectual curiosity the book may engender is not to be found in its last third.

True to Romance, *Madrid, de corte a checa* provides plenty of risk-taking, sometimes to demonstrate the nobility of the hero and other times, seemingly, because of a childlike passion for violence and danger. Is not Romance the favorite narrative mode of the young? One of the constant attributes of fascism in the eyes of Spanish fascist authors is youth. Foxá underscores it in his descriptions of José Félix and José Antonio; García Serrano and Alfaro employ very young protagonists.

The fictional plot presents the theme of regeneration expressed in the form of José Félix's spiritual development. In the first part of the novel, José Félix lives in a decadent world born out of a desperate but futile search for a meaningful existence. Life lacks adventure and drama and, therefore, pleasure takes on the immediate forms of sex and drugs and more excessively refined cravings such as reading poetry in cemeteries. This world is presented as focusing on the style of the moment but lacking a true sense of eternal values.

Against the failings of modern society is contrasted another way of being—the way of the fascist. The novel's ultimate message for a fascist is locked in its testament to what constitutes an ideal man. That ideal—one need go no further—is locked in the character of José Antonio Primo de Rivera. He mediates between history and Romance; he is a character from history who also represents the ideal. In contrast to all that is decadent in the fictional plot and unpatriotic in the historical plot, José Antonio and the Falange Española offer "the Truth" and "the eternal values of the heavens, of war and love" (134-35).

A questioning reader may desire some explanation of the offerings. After all, "the eternal values of the heavens, of war and love" seems rather vague. As has already been indicated, it is not in Foxá's discursive design to offer profound explanations. Indeed, much of José Antonio's program is vague, and he admitted it, and justified it, in his "El hombre es el sistema."[10] José Antonio was well-read, and could certainly have been a complex thinker, but simplicity of thought was viewed as a virtue by European fascist thinkers, many of whom were rebelling against what they perceived to be an excess of tired and exhausted civilization. Excessive thought was viewed as reducing the will to act, and the inability to act, to live life heroically, was precisely what many fascists viewed as the major fault of modern man.[11]

This strong visceral attitude towards existence, which places intuition and daring above pensiveness and caution, is, in José Antonio, linked by the narrator to some other important qualities. José Antonio is "young, decisive, and a poet, and he had a manly presence that bowled the female Falangists over. He was the epic and the lyric combined; his eyes were clear and slightly sad. He brought together tenderness and the impetus to fight" (153-54). An example of José Antonio in action, and certainly living up to these qualities, is given:

> José Félix recalled a night on Recoletos Street. [José Antonio] was commenting on the most subtle essence of a delicate poem by Juan Ramón Jiménez. Suddenly he turned around.
> —They are following us.
> When [José Félix] realized what was going on, [José Antonio] already had the two gunmen in the sights of his pistol. (154)

This type of man is the ideal, and the novel's resolution lies in José Félix's achieving that combination of poetry and action that is fascist man; that is, to be subtle without losing clarity, to be refined without losing the love of adventure.

It is not unusual for traditional Romance to reveal truth through magic, but this is too much to ask of a political novel of the twentieth century; hence, in *Madrid, de corte a checa*, truth is revealed through coincidence. Coincidence can be thought of as a type of magic. In lieu of finely traced psychological growth, coincidence neatly does what magic used to do. It makes things happen whenever a writer feels like having them happen, without any special development. Thus, after wandering adrift for pages in a café life of alcohol and women, José Félix, quite accidentally, finds himself, by coincidence, outside the Teatro de la Comedia on the day José Antonio gives his famous "Discurso de la fundación de Falange Española." The speech is a moment of epiphany for José Félix. It leads him to make contact with José Antonio and to become a fascist. This circumstantial union with fascism raises the issue of character development.

The notion of spiritual growth can only be loosely applied to the molding of José Félix's character. The text does not accept the possibility of development in the normal sense of the word. While the plot shows José Félix moving through several decadent situations involving women and alcohol, the descriptive language reminds us of the character's essential stability. José

Félix's qualities are fixed from the start. At the beginning of the novel, the reader receives the following description of him: "He was a boy of some twenty-two years, tall, romantic and gener-ous . . . he possessed a keen and finely-tuned mind" (10). His powerful internal struggle, which is the essential conflict and could have led to an intense psychological and spiritual novel, is summed up by the narrator in the following way:

> [José Félix] was a Republican because of the elegance of the moment. . . . He had been born in the century of the automo-bile and of the dehumanization of Art and had to abandon God in the sordidness of the Ateneo . . . [but] the Ramiros and Berengueres of his genealogical tree weighed in his blood. (11)

Like many heroes of Romance, José Félix seems to be pos-sessed of the necessary natural qualities. The text, therefore, comes close to being determinist. José Félix is shown to be too intrinsically good. Indeed, the statement above is reactionary in a blatantly aristocratic sense: he is superior because of his ancestors. Not as aristocratic as Foxá but susceptible to the same notion of natural superiority, García Serrano has his narrator refer several times to Eugenio as "well-engendered." This type of determinist discourse plays intratextually with the concepts of decadence and regeneration/degeneration. José Félix is never really a decadent and thus never really has to regenerate his spirit; his only fault is that he is too susceptible to alcohol and women at an age when, indeed, many men are. Decadence in *Madrid, de corte a checa* is more like a college weekend than a deep pit, escape from which can be obtained only through fierce commitment. In a text that views its protagonist as inherently and undeniably superior, the turn toward fascism hardly needs to be prolonged; and, in fact, as soon as the message of José Antonio is heard, the turn takes place, thereby creating the effect of coincidence.

Questions of discourse must of necessity also focus on the narrator's voice. In *Madrid, de corte a checa*, it is a powerful, constant, and controlling influence. It has been heard in pre-vious quotations, offering not only description but full-blown judgments. Its tendency is to close situations rather than to leave them open. It is the voice of vertically arranged values and clearly stated preferences. It describes and judges, but it does not explain. It arranges its narrative world according to fascist ideals. It does not doubt itself. To believe it is to know that there is an answer to the world's problems. Not to believe it is to know an enemy.

In criticizing Foxá, some may point to the French fascist novelist Drieu La Rochelle in whose works the fascist response to life and politics springs from a carefully delineated spiritual crisis. For him, fascism is linked philosophically to a sense of salvation in the face of what is perceived as an existential abyss. Drieu is a writer who, despite his fascism, does those things the refined, modern European and American demand.[12] When Drieu chooses fascism, he does it very intellectually. Foxá does not. The environments of Spain and France were radically different. French and Italian writers saw other possibilities.[13] Spain's fascism was less delicate in its examination of motive, because it was immediately polarized by street conflict and war. Values in *Madrid, de corte a checa* are presented quickly. They are givens rather than issues to be debated. *Madrid, de corte a checa* is not oriented as a search for truth, i.e., the achievement of proper values, because truth from the start is not up for debate; it is known. It is clear that the novel was not written to convince antifascists of the incorrectness of their position. It was written for those who were already converted. It is, in part, propaganda. This pejorative term, however, does not explain the complete human impulse operating within a text. Foxá was writing in a time of war. His discourse of moral and political verticality and justification of militant action would have been understood by his rivals, most of whom thought in the same way. Foxá's discourse, in short, reflected his world. It did not try to convince but to inspire, within an environment focused on heroic acts, a world in which Romance could flourish.

To summarize is to become fully aware that *Madrid, de corte a checa* contains the essential trappings of Romance: a hero who searches for the proper way, a struggle between good and evil, a need to regenerate the world, a love of adventure,

Antonio Varela

characterization based on essential traits rather than psychology, a vertical ordering of people and ideas, and a simplicity of motive.

A significant question is whether *Madrid, de corte a checa* is a good Romance. The answer is next to impossible to give. The problem is that quality in Romance is hard to judge. Romance is that literary form which least obeys careful structuring and development. It is the most prone to rambling and seemingly mindless enumeration of characters and events. Individual lovers of Romance eventually respond to it because they find in it an agreeable heroic impulse and perhaps, in some cases, language that can be fascinating. Ultimately, for a Romance to be really liked, it must connect the reader's heart and soul with its vision of life. This should be remembered carefully when *Madrid, de corte a checa* is read. Spanish fascism did not provide sensible structures in the democratic, capitalist, or communist sense. It provided, instead, a quickening of the blood, a clarion call to battle against the dark, a sense of grasping the future with the muscular arms of the nation's heroic forebears. It was reality in the mode of Romance. And, although all European fascism, as a significant force, died on the battlefield, its basic impulse lies imbedded in all humans. It only waits for a cause large enough to summon forth the need for desperate victory.

The University of Toledo

NOTES

1. Agustín de Foxá, *Madrid, de corte a checa* (Madrid: Editorial Prensa española, 1962); originally published as *Madrid de corte a cheka* (San Sebastian: Librería internacional, 1938). A comma was added and the spelling of *cheka* changed in later editions. Further references to this work will appear in the text. All translations are mine.

2. Rafael García Serrano, *Eugenio o proclamación de la primavera* (Barcelona: Planeta, 1982); José María Alfaro, *Leoncio Pancorbo* (Madrid: Editora Nacional, 1942). *La fiel infantería* of García Serrano, *Leoncio Pancorbo*, and

108

Madrid, de corte a checa are generally considered the best novels voicing the Nationalist cause's view of events surrounding the Spanish Civil War.

3. Anthony Geist, "Popular Poetry on the Fascist Front During the Spanish Civil War," in *Fascismo y experiencia literaria: reflexiones para una recanonización,* ed. Hernán Vidal (Minneapolis: Institute for the Study of Ideologies and Literature, 1985), 146.

4. Hayden White, *Metahistory: The Historical Imagination in Nineteenth-Century Europe* (Baltimore: The Johns Hopkins University Press, 1973), 8-9.

5. Hayden White mentions three other modes: satire, comedy, and tragedy. It can be said, in the briefest of fashions, that from the perspective of fascism, satire is too cynical, comedy is too prone to compromise, and tragedy, too fatalistic.

6. Hans Hinterhauser, *Los "Episodios Nacionales" de Benito Pérez Galdós,* trans. José Escobar (Madrid: Editorial Gredos, 1963), 233-47.

7. Juan Ignacio Ferreras, "La generación del silencio: Ensayo sobre un novelar de la posguerra española," in *Fascismo y experiencia literaria: reflexiones para una recanonización,* 156-57, 161-63.

8. Hernán Vidal, "Hacia un modelo general de la sensibilidad social literaturizable bajo el fascismo," in *Fascismo y experiencia literaria: reflexiones para una recanonización,* 35.

9. Stanley G. Payne, *Falange: A History of Spanish Fascism* (Stanford: Stanford University Press, 1961), chap. 15. See also his "Social Composition and Regional Strength of the Spanish Falange," in *Who Were the Fascists: Social Roots of European Fascism,* ed. Stein Ugelvik Larsen et al. (Bergen: Universitetsforlaget, 1980), 423-34.

10. José Antonio Primo de Rivera, "El hombre es el sistema," in *Obras completas* (Madrid: Editora Nacional, 1942), 405-7.

11. The history of fascist attitudes towards European civilization and culture is traced by Zeev Sternhell, "Fascist Ideology," in *Fascism: A Reader's Guide, Analyses, Interpretations, Bibliography,* ed. Walter Laqueur (Berkeley: University of California Press, 1978), 315-76.

12. See the excellent study of Frédéric J. Grover, *Drieu La Rochelle and the Fiction of Testimony* (Berkeley: University of California Press, 1958).

13. For an overview of Italian fascist fiction, see Alberto Traldi, *Fascism and Fiction: A Survey of Italian Fiction on Fascism (and Its Reception in Britain and the United States)* (Metuchen, N.J.: Scarecrow Press, 1987). Italian fascist literature has been far more thoroughly discussed than its Spanish counterpart.

NARRATIVE VOICE AND THE TOLL OF WAR IN RAMÓN SENDER'S *CONTRAATAQUE*

Mary S. Vásquez

Remember that in our attacks all goes well in the morning,
but the afternoon usually belongs to them.[1]

Contraataque is Sender's novel of wartime Spain. Written under
what must have been particularly intense circumstances of
Republican involvement and deep personal sorrow, the work
was hurriedly translated into English by Sir Peter Chalmers
Mitchell and published in London in 1937 as *The War in Spain*.
Less than a year later, the same translation of Sender's book
appeared in an American edition as *Counter-Attack in Spain*. A
French edition, published in Paris, also bears a 1937 date. Only
in 1938 did the complete work appear in Spanish and in Spain,
published by Ediciones Nuestro Pueblo, publishing arm of the
Spanish Communist party; the Republican Fifth Regiment had
issued Chapter VIII, "Primera de acero," in pamphlet form
in 1937.

It seems natural that the early reviewers of *Contraataque*, in
commentaries appearing primarily in July of 1937 in London
and in November of that year in the United States, should prize
Sender's book for its vivid reportage of the conflict which the
intellectual world in the Western democracies was following
with intense interest. The pages of the magazines in which the

reviews appear—*The Saturday Review of Literature, The Nation, The New Statesman,* for example—contain numerous articles on the war in Spain and its context. Some reviewers, like the book's translator himself—a resident of Málaga when the war broke out—had a profound personal involvement in the fate of Spain. Ralph Bates, who was on a United States lecture tour when he composed his review for *The Saturday Review,* had been on the front as an officer of the Fifteenth International Brigade.

Contraataque is for these early reviewers a source of "the truth," a view directly from Spain by a Spaniard of intelligence, idealism, and sensitivity, which lends comprehension to the chaotic, conflicting, and always incomplete reports from the fronts and the politicians, helping to supply many of the "important pieces missing from the mosaic of [the war's] first days."[2] The commonality of humankind which was very much a part of the idealism of the times is seen in at least one review as an implicit affirmation of Sender's book: "that is not a dream, or a fantasy of Wells's, but a town not far away."[3] Some reviewers refer, too, to the book's lyrical passages, and for Mildred Adams, *Counter-Attack in Spain* is both "a moving piece of first-hand testimony" and "the work of an artist" (537).

Following the 1938 Spanish edition, of which few recorded reviews exist, there was no reissue of *Contraataque* until the somewhat flawed Aymar edition of 1978. A reissue of *Contraataque,* with its passionate defense of the Republican cause and equally fervent indictment of the fascists and the Falange, would not, of course, have been likely in Franco's Spain, save perhaps in a clandestine printing; and most of Sender's well-known novels of his early period also existed for many years—though not usually quite so many—in their original edition only.[4] Those Cenit, Zeus, Balagué, Pueyo, and Espasa-Calpe editions, however, remained more available over the years than *Contraataque,* published under such particular circumstances; Sender claims in his 1978 foreword that he himself had no copy of the original edition (12). This inaccessibility goes far toward explaining the almost total lack of critical attention devoted to *Contraataque* in the years since the war, an inattention clearly shown in the authoritative King and Espadas bibliographies on Sender.[5] Critical interest has hardly been more abundant, however, since *Contraataque's* 1978 republication, and this despite the work's subject matter, surely a topic of enduring interest.

Not even the deep social concerns of the sixties provoked the curiosity of Hispanists in the United States with respect to *Contraataque*. Even so major a Sender scholar as Marcelino Peñuelas gives the book short shrift in his study of Sender's narrative works,[6] as well as in the commentary of his *Conversaciones con R. J. Sender*.[7] Though Peñuelas includes *Contraataque* in his list of Sender's novels at the conclusion of the *Conversaciones* book, it does not figure among the twelve works, plus the nine-volume *Crónica del alba*, singled out for special dialogue in the text proper, nor does he mention the work in his forty-six-page introduction. In *La obra narrativa*, Peñuelas refers to *Contraataque* as a propaganda work,

> a war tale written with a clear propaganda intent which the author does not trouble to hide. But this is a work of circumstances, written with the sole purpose of presenting the Republican cause to a foreign public at a critical time in which political propaganda about Spain's war was an important weapon. (97)

The term "propaganda" has, of course, taken on in recent decades a highly pejorative connotation, moving from an older sense of the term as literature in the service of a cause, with an intent to persuade and convince, toward the current popular usage implying gross manipulation and distortion. An anti-propaganda bias has in all likelihood dissuaded those readers who have heard of the obscure *Contraataque* from an attempt to gain direct knowledge of the text, a likelihood combining with the book's longtime inaccessibility to make this lengthy work (390 pages in the present edition) probably the least read and least known of Sender's novels of the thirties.

Contraataque possesses, certainly, an important documentary value. Yet the novel—which *Contraataque*, in my view, most definitely is—is this and more; it is a complex, ambiguous, and ambivalent work, one built on essential conflict and counterposition, which contains many passages of remarkable beauty and power, its complexity having much to do with its literary treatment precisely as a novel. Though the work does contain propaganda, these passages are an integral part of the point-counterpoint structure which yields a multiple and contradictory vision quite distant from the single-mindedness of propaganda.

The vehicle that conveys this complex vision, and contributes to the creation of it, is the permutation of narrative voice. I find four distinct narrative voices in *Contraataque*, all of them expressions of one theoretical entity. The first narrator, who describes the period from May to the fateful July 18th of 1936, though he employs the first person, largely hides behind the currents evoked and behind an anonymous character whose interpretation is, however, filtered through him. Once the war has begun, a change in narrative function occurs; for the bulk of the novel, two narrative voices operate in opposition. The primary one, strongly linked to the implied author, is that of an actor-teller, a soldier-chronicler who, as participant in the events recounted, evokes at the same time the texture and feel of his ambience; he fits himself into this vitally evoked context, which he interprets as he goes. This is the novel's dominant narrative voice. Counterposed to it is what I will term an exhortatory narrative voice, exclaiming, insisting, pretending to lift us above the trees so that we may see the forest full and complete. This voice is contradicted and subverted by the content of the predominant narrative voice's tale. Finally, at the novel's end, a fourth narrative voice, that of the implied author himself, narrates, in a spare, unadorned prose greatly in contrast to the lush phrasing and wealth of metaphor of the major portion of the novel, the harsh personal tragedy of the deaths by assassination of his wife and brother in the fall of 1936. This portion of *Contraataque* constitutes a sub-text which demands a re-reading and reinterpretation of all that has gone before. The reader's conclusions are likely to affirm the correctness of the themes implicit in the first section of the text, as well as in the tale told by the predominant narrative voice in the major part of the novel, with added generic implications of the kind that come best from experiences of the most deeply personal nature.

In *Contraataque's* first segments, the character behind whom the implied author's prescience tends to hide is an obscure and unnamed Army captain posted in Africa who has come to Madrid to warn of a planned insurrection soon to erupt in Africa; it must, he insists, be stopped while there is still time. The captain excitedly shares his evidence with all who will listen, but those listeners are few and unconvinced. Finally, the narrator secures an appointment for the captain with a colonel in the War Ministry and accompanies him on the visit. The colonel listens in boredom, rejecting all that he hears. Events, of course, make of the captain a seer and a prophet—as, Sender strongly implies, nearly all could and should have been.

In this first segment of *Contraataque,* a momentum of inevitability is established, not only of the war's arrival but containing as well the suggestion of ultimate defeat. There is an air of tragedy, and, as in tragedy, fatal flaws play a part, and the hero is blind. As Peñuelas notes in the *Conversaciones,* Sender tended always toward a tragic view of humankind (40).[8] This segment portrays all too convincingly the first of a series of errors and flaws of the Republic which *Contraataque* shows: that of over-confidence and a removal from reality. This attitude appears in the narrative to have three aspects: first, idealism and a conviction of being right, with the implicit thought that rightness bestows its own protection; next, a euphoria felt at the Republic's very existence; and, finally, lack of vision.

As the novel moves with the outbreak and early days of the war itself into its second and by far most extensive portion, this tragic view is expanded to include confusion and bungling; betrayal from within, a theme that runs throughout the novel; and an excessive decency, a quality seen by the exhortatory narrative voice as evidence that the Republic will triumph, since it is good, and by the predominant narrative voice as a possible weakness: the Republic is too good to triumph militarily, particularly against the forces in question. Yet it is a "weakness" which for this narrative voice, too, renders it morally superior. *Contraataque's* portrayal of the Fascist Beast, a mad animal severing its own tail, and the complementary view of the irrevocable loss that lies at the heart of all civil war—and of all war of whatever nature—completes the picture.

In this major portion of the novel, the two narrative voices, the dominant and the exhortatory, move in separate but interlocking concentric circles, the dominant voice moving from the personal to the communal and back to the personal and the exhortatory voice progressing from the immediate to the remote, returning then to the immediate. These circles intersect at two points: in the chapter dealing with the "Primera de acero," the volunteer company with spirit and the beginnings of organization which is in the novel the first heartening and productive response to the waste and chaos of the war's first days, and again in the discussion of the late-1936 defense of Madrid. For the bulk of this major narrative segment, the two voices exist in a relationship of opposition and counterpoint.

When the war begins, the narrator is summering with his wife and two tiny children in San Rafael in the Sierra de Guadarrama. Leaving them with relatives and friends, the narrator crosses enemy lines and joins the confused and milling Republican groups who are yearning for leadership and direction. He chronicles the formation of the "Primera de acero" and the initiation of the Republic as a democratically based and morally guided war machine, fighting for its survival, fired by a dream. He is present at the defense of, and eventual attack upon, a post at Cabeza Lijar. Asked by a group of soldiers to be their officer, the narrator then departs for the fronts to the south. He shares his experiences of the war at the individual and small unit level. In his praise of officers who have sprung, almost without exception, from the humble, the narrator distinguishes clearly between the Republic as the expression of an ideal—the people's voice, its hope, its autonomy—and the conduct of the Republic as a government, carefully affirming his own fealty to the popular cause despite his more privileged background. In the unprepared government, there is bungling and mistaken judgment. More poisonous than error are the real and suspected betrayals from within. There is mention of a highly placed war minister, in the early days of the war, who proved to be a traitor to the Republic and, later, of a disloyal supply officer at the front. The placement of references and their accumulating effect suggest that error, too, may at times have been something worse. Then there is the character self-dubbed "el Negus," a strange, repulsive man who mysteriously appears at almost every post the narrator visits. Always watching, listening, "el Negus" is possessed of information he decidedly should not have. His claim to "weak-headedness" is an unconvincing defense. Ultimately, "el Negus" is caught in unmistakable treachery and shot. Filled with self-loathing, he is the fifth column, the ubiquitous traitor who is here, there, nowhere, and everywhere. He might be a neighbor, or even a friend; such is the incipient paranoia based on fact, experience, and fear.

There are propagandistic elements in this section of the novel. Stronger, however, is the balanced and often critical vision discussed above and the evocation of the march of events in a gathering tragedy. Tacitly echoing the theme suggested in *Contraataque*'s opening segment, for example, soldiers wonder aloud: "We all wondered if the enemy would eventually take Madrid" (279). They recall Talavera; the same question had been asked there. And at Toledo. Momentum accelerates. As "el Negus" counters the decent and heroic officers who have sprung from the people, so, too, does the theme of fratricide begin to override questions of triumph. Again and again, the reader encounters images of "the wound-ed land" and of pines bleeding from their wounds. The land fought for is being weakened and torn. It is Mother Spain who lies in suffering. In this sense, any victory would be a Pyrrhic one.

The second, exhortatory narrative voice operative in this major portion of the novel would have it otherwise. This voice intrudes into the text at numerous points, in passages ranging from a sentence or two to as much as a page. Categorical, impassioned, insistent, it speaks in a mode quite distinct from that of the dominant narrative voice; in the longer passages the prose builds to a crescendo of rhetoric, and exclamation marks are frequent. The dominant voice speaks nearly always in the imperfect and, to a lesser extent, the preterite; rarely does a present-perfect or present-tense verb bring the action to the present plane of the telling of the tale. The intruding voice, on the other hand, speaks almost exclusively in the present. It seeks to sum up, to synthesize, to draw the generality from the sequence of narrated parts. It exhorts to faith, to belief in the triumph that surely will come. Following its intersection with the predominant voice in the recounting of the hopeful days of the founding of the "Primera de acero," however, this voice separates markedly from the major one. Its intrusions seem increasingly extraliterary, more and more divorced from the integrity of the text, becoming a corrective to the text rather than a complement to it. As the sense of tragedy deepens, the exhortatory voice is subverted and contradicted by the stronger narrative voice. Stated differently, the corrective voice fails to correct, the breach continuing until the segments detailing the popular defense of Madrid, the deeply moving miracle that inspired much of the world. At this point, the two narrative voices meet briefly once again; if the enemy could be stopped in the Ciudad Universitaria and in the streets of Carabanchel, perhaps military victory could belong to the Republic after all. By this point in *Contraataque,* however, the sense is strong that a win is still a loss, in the sense discussed above. The dark street corners of Madrid, "around each of which the unknown wind waited, cast poisonous shadows" (376). Houses where families had lived and children had played are sometimes gutted within, though intact in external appearance. Their former inner structure lies in heaps in the street. "The ruins . . . were like innards vomited from the mouth" (376). The "poison" frequently evoked in these sections of the narrative is more than the breath and spirit of the "Bestia," as the gutted homes are metaphors, too. Hate, violence, and destruction have taken their toll.

One day in the deserted streets of Moncloa, in a December cold so sharp that the ground creaks under his boots, the narrator meets an old man who appears to be in his seventies. The man's expression is of "an innocent hardness."

> Scraggly white beard, which wasn't a beard but physical misery. His hands were hidden, and his head, which looked a little like a turtle's, protruded from his narrow shoulders. He looked around, uncomprehending, but the movement hurt the back of his neck. His clothing bore shards from several windows, and dust that had been carried back and forth by the winds at street intersections. (350-51)

Hesitatingly, the old man approaches a door, starts to enter it, then steps back out, "with a child's fear in his eyes" (351). "There's no one there," he murmurs (351). The scene is repeated several times as the old man shuffles along, a purpled toe protruding from a sandal. Seeing the narrator, he steps aside, extending his hand in a somehow surviving courtesy. The narrator asks where he is going.

> "Around, at God's mercy."
> "God no longer exists."
> "What?" he asked, not understanding.
> "They've killed God."
> "That's not right. Who's going to kill God?" (351)

The magnitude of the loss links the old man to a young enemy prisoner taken earlier, in October, near Seseña. In a lamentable physical state and half-mad, the soldier is brought to the narrator. A disjointed letter to his parents is found in a pocket. The narrator offers it with the disclaimer that it has "documentary interest" (314):

> "Dear Parents:
> For days I've wanted to write to you, but I don't have anywhere to put the paper, which gets dirty everywhere. . . . And after looking for so long, now I find that I have nothing to say to you because, once I've said 'Dear Parents,' I can't think of anything more. Life is bad. I'm afraid of the dead at night, but during the day I envy them because, even though they are so dirty and so torn apart, they can't see or hear anymore. I don't

envy the wounded, because even though they leave, they still have to come back here. . . . I put the paper on a dead man and, since his shirt was dirty, it got dirty, too. I have taken off his shirt and placed the paper on his back. His skin is clean, but very cold. It's also a special kind of coldness, that freezes you without being very cold. The paper won't get dirty anymore. . . .

Now don't feel happy about that or about anything else, because you will damn yourselves. Though my memory is going I haven't forgotten you, since you are my parents. Forget everything and forget me, too. The best thing would be to forget everything forever." (314-15)

The soldier closes with a request for money, "'because without money a person is nothing,'" adding an "'¡Arriba España! ¡Viva el caudillo!'" and signing his letter "'Your son – Ceferino'" (316).

Here it need not matter, until the letter's final sentences, on what side this young soldier has fought or what his political philosophy, if any, may be. Ceferino is many combat soldiers of many wars, brutalized by war and, perhaps, by his own brutality.

As these moments in the narrative approach, the exhortatory voice has altered its message, forced perhaps by the weight of events to bend the line of its circle. As the circle of the dominant narrative voice has moved from the immediate and personal context to the ever more generalized one of the war's progress and the Republic's fight for survival, returning once again to the personal as it cedes to the fourth narrative voice, so, too, does the exhortatory voice move in a cycle. Its progress is from the immediate to the distant and remote, then, at the defense of Madrid—the point at which the two circles again intersect—back to the immediate. This voice's early insistence on the certainty of a proximate victory yields gradually to affirmations of the guarantee of an eventual triumph for the popular cause in Spain, retreating finally to declarations that someday in the course of time and human events, in another generation and another place, the Republic's cause will emerge victorious. Only with the miracle in Madrid does the surety begin to return of a victory not removed in time but at hand.

The very existence of the exhortatory voice, as well as its functioning and evolution, raises the question of the identity of the intended audience. *Contraataque's* 1937 publication in English and French, prior to its appearance in Spanish and in Spain, suggests that the book formed part of the Republic's efforts to generate support in the Western democracies—efforts in which Sender was active in other ways as well. The book's praise of Republican officers; its celebration of anonymous popular types in their devotion to and sacrifice for their cause; its expressed admiration for the Communists who came to dominate the resistance effort—though Sender clearly speaks primarily of non-Russian Communists and of local organization; and its eventual affirmation that all were united behind the Republic's president, Manuel Azaña, all point in this direction. There is, without question, a good deal of gloss and a hefty dose of propagandism in the last two of these elements, as in the total dichotomy portrayed between rebel bestiality and loyalist decency-to-a-fault.

Yet, as a propaganda instrument, *Contraataque,* with its depiction of government bungling and its insinuation of a persistent fifth column, in addition to its counterposed vision, would surely be a strange and divided one. The one major Republican offensive depicted, that of Seseña, fails by reason of multiplied error; and a war effort at the official level which would leave four trainloads of troops throughout the night—still in the close-clustered railroad cars—could hardly be expected to inspire foreign confidence in a government. The tension between this exhortatory voice and the dominant narrative one, the tone in which this voice speaks, and the changes in it suggest a quite different audience: the reading public of Republican Spain. It is certainly possible that authorial intentions were multiple; if not, the distance between plan and realization could well have rendered the product so. Sender's book may be seen as a call to faith and a shared cry for the fate of a beloved homeland. The praise of the Communists, with whom Sender was, well before *Contraataque's* publication, engaged in bitter dispute, may represent an attempt to present a united front for the good of the Republic, though an effort at conciliation with forces viewed as negative would not have been characteristic of Sender. In this light, these long and deep-seated difficulties may be a reason for the delay in the book's publication in the country it most immediately concerned and in the language in which it had been written.

Questions of intentionality aside, the terse, dramatic, and profoundly affecting prose of the novel's final section posits the possibility that Sender was writing ultimately to and for himself, his novel serving, perhaps, as one means of bearing grief. In this section of *Contraataque*, a fourth narrative voice details the assassinations of Sender's wife and brother—here the implied author and the narrator become one—and the subsequent rescue of his children and removal of them to southern France with the aid of the Red Cross. The narrator's wife was killed in October of 1936 in her home city of Zamora, where she had gone with her children to be with her family; he learned of her death, he states, in January 1937—after the events described in the novel, yet before its writing. Sender has stated in the *Conversaciones* (88-91) that these sections of *Contraataque* contain a factual account of the circumstances surrounding his wife's murder. Sustaining this idea is evidence in the book that it was written in part from notes made during a military campaign: scant references in the present tense to positions still held, for example, and the use of a date, 14 June, that obviously could not belong to 1936, the one year encompassed in the novel's plane of action. These notes of the implied author may well have been Sender's, made for himself; it would not then need to matter that embarrassing information harmful to the image of the Republic was included. Finally, in the last section of *Contraataque*, the narrator/implied author, here closely joined to Sender, addresses the collective implied listener/implied reader several times in the familiar plural. There is an intimacy to this portion of the work not found elsewhere in *Contraataque;* its powerful emotion is at once contained and shared. There are suggestions in the last section, too, that the book was written, wholly or in part, in one or more intense periods of removal from direct military involvement in the war. "When my children are recovered and re-established, when happiness—and that is divine—has returned to their eyes, I will return to the front" (390), Sender writes on the last page of his novel. Sender did, in fact, spend one brief and a second lengthy period outside of Spain in 1937.[9]

The book, then, may well be a part of Sender's own coming-to-terms with a personal tragedy, which emerges as a metaphor for a national and global loss far deeper than military and political defeats or gains. A hymn of praise to a dream, and to those who defended it, *Contraataque* is also, and at a still more fundamental level, a profound lament. The very elements that make the work a novel go into the creation of this lament: wealth of image; vividness of character portrayal; multiplicity of narrative voice and of the vision attained; creation, in sum, of a literary world. Transformations within the text through the vehicle of narrative voice make any single definition of victory—or defeat—an impossibility. The novel's final words are telling: "Soon I'll be able to tell you what the victory was like, though for me, in the sphere of my private joys or sorrows, it will no longer be a victory but instead a compensation" (390). So it might have been for many.

Arizona State University

NOTES

1. Ramón J. Sender, *Contraataque*, 2nd ed. (Salamanca: Ediciones Aymar, 1978), 263. All quotations are from this edition and will hereafter be identified by page number within parentheses in the text. This and all other translations from Spanish are my own.

2. Mildred Adams, "Memoirs of a Fighting Writer," review of *Counter-Attack in Spain*, *The Nation*, 13 November 1937, 536. Further references to this review will appear in the text.

3. David Garnett, Untitled review of *The War in Spain*, *The New Statesman and Nation*, 31 July 1937, 187.

4. These are *Imán* (Madrid: Cenit, 1930); *O.P.* (Madrid: Cenit, 1931); *Siete domingos rojos* (Barcelona: Balagué, 1932); *Viaje a la aldea del crimen. Documental de Casas Viejas* (Madrid: Pueyo, 1934); *La noche de las cien cabezas* (Madrid: Pueyo, 1934); *Mr. Witt en el cantón* (Madrid: Espasa-Calpe, 1935). Less known is *El verbo se hizo sexo* (Madrid: Zeus, 1931), rewritten and published as *Tres novelas teresianas* (Barcelona: Destino, 1967).

5. Charles L. King, *An Annotated Bibliography of Ramón J. Sender, 1928-1974*, (Metuchen, N.J.: Scarecrow Press, 1976); Charles L. King, "Una bibliografía senderiana española (1928-1967)," *Hispania*, 50 (1967): 630-45; Elizabeth Espadas, "La visión crítica de la obra de Ramón J. Sender: Ensayo Bibliográfico," in *Homenaje a Ramón J. Sender, 1901-82*, ed. Mary S. Vásquez (Newark, Del.: Juan de la Cuesta Hispanic Monographs, 1987), 227-87.

6. Marcelino C. Peñuelas, *La obra narrativa de Ramón J. Sender* (Madrid: Gredos, 1971). Further references to this work will appear in the text.

7. Marcelino C. Peñuelas, *Conversaciones con R. J. Sender* (Madrid: Magisterio Español, 1970). Further references to this work will appear in the text.

8. "Sender is always drawn to what directly confronts or touches the tragic sense of existence" (Peñuelas, *Conversaciones con R. J. Sender*, 40).

9. Sender spent two months with his children in Pau in early 1937, after being denied permission by the Communists to be sent to the Segre River on the Aragón front to join CNT troops there, then gave a series of lectures promoting the Republican cause in the United States before returning to France to found and edit, in Paris, the magazine *La voz de Madrid*. He later rejoined the military effort in Spain. *Contraataque* was published in England in mid-1937 (*Conversaciones*, 58-59, 88-89).

THE LANGUAGE OF MEMORY:
THE SPANISH CIVIL WAR
IN THE FILMS OF CARLOS SAURA

Kathleen M. Vernon

The enormous impact of the Spanish Civil War on contemporary Spanish narrative, both written and filmic, is undeniable. Maryse Bertrand de Muñoz, editor of a two-volume catalogue of novels on the Spanish Civil War, counts over 400 novels written by Spaniards through 1981 in which the war figures as a major or partial subject. Román Gubern, preeminent Spanish film scholar and scriptwriter, identifies some sixty-five films made in Spain between 1936 and 1986 which deal with the Civil War as a central theme or important element of the plot.[1] But numbers alone cannot indicate the extent to which the war has informed and altered the consciousness of at least three generations of Spanish writers and directors.

While a number of the essays in this volume will deal with the artistic response of the "first" generation of writers, who knew the war as adults, I am particularly interested in the work of the second generation—those writers and filmmakers born between 1925 and 1933 who experienced the war as children. In the works of these artists—I am thinking, of course, of Carlos Saura, but also of his novelist contemporaries, in particular, Juan Benet and Juan Marsé—the war appears through the highly subjective and frequently distorting filter of memory.[2] In thematic terms, these artists' portrayal of the war centers around a vital complex dominated by the family and comprised of characters whose psychic organization has its roots in childhood experiences in which wartime violence and personal trauma are often indistinguishable.

Born in 1932, Saura did indeed experience the war as a young child, and his films portray the conflict through a mixture of direct recollection and hearsay, combined with the clearly creative effects of adult reworkings and re-elaborations of earlier events. For Saura, the past is never simply past, safely confined to the realm of history, but rather it impinges on the present, just as the present exercises its own revisionist power over the past. Saura's accomplishment, in thematic and formal terms, lies in his ability to represent that intermingling of past and present on the screen. Turning from classic narrative cinema's conventional evocations of past memories through flashbacks which evoke the past in a contiguous but isolated relation to the present, Saura fashions a flexible and highly original cinematic language of memory whereby character and spectator are challenged to confront the essential but destabilizing role of remembrance in determining our sense of self in history.

Of the four films where the war appears as a central theme, beginning with *La caza* in 1965, and followed by *El jardín de las delicias* (1970), *La prima Angélica* (1973), and *Dulces horas* (1981), I propose to concentrate on the last three, which constitute what might be called Saura's trilogy of memory. Through their double framing of the war and the memory process itself, they offer a profound meditation on the role of film in representing—and manipulating—the link between individual and collective memory.

The first of the three films, *El jardín de las delicias*, chronicles the efforts by the family of Antonio Cano, a rich industrialist of the sixties' "boom" years, now the semi-paralyzed, amnesiac victim of an auto accident, to stimulate the recovery of his memory, most notably of the number of the Swiss bank account where he has stored the profits from the family construction business, far from the eyes of the tax collector and even his business partners. To that end, they recruit family members and even professional actors to dramatize a series of scenes from the past of this business magnate and *pater familias*. During the film, childhood traumas, his first communion, the sights and sounds of his triumphant business career are paraded before the eyes of the protagonist, now the hapless spectator of his own life. In their attempts to jump-start the recall mechanism of Antonio's broken consciousness, the avaricious family has recourse to a mechanistic parody of Freudian therapy. The second sequence of the film reenacts a moment from Cano's early childhood where the five-year-old Antonio is punished for touching himself by being locked in a room with an enormous pig which, they threaten, will "eat his little hands off." Through their re-creation of a literal castration trauma, the family seeks to use the cathartic incident to effect a dramatic cure.[3] "The subconscious, let the subconscious work," shouts the grandfather as he stands guard over the darkened room where the invalid Antonio is shut in with the pig.

Abandoning their reductive Freudianism for a more behaviorist approach, the family subsequently has recourse to a range of sensory stimuli in their carefully calculated efforts to awaken his dormant memory. Newsreel footage, family photos, a recording of the industrialist's triumphant speech marking the successful expansion of the family's construction business, the evocative music of the "Concierto de Aranjuez" popped into a cassette recorder as the patient strolls through the gardens of the Aranjuez Palace with his wife—these are the pieces of a patchwork past marshalled by Cano's nearest and dearest in their efforts to trigger the memory process.

The principal dynamic of the film is ultimately Spanish history itself. The family's self-serving *mise en scène* of key moments in the life of Antonio Cano offers up an esperpentic version of the last fifty years of Spanish history. Antonio's first communion, for example, takes place on 14 April 1931, the day the Republic was proclaimed, and thus in the midst of the recreated service, the organist breaks into the Republican hymn as supporters of the new government burst into the church. Other events in Antonio's private story are explicitly tied to history as well. In a later sequence, the character sits before a movie screen as the same documentary footage of the war is projected over and over again to the verbal accompaniment of Rubén

Darío's martial epic, the "Marcha triunfal." Suddenly the amnesiac's father comes bursting through the screen announcing his "return" from the war. Despite the patient's protests that he wants to keep watching "the movie," his father drags him off to watch a histrionic reenactment of another of his life's events. Finally, with an irony that escapes the family's distorted re-creation of Spain's immediate past, the story of the development of the family business from a small quarrying firm to a major industrial concern recaps the more generalized history of the profits made by the sons of the victors who grew wealthy rebuilding the country their fathers had helped to destroy.

El jardín de las delicias offers a particularly imaginative solution to the problems of representing memory, and its collective supplement, history, on the film screen. From the family's clumsy historical re-creations to the epic film within a film cited above, Saura's black comedy serves up a parodic reflection of an entire tradition of Francoist historical films—from Franco's own idealized reenactment of the Civil War as lived by a heroicized version of his own family, *Raza*, to the 1948 reworking of Columbus' voyages, *Alba de América*.[4] Antonio, the privileged spectator of a similarly biased projection of the past within the film, once the active embodiment of the Francoist legacy in its sixties' technocrat version, now appears as the cumulative product of Francoist history: rendered childlike, the passive victim in a world manipulated by others.[5]

This ambivalence in the portrayal of the Cano character—the victimizer turned victim—seems entirely deliberate, as one persuasive interpretation of the film makes clear. In the portrait of the formerly authoritarian father and business leader, now reduced to abject physical and mental infirmity, a number of critics have seen a pointed reference to Franco himself.[6] Though he was not to die until November of 1975, Franco's health and attention span were already failing in the late sixties and early seventies. At least one obvious parallel between the character created by Saura and the "Caudillo" occurs in the scene depicting the hunting party staged for Cano with birds wired in the air to make them an easy target. John Hopewell, in his recent book on Spanish film, recounts the tale of Franco fishing expeditions where frogmen were sent under the boat to attach fish to Franco's hook.[7] Indeed, the final scenes of the film would seem to confirm the identification between Franco and Cano, for, despite the family's elaborate efforts, their father-patient makes scant progress toward recovery. Neither fully functional nor entirely helpless, he continues to exercise control over their lives. The last sequence shows Antonio in the foreground in his wheelchair as the other members of his family, also in wheelchairs, circle around him aimlessly. *El jardín de las delicias* ultimately offers a pessimistic view of Spanish society still in thrall to the paralyzing effects of thirty years of the Franco regime.

As is often true in Saura's works, the visual seeds of a later film, in this case *La prima Angélica*, are already present in the earlier 1970 work. While the main thrust of *El jardín de las delicias* is directed toward the exteriorized dramatization of memory and history as the stage on which past and present meet, it is in this same film that Saura conducts his first experiments in the representation of the subjective and often involuntary workings of memory that he will pursue more fully in *La prima Angélica* and *Dulces horas*.

The fourth sequence of the film, while initially appearing to follow, in plot and chronology, the actions of the previous scene, which show the helpless Antonio being prepared for bed by family and servants, in fact, projects the spectator into another world, a subjective realm where memory and fantasy mingle. Although no explicit cuing takes place, a number of indications alert the viewer, especially one whose cinematic competence includes a general familiarity with the rhetoric of art cinema narration, to a shift in space, time, and narrative mode.[8] Eschewing the classic cinema's use of cutting between scenes presumed to occur at different places or moments, the director relies on non-diagetic music (that is, music with no source in the action of the scene itself, as in a band playing or a radio switched on) to signal the break with the previous scene. The camera lingers through the transition from one sequence to the next on the image of the (one hesitates to call him) protagonist's face and then pans from the immobile

Cano to the pastel walls of a 1940s boudoir, complete with filmy curtains and the chirping of birds. As the strains of the Imperio Argentina tune "Recordar" (a recording of which [hence diagetic] is enlisted by the family/actors in their initial staging of a scene from Antonio's childhood) rise on the sound track, a woman dressed in a white peignoir approaches the adult Cano with greetings for his eleventh birthday. In the absence of definitive cinematic cues, it is, finally, the previously aphasic Antonio's childlike words of response (as well as his infantile facial expression) which provide the confirmation that, rather than another "objective" scene with its dramatized re-creation of childhood, we are witnessing genuine subjective recollection.[9]

With this sequence, Saura seems to have tapped a fundamental intuition about the nature of remembrance and mental re-creation of the past and past selves.[10] The adult Antonio returns to his youth, but in contrast to the family's theatrical reenactment of his first communion where a child actor is hired to play his role, the "I" he sees in his mind's eye is his present "I," the only one he knows. The originality in Saura's representation of memory (in contrast to directors such as Bergman or Resnais) lies in his use of the adult actor to embody both the (adult) remembering and (child) remembered selves.[11] This same technique, entrusted to the same actor, José Luis López Vásquez, will provide the central device for representing memory in Saura's otherwise quite different 1973 film.

La prima Angélica, in its departure from the *grand guignol* theater of *El jardín*, chooses to tell a more personal and yet familiar story. In her account of the Civil War novel, Bertrand de Muñoz characterizes the period of the sixties and seventies as a time of return for many exiles of the war. Not surprisingly, she finds this theme reflected in the novels written during the period.[12] Like Marré Gamallo, the "traveler" of Juan Benet's *Volverás a Región*, and the narrator of his *Una meditación*, in Saura's film, the protagonist's return to the places and people of his childhood sets in motion a series of past recollections that threaten to engulf the present.[13] Luis, played by López Vasquéz, has returned to Segovia from Barcelona, to the home of his maternal relatives, where he spent his summers as a child, and most notably the "long vacation" of 1936, in order to deposit his dead mother's remains in the family pantheon. In Segovia, he meets the relatives he has not seen in years: cousin Angélica, his first love of almost thirty years ago, and tía Pilar, his mother's sister. He also meets others for the first time: Angélica's daughter, also named Angélica, and his cousin's husband, Anselmo.

Once again, in memory's reprise of the protagonist's life, personal story and public history coincide. The film opens with a dreamlike sequence, repeated towards the end of the film where it is identified as the memory of the bombing of a school classroom. As Luis' literal journey gives way to interiorized temporal displacement, he relives a further series of wartime events. Far removed from the idealized vision of official Francoist accounts, Luis' memories of the war reveal no evidence of heroism among the victors. The outbreak of the conflict finds his relatives cowering in a darkened room until a radio broadcast informs them that their side, the Nationalists, has gained control of the region. Luis, the son of a "red," is treated as an outcast, in particular by his uncle, Angélica's father. For the child of a Republican living in the insurgent-controlled zone, Nationalist "culture" is repression writ large, most notably at the hands of the Church. A parish priest twists Luis' pubescent love for Angélica into the stuff of mortal sins while the picture of the mortified nun on his bedroom wall inhabits his nightmares and even edges over into daily life. A particularly striking scene portrays a priest's harrowing sermon on a young boy's death under "enemy" bombardment. Saura has acknowledged the autobiographical origins of many sequences in the film.[14] For him, as for many other Spanish writers and directors of his generation, childhood is a painful time, anything but the lost paradise evoked by earlier literary explorers of the shifting geography of memory.

Perhaps because of these personal roots, images speak an especially powerful language in *La prima Angélica*. The linear narrative causality of conventional cinema is replaced by the associative logic of memory, dreams, and nightmares. The film proceeds in a series of alternating sequences of objective and subjective scenes, present and past events, that succeed one another without warning. Film analysts have long noted that cinematic language knows no past tense.[15] Instead, it must make use of verbal or visual clues (a title with a date superimposed on the screen or a verbal reference by a character or off-screen narrator) to establish the pastness of a scene. In Saura's film, however, we are far from the conventional structure of the flashback as the usual articulation between past and present, for one of the fundamental characteristics of the flashback, and the aesthetic of classic narrative cinema in the context of which it developed, is the neat separation between the two moments in time and the total distinctness of both. If we think of the disordered, confused, and highly subjective past evoked by the narrators of Benet or Marsé, for example, and we contrast it with the ordered, unambiguous, technicolor past of a film like *Rebecca*—"Last night I dreamed I went back to Manderly"—we perceive the importance of Saura's discovery.

In *La prima Angélica*, past and present intermingle, not only through the dualistic performance of López Vásquez but also through the presence of the same actors/characters in both the 1936 and 1973 planes of the film. The result is the further confusion of the spectator, who sees the events through the eyes of Luis, as Angélica's mother of '36 becomes the adult Angélica of '73, Angélica child of '36 is Angélica daughter of '73, the grandmother of '36 appears as tía Pilar of '73, while Anselmo, the husband of the adult Angélica is seen as her blue-shirted father in the past sequences. The projections of Luis' fallible visual memory insistently confuse Anselmo with Angélica's fascist father, despite the proof to the contrary in photos from the era. If memory errs on a superficial level of physical resemblance, the film seems to say, it rightly identifies a stratum of continuity between Angélica's despotic father, incapable of forgetting Luis or his father's adherence to the opposing side in the war, and the unfaithful, unscrupulous, apolitical husband of his grown-up cousin Angélica. Saura, who began his professional career as a photographer, seems to champion the fluid, equivocal nature of memory, represented in film, over the objective past recorded by still photography, contrasting the subjective power of the moving image to transport both characters and spectators to other places and other selves with the depersonalized having-been-there of the photograph, identified by Roland Barthes.[16]

If psychology—both Freudian and behaviorist—supplies the (playful) model of memory in *El jardín de las delicias,* the inspiration for *La prima Angélica* is literary. Saura's allusions to literary works in his films from Garcilaso to Machado and Mérimée are well known.[17] In *La prima Angélica,* these references, evoked by Luis in the sixteenth sequence of the film, serve to contextualize Saura's experiments with the process and thematics of memory. Luis mentions Proust, in his desire to explain to others and to himself the mechanisms of his own memory, noting: "Proust, a writer, one day dips his *madeleine* in his tea . . . and suddenly his mouth is filled with the aroma of geraniums and orange blossoms . . . his grandfather's garden." In the sequence that follows, it is hot chocolate rather than a *madeleine* that transports the character from a present-time afternoon tea to a summer's day some thirty years earlier when his mother took leave while his father waited by the car outside.[18]

Yet Saura exploits the cinematic value of the Proustian aesthetic of involuntary memory without embracing either its context or conclusions. Luis' re-immersion in his past is sterile and unproductive. When, near the end of the film, his grown cousin Angélica appeals to him for solace from her loveless marriage, he is incapable of response toward the adult woman. He leaves Segovia as he arrived there, a solitary figure, a man lacking the capacity for vital connection to his fellow human beings. Like the earlier López Vásquez character, Luis is left damaged, in this case emotionally impaired, by his experiences in wartime and postwar Spain. While some critics have attacked Saura for his satiric and simplistic portrayal of the victors of the war in the double characterization of Angélica's fascist father and her uncultured, materialist husband, Saura's vision of the *dos Españas* is ultimately no kinder toward the representative of the Republican defeated, Luis.

With *Dulces horas* (1981), his sixteenth feature-length film, Saura returns self-consciously to the themes and techniques of his earlier works: the predominating role of memory, especially memories of the Civil War; the family setting; the use of auto-biographical materials; and the theatrical representation of the links between past and present. The film's protagonist, Juan Sagahún, a fortyish *madrileño* art gallery owner and sometimes writer, is a man obsessed with his past, and at the center of that past, his relation to his mother who committed suicide when he was quite young. When his sister challenges his idealized view of their mother and her suicide by giving him a packet of letters written between their father and mother in the months before her death, Juan is motivated to write a dramatization of his childhood, *Dulces horas*, in an apparent attempt to puzzle out the real nature of his personal history. Rehearsals take place in an apartment across from the Retiro Park (in fact, the site of Saura's own family apartment in the thirties). Professional actors play the roles of his mother, young sister, aunt, uncles, and grandmother, with Juan himself interpreting the part of his childhood self, Juanico. But, unlike *El jardín de las delicias*, here, the theatrical character of these past scenes remains unannounced until well into the film. Instead, they risk being taken as instances of "real" memory, especially by experienced Saura watchers who are likely to connect the adult Sagahún's childlike character with the dramatic conceit employed by López Vásquez in the two previous films.

The director will exploit this potential ambiguity as the film progresses, with the viewer's confusion doubling that of the actor/characters. Chronological anomalies abound in the family drama, set sometime in the 1940s. Newspaper and radio reports on the Battle of Stalingrad overlap in the same scene with references to the scandal created by the Madrid debut of the film *Gilda* in 1947; lines of dialogue are repeated; the performers seem unable to resist the temptation to add personal reminiscence to dramatic reconstruction. Clearly, historical accuracy is not the goal here. While the subsequent disclosure of the theatrical origin of the scenes helps to explain some of these inconsistencies, there is never any specific indication as to what the group is rehearsing for—a play, a movie?

Juan tells Berta, the young actress chosen to play his mother because of her apparent resemblance to the original, that he wrote *Dulces horas* out of his conviction that nothing important happened to him after his adolescence, and because "I was in love with my mother." Juan's projection into an archetypal Oedipal search for origins is staged in the film as a literal dramatization of his own "family romance." This private theater becomes a means of self-discovery, a personal time machine that works to stimulate genuine recollection.[19] Losing control of the memory process, Juan experiences an involuntary re-immersion in the past as the central images of his childhood traumas play before his eyes: wartime air raids; the privations of cold and hunger; an exacerbated closeness to his mother and rivalry with his father, never resolved due to the latter's departure and her early death. In the course of his memories, he comes to see his original image of the beautiful, talented, all-loving, self-sacrificing mother abandoned by her husband displaced by a revised view of her as a willfully manipulative woman who, in the words of Juan, made him an accomplice in her death, since he himself brought her the poison from the pharmacy and watched her take it. Two symmetrical scenes at the beginning and end of the film, each depicting his mother's death but from opposing camera angles, frame his conscious and unconscious interrogation of the past, offering a visual representation of its conclusions. The therapeutic value of this experience would seem to be confirmed by the changes wrought in his present life as he falls in love with Berta.[20] Furthermore, the rehearsals of *Dulces horas* are suspended, in large part because the characters appear unable to separate life from art, past from present. Paradoxically, Juan's "cure" consists not in his escape from past obsessions into present "reality," but rather in his successful realization of his Oedipal fantasy by marrying Berta, the mother who escaped from his grasp in childhood.

Ultimately, however, the ironic effects of the play within the film and the burlesque character of Juan's Oedipal fantasy extend beyond the boundaries of the fiction. The pervasive theatricality of the film, evidenced in the use of exaggerated camera movements and the intrusive effects of the film's two

principal musical themes, Ravel's "La Valse" and, in a reprise of
El jardín de las delicias, the Imperio Argentina song "Recordar,"
points behind the protagonist Juan to the director Saura and
to the role of the film medium itself. Saura further signals his
own presence in a number of ways—through the incorporation
of some of his own wartime memories into Juan's dramatically-
induced reveries and by the appearance of his brother, the
painter Antonio Saura, in an early scene, as well as the latter's
paintings on the wall of Juan's apartment. Are we to take these
references as gratuitous personalism? I think not.

In the eight years that intervened between the making of
La prima Angélica and *Dulces horas,* much was happening in
Spain—Franco's death, the transition to democracy, and the
disenchantment among Spaniards on both the right and the
left, unhappy with too much or too little change. Rather than
yielding to intimist self-indulgence as some of his Spanish critics have charged, in his 1981 film the director interrogates the
impulse on the part of many of his contemporaries to indulge
in nostalgic evocations of the war and postwar years.[21] In one
striking scene, Juan relives an intrauterine memory of a stroll
through the Retiro by his parents-to-be. Standing in front of the
Crystal Palace, his mother exclaims that she wants her unborn
child to remember such a perfect moment, but her husband
undercuts the idyllic vision with his comments: "The pond is
artificial, the Palace a tasteless gewgaw, and the poor ducks are
dying of hunger." Juan's evocation of his mother's rose-colored,
movie version of reality points up the pervasive influence of
second-hand memories and dreams.

A primary medium of those second-hand memories is, of
course, film itself. A crucial earlier sequence highlights more
explicitly the role of cinema as a source or even substitute
for personal remembrance. Juan has accompanied Berta to a
dubbing session where the actress records her voice over the
image track of an American movie. As Juan sits at the back
of the darkened projection room, the flickering lights on the
screen trigger a recurrent memory of a wartime air raid, as a
voice from the past shouts a command to turn off the lights. In
the succeeding frames, wailing sirens and the sounds of aerial

bombardment accompany actual documentary footage showing people fleeing or falling amid the destruction in the streets of Madrid. Intercut with the genuine documentary images are shots of Juanico and his mother scrambling through the smoke and rubble. That Juan should see his memories in the form of movie images points to the impossibility of ever recovering pure past, uncontaminated by mediating representations, fabrications whose origins are not always so easy to discern. The ironic juxtaposition of two so apparently different types of filmic fabrication—American entertainment film versus newsreel documentary—hints at the ambiguous status of Saura's own project. Film is not the innocent recorder of history, public or private, as was demonstrated in *El jardín de las delicias*, but instead must create and recreate history as a story often more persuasive than the real or imagined original.

The final sequence of *Dulces horas* offers the ultimate testimony to the double-edged power of the film medium in its refashioning of reality. Presented by way of epilogue to Sagahún's memory quest, the scene opens with the sight and sound of Berta, now a visibly pregnant mother-to-be, straightening up the living room of Juan's apartment as she lip-syncs the film's theme song "Recordar" (also the source of the film's title with its, here ironic, invitation to remember "yesterday's sweet hours . . . that love of yesteryear"). Her song continues as she enters the bathroom and pauses to address an unseen figure in the bathtub as "mi niño." As she picks up a sponge and approaches the tub, the camera discovers her "little boy" to be Juan himself. The two engage in a (perhaps ritual) exchange between mother and son that, in its erotically charged playfulness, mimics Juanico's original relation with his "real" mother. However, any remaining shred of fictive autonomy is irremediably broken when Berta turns from her tender caresses to finish her song, singing directly to the camera in the best manner of the Hollywood musical, as the film's closing credits roll over the image of her face in close-up.

By means of such a self-reflexive, fiction-shattering finale, Saura seems to point, on the one hand, to the collusion between

the clichéd movie "happy ending" and the improbable realization of Juan's childhood fantasy. On the other hand, the director's comic turn on Oedipal tragedy provides "dramatic" proof
of film's power to turn personal, and even national, tragedy to
comedy. Saura uses the magic of the movies to rewrite the
conclusion to his own trilogy of memory, in the tradition of
the classic Hollywood film comedies of the thirties and forties.[22]
This last parallel is reinforced by the source of the theme song
"Recordar," which comes from a Spanish remake of an American
film comedy from the early thirties—*Her Wedding Night*. The
Spanish version of the film, *Su noche de bodas*, perhaps not
coincidentally, had its debut in Madrid on 14 April 1931, the day
of the proclamation of the Spanish Republic.[23] Thus, I suggest,
it would be a mistake to take Juan Sagahún's happy resolution
of his personal trauma as a purely private matter. Taking a
page from Spanish history's perhaps equally improbable happy
ending to nearly forty years of Francoism, Saura's film affirms,
not without irony, a nation's capacity to rewrite its relationship
to a traumatic past in terms of a more promising present.[24]

Cornell University

NOTES

1. The figures cited are drawn from Maryse Bertrand de Muñoz, "The Span-
ish Civil War in the Recent Spanish Novel, in *Red Flags, Black Flags*, ed.
John Romeiser (Madrid: J. Porrúa Turranzas, 1982), 199-252; and Román
Gubern, *1936-1939: La guerra de España en la pantalla* (Madrid: Filmoteca
Española, 1986). Other major studies of the war in Spanish novel and film
include Malcolm Alan Compitello, "The Novel, the Critics and the Spanish
Civil War: A Bibliographic Essay," *Anales de la Narrativa Española*, 4 (1979):
117-38, and his *Ordering the Evidence: "Volverás a Región" and Civil War
Fiction* (Barcelona: Puvill, 1983); and on film, Carlos Fernandez Cuenca, *La
guerra de España y el cine*, 2 vols. (Madrid: Editora Nacional, 1972); Marcel

Oms, *La guerre d'Espagne au cinéma* (Paris: Editions du Cerf, 1986); and Marjorie Valleau, *The Spanish Civil War in American and European Films* (Ann Arbor: The University of Michigan Press, 1982). See also Maryse Bertrand de Muñoz, *La guerra civil española en la novela: bibliografía comentada*, 2 vols. (Madrid: J. Porrúa Turranzas, 1982).

2. Jean Tena identifies *memoria* (and/or *recuerdo*) as the "mot-clé d'une génération," citing not only Marsé and Benet but also a number of poets from the same age group: J. M. Caballero Bonald, Carlos Barral, Jaime Gil de Biedma and José Angel Valente, among others ("Carlos Saura et la mémoire du temps escamoté," in *Le Cinéma de Carlos Saura*, Actes de Colloque sur le Cinéma de Carlos Saura des 1 et 2 février 1983 [Bordeaux: Presses Universitaires de Bordeaux, 1984], 17).

3. The family's version of psychoanalytic therapy corresponds to what authors Krin Gabbard and Glen Gabbard in their *Psychiatry and Cinema* (Chicago: University of Chicago Press, 1987) have identified as the typically reductive movie view of the uses of psychiatry.

4. Virginia Higginbotham discusses the legitimating function of the "official" Francoist historical film *(Spanish Film Under Franco* [Austin: University of Texas Press, 1988], 18-23), which she describes as "the only images most Spaniards had of their country's . . . history" (18). Saura is not the first to parody the Francoist historical film. Of the four dream sequences, each based in film imagery, of Luis García Berlanga's brilliant *Bienvenido, Mr. Marshall* (1953), one is an obvious send-up of the *carton-piedra* historical epic which dominated the Spanish productions of the previous decade.

5. For a full analysis of the rhetorical role of the spectator within the film, see Nick Browne, "The Spectator in the Text: The Rhetoric of *Stagecoach*," *Film Quarterly* 29, no. 2 (1975-1976): 26-37; for its function in Saura's films, consult Marvin D'Lugo, "Carlos Saura: Constructive Imagination in Post-Franco Cinema," *Quarterly Review of Film Studies* 8, no. 2 (1983): 35-47.

6. Marcel Oms seems to agree with Gubern's affirmation of the link, for he quotes the latter's opinion to that effect in his own discussion of the film *(Carlos Saura* [Paris: Edilio, 1981], 47). Peter Besas also alludes to this association, although he cites Saura's disclaimer in a later section *(Behind the Spanish Lens* [Denver: Arden Press, 1985], 123, 237).

7. John Hopewell, *Out of the Past: Spanish Cinema After Franco* (London: British Film Institute, 1986), 78.

8. A lucid account of the techniques of the European art film, in contrast to classic Hollywood style narration, can be found in Chapter 10 of David Bordwell's *Narration in the Fiction Film* (Madison: University of Wisconsin Press, 1985).

9. The interaction between the solicitous but seductive aunt and her man-child nephew Luis projects an ambivalent eroticism that confirms a largely Freudian view of childhood that Saura exploits in many of his films.

10. See Saura's remarks to Marsha Kinder: "The mechanisms of memory are different in every person. One day I looked in the mirror and said, 'My goodness, what did I look like as a child?' I can't remember myself as a child in the mirror. I have photographs, but when I look at them, I feel it's someone I don't know. When I've tried to reconstruct my past, I don't do so with the mentality of a child. Mostly I see myself as I am now, but going back 20 or 30 years. That was one of the fundamental ideas that made me make this film [La prima Angélica]—that you cannot see yourself as a child." (Quoted by Marsha Kinder, "Carlos Saura: The Political Development of Individual Consciousness," *Film Quarterly* 32, no. 3 [1979]: 20.)

11. For a discussion of such "mental cinema" in Bergman and Godard, see Bruce Kawin, *Mindscreen* (Princeton: Princeton University Press, 1981). However, let me add that despite the possible antecedent of Saura's device in Bergman's *Wild Strawberries*, where Professor Isaac Berg revisits the scenes of his youth in the body of an old man, Saura's treatment differs in its attack at the heart of the traditional filmic view of the past as intact and autonomous. López Vásquez's performance in both *El jardín* and *La prima Angélica*, through his corporal and physical expression, shows us the man as child, while Victor Sjöstrom's uniform performance serves to emphasize the distance between the present man and his faraway and irrecoverable past.

12. "The Spanish Civil War in the Recent Spanish Novel," 213-14.

13. Eduardo Haro Tecglen, in his introduction to the published screenplay of *La prima Angélica*, writes: "Luis es un personaje conocido del cine, de la literatura: es el hombre que regresa. Vuelve al lugar de su infancia, a los puntos y a las personas en que o con quienes sucedío su infancia. Evoca sus recuerdos: evoca los nuestros" (Carlos Saura and Rafael Azcona, *La prima Angélica* [Madrid: Elias Querejeta Ediciones, 1976], 10). According to Saura, Luis has not sought out this reencounter with his past: "En cierta forma, ha llegado un momento en que, después de haber estado huyendo de su pasado, tiene que enfrentarse con una parcela de su vida que hasta ahora ha querido olvidar. Entonces, en un primer estadio hay un leve rechazo por él de su pasado, o por lo menos no existe un deliberado intento de reincorporarse a ese pasado; pero a lo largo de la película el pasado va adquiriendo cada vez más fuerza hasta terminar dominándolo todo. Realmente la trayectoria del film aparece definida en el sentido de que si el presente pesa más en la primera parte 'Luis' acaba

al final devorado por su pasado. La fuerza de esos fantasmas, de esos personajes del pasado, de esas vivencias, de esas imágenes sobre todo, la fuerza de los recuerdos es tal que termina por devorar al personaje" (cited by Tecglen, 21).

14. A primary source of information on Saura's own wartime memories is his "Recuerdos de la guerra civil," *Penthouse* (Spanish edition), November 1978, reprinted in Oms, *Carlos Saura*, 99-103.

15. As David Bordwell puts it: "The cinematic signifier does not have formal marks which could characterize its temporality, not even equivalents of autonomous monemes, the specialized lexical items of language (yesterday, today, tomorrow, etc.)" (77).

16. Roland Barthes, "The Rhetoric of the Image," in *Image, Music, Text*, trans. Stephen Heath (New York: Hill and Wang, 1977), 44-45.

17. Garcilaso's sonnet "Elisa vida mía" and Calderón's *Gran teatro del mundo* provide the inspiration for *Elisa vida mía* (1977). Machado makes an appearance in both *Peppermine frappé* (1967) and *La prima Angélica*, while Mérimée is one of the sources for *Carmen* (1983).

18. This scene offers an exemplary instance of Saura's representation of memory through both theatrical and cinematic means. As Luis (López Vásquez) raises the cup of chocolate to his lips, his expression changes imperceptibly. To the strums of guitar music off-screen (non-diagetic music is a frequent clue to shifts in time and/or space in Saura, as noted in *El jardín*), Luis looks off to his left, and the next image, a subjective shot in more than one sense, shows his mother adjusting her hat in a large mirror, with Luis watching her in the background. The reflexive gesture of the mirror shot marks it as an emblematic image of the film as a whole, where past and present are shown to coexist in the mind of the perceiver through the agency of film.

19. Notes Saura: "Juan es a la vez autor, actor, y espectador" (quoted by Miguel Hidalgo, *Carlos Saura* [Madrid: Ediciones J C, 1981], 18).

20. Jean Tena sees Juan Sagahún's investigation of the past as an exorcism that enables him to sweep aside the lies and evasions that block his development (and, by extension, that of all Spaniards): "Une fois de plus, la mémoire apparaît comme le seul moyen d'exorciser tous les escamotages, individuels ou collectifs" (20).

21. Manuel Palacio observes that: "*[Dulces horas]*, hasta el momento, de su filmografía es sin ningún tipo de dudas la que peor críticas ha recibido de toda su carrera" ("La obra de Carlos Saura en la crítica especializada española," in *Le Cinéma de Carlos Saura*, 62). For a survey of opinions from various Spanish critics, see 62-63.

Kathleen M. Vernon

22. For an extremely suggestive study of the Hollywood "comedy of remar-
riage" as part of a tradition of comedy going back to Shakespeare, see
Stanley Cavell, *Pursuits of Happiness* (Cambridge: Harvard University
Press, 1981).

23. Hopewell, 15. Fernando Méndez-Leite, in contrast, shows the film as having its debut on 4 April of that year *(Historia del cine español*, 2 vols.
[Madrid: Ediciones Rialp, 1965], 2:776). This small discrepancy should
not obscure the association of this film in particular with that important
moment in Spanish history. Saura's brilliant use of music in films, whether
as a device used in characterizing individuals or settings, or as a trigger to
the spectators' own memories or associations, deserves study in its own
right.

24. The comic revisionism offered by *Dulces horas* with respect to the earlier
two films recalls the sequel, *Mama cumple cien años* (1979), to his dark
allegory of postwar Spain, *Ana y los lobos* (1972). The family of "wolves"
who enact real or symbolic murder on the foreign governess, played by
Geraldine Chaplin, return for the 1979 film, a comic-satiric fantasy, while
Ana herself is resuscitated. Oms cites a remark by Saura concerning the
relation between those two films that is equally relevant for the discussion
of *El jardín de las delicias, La prima Angélica*, and *Dulces horas:* "Ce qui est
peut-être le plus important, bien que ce ne soit pas mentionné dans le film,
c'est le fait que Franco est mort il y a quelques années . . . et il y a eu, en
Espagne, de grands changements politiques et d'autres" *(Carlos Saura*, 78).

PART II
THE
INTERNATIONAL RESPONSE

NARRATIVE DISCONTINUITY AND THE WARRING IMAGE:
THE ROLE OF THE SPANISH CIVIL WAR IN THE NOVELS OF CLAUDE SIMON

Mark W. Andrews

The Spanish Civil War occupies a moment in history and a place in Claude Simon's fictional production which function as mirror sets of coordinates. Cross-referenced, they serve to locate twin foci of conflict, binocular images of war, but where each perspective, as through a looking glass, is the inverse of the other, at odds with its counterpart. World and stage are in anarchy, usurping the other's frame. Barcelona is in turmoil in July 1936, yet some of the frenzy of activity is no more than mere form, pointless on the surface yet fulfilling a deeper need for order. The formal representation of discontinuous events is achieved by the staging of more such events. This activity is dangerously mimetic, and purposefully utopian; it seeks to normalize an anarchic state of affairs, to impose standards of frenetic behavior. It is also unproductively parasitic, fated to fail and to induce failure. The anarchists turned out to be a thorn in the side of their allies, placing their own idealistic programs above the Loyalist cause, and losing themselves in the pursuit and perpetuation of ephemeral local conditions, effects, and opportunities.

Simon's novel, *Le Palace*, retraces the upheavals of the early months of the war, but a radical inversion has occurred; form is now presented in disorder, and history has become the potential guide. The narrator returns to Barcelona some fifteen years after the war to retrace his own itinerary as a student revolutionary and to try to impose a sense of history and of place on a chaotic series of impressions and experiences. However, the story retold still lacks a plot. The narrator's very failure to concatenate his recollections in a relationship of cause and effect accounts for the novel's success: the unfolding of a narrative is taken over by the enfolding of history within a structural complication. History itself is revealed to be a form of representation, elusive of authenticity and reluctant to originate meaning. History and fiction exist as contradictory forces, at war with each other and with themselves; they reflect balance without harmony, symbiosis without nourishment.

Le Palace is a deceptively simple novel in terms of its formal design. Unlike many of the novelist's later works, it deals with only one setting and issues from a single and identifiable narrative source at two points in time. The novel's surprising resistance to critical elucidation resides in large measure in the breakdown of causality it espouses. The novel accelerates the sequencing of events; the rapid succession of impressions outpaces the narrator's perception, setting up a stroboscopic disjunction of the image. What is retained is an effect of stationary, disconnected moments, most strikingly conveyed by the image of the pigeon landing on the balcony in the opening lines of the novel. The bird simply materializes, motionless, its arrival too swift for the eye to follow.

The loss of flow similarly occasions frames of reference to career, collide, and collapse like the taxis which speed around the city. The resulting disorientation creates a vacuum, an absence of continuity, which is invaded by representations of the process of acceleration itself, space traversed by pigeons and by taxis. In order to clarify the relation between events and their representation, between history and its fictions in the novel, *Le Palace* may be approached intertextually from the direction of an earlier, more explicit novel, *La Corde Raide.* This latter work, more naively, and ultimately less interestingly in its own right, chooses to explain rather than to show the forces at work in the first days of the war in Barcelona. It can, therefore, serve as a valuable hermeneutic tool with which to explore the representational space of *Le Palace*.

La Corde Raide, published in 1947, is Claude Simon's second novel and his first venture into autobiography. In the opening pages, the Spanish Civil War poses a problem of pictorial representation for the protagonist: how can he tell the story of his involvement to his Russian-speaking girlfriend through the medium of his drawings?[1] The manner in which war is to be represented is, for Simon, critical to its interpretation; he sees the meaning and experience of war for those who are at the center of the action as being largely determined by their particular situation, by a semiosis that is immediate and local. There is a circularity of signification here that feeds upon itself, creating its own forms of urgency and, as its antidote, making the creation of form a matter of urgency. History is in the making; the task of soldiering as perceived by Simon is "artisanal" in nature, and the creation of provisional forms is required not merely to mirror but to help determine the outcome of events in process.

Sitting in Gorky Park with Vera, trying to communicate by drawing for her in his notebook, the youthful protagonist of *La Corde Raide* notes that just behind the bench on which they are seated there is a large poster representing a map of Spain. He reminisces that he has been in Spain and seen a little of the Revolution, that he has done some gunrunning, has met some splendid people, and has witnessed some rather ugly situations. All of this is much too complicated to relay in images to someone who speaks a different language. War has just broken out between China and Japan; it is, presumably, the summer of 1937, and he is in love. The problem of representation can safely be deferred as far as he is concerned. It will be a task for the older narrator-turned-writer for whom coming to terms with the past has become the more pressing matter, and for whom, also, the representation of Spain is problematic, because, as it turns out, the Civil War is itself an exercise in representation.

In 1936, the narrator had been in Barcelona, a witness to the events of July in the Plaza de Cataluña. It was at this time that the Nationalist strongholds in the Telefónica and the Hotel

Colón, held by the Guardia Civil and rebel army units, were stormed by loyalist guardsmen and leftist militias. The narrator of *La Corde Raide* remembers in particular the speeding black cars of the anarchists, which carried the message "Viva la Muerte" daubed in white paint on their sides. He wonders what was achieved by such urgency, and by the senseless waste of life that frequently resulted. The acclamation of death, whether from the heroic storming of one of the machine guns of the Hotel Colón or an ignominious collision at a crossroads, seemed to stem from a "desperate attempt at deliverance,"[2] a "dream of liberation" (*CR*, 35).

The attempt and the dream appear, to the narrator, to be self-generated and self-sustaining, fed by a desperation that interprets action as an end in itself, a means of immediate liberation. "Certainly Barcelona," muses the narrator, "was a place for that. I mean for this revolt which found its goal and its justification in its own substance, feeding off it, exalting in the spectacle of its own representation, sufficing unto itself, disenchanted. And, definitively, I think that it was like that: these fellows gave themselves their own representation" (*CR*, 46). As the narrator concedes, an unselfishness was also at work, perhaps even as a concomitant of this activity of representation; there was a sense of higher purpose in quest of something "too perfect ever to be achieved" (*CR*, 46). While he views the ultimate global significance of the causes that are at stake as playing its part in determining the course of events, the narrator has no quick response to the indignant question of his friend Carl, who feels that the revolutionaries hold life in too low a regard: "Do you believe those people will achieve anything?" (*CR*, 46).[3] Only later does he see that the use of the future tense begs the question. These people were doing something at that time. Their vision of the future, their contribution to history, civilization, and progress must not be considered in isolation, as Carl wanted to do; their concerns must be viewed as conditioned by the exigencies of the here and now, by an aesthetics of immediacy and urgency.

The narrator says of the cars which race around the city that "the excess of speed also had a meaning at this moment"

(*CR*, 35). In *The Passionate War,* Peter Wyden presents a dialogue between Koltzov and Durruti in which the latter explains possession of a Hispano-Suiza convertible by claiming to need a fast car so that he "can get quickly to all sectors of the front."[4] Koltzov, Stalin's personal envoy, has come to see Durruti's anarchosyndicalists and their allies, the anti-Stalinist *Partido Obrero de Unificación Marxista* (POUM), as a present danger. In his eyes, they have become increasingly carried away with the trappings of self-representation, intoxicated by images of dictatorial power. Yet Durruti's explanation is perhaps more sincere than it appears from the exchange. The anarchists' urgency and need for speed is to be understood in terms of the desperateness of their attempt to dream. Not for them the drawn-out conflict of war, for their revolutionary program is as disdainful of the war as is Simon's own critique of Malraux's work:

> *Man's Hope?* For me it's a bit like TinTin carrying out the revolution. . . . Besides, Malraux speaking about the Spanish Civil War is like a warrior describing acts of war. My book is taken from confused memories of what was going on in Barcelona when I was there. That is to say the revolution properly speaking and not the war.[5]

The sense of urgency that attends the anarchists' project of *communismo libertario,* as Wyden points out, undermines the Republican cause, and that of the Communists themselves, in that it assigns a higher priority to the anti-capitalist revolution than to the winning of the war (58). The incoherence of the actions of those "apocalyptic conquistadors in their delirious cars" (*CR*, 36) was incomprehensible to those who had not been in Barcelona to witness it, and belonged to a discontinuous, disjunctive order of events, as unpredictable and volatile as the government-issue grenades used by Orwell and described by Simon in his latest work, *Les Géorgiques:*

> The drawback of these bombs put together more or less by artisans (although it was the government which supplied them now—which led one to believe that it was a government more or less put together by artisans) was that they were as

likely not to explode when you threw them as they were to
explode without any warning.[6] (G, 293)

Historic actions become possible under such conditions, if
only because existence itself takes on a numbing "artisanal"
quality. Fatigue and constant vigilance create a condition of half-
sleep which, according to the narrator of Les Géorgiques, has
the same characteristics of improvisation and approximation,
of what he identifies as "bricolage," as do the hastily assembled
bombs; the inhibitions and psychic safeguards that normally
protect against suicidal risks are depressed, creating a dangerous tolerance of the extraordinary, a predisposition towards
heroism. Life at such moments has an accelerated character.
Writing as Simon characterizes it in La Corde Raide obeys similar
dictates; speed is all. At the conclusion of the novel, the narrator
identifies his autobiographical endeavor as a race. It is a sprint
to keep up with fleeting impressions, memories, and ideas; an
attempt, he says paradoxically, "to remember what happened at
the moment I was writing" (CR, 178).

If the traditional narrative of La Corde Raide does not
address this problematic of writing in terms of its own techniques of representation, it is because the fledgling novelist,
despite his penetrating insights into the nature of representation for the anarchists of POUM and Durruti, has not yet
begun to implement a formal preoccupation with "bricolage"
in his own writings. When he does eventually characterize his
writing as "bricolage" at the Cerisy Colloquium on the French
New Novel in 1971, he will compare his practice to a chapter
title in a mathematics textbook: "Arrangements, permutations,
combinations."[7] In La Corde Raide the narrator still takes the
mathematics of Riemann to be as incomprehensible to the artist
as is the work of Picasso to the mathematician.

This attitude will undergo change as Simon's art evolves
toward an emphasis on formal design, as may be illustrated by
a juxtaposition of the epigraphs from Le Sacre du printemps, a
more conventional novel, which appeared in 1954, and its laby-
rinthine counterpart, Le Palace, Simon's only novel fully devoted
to the Spanish Civil War, published in 1962. The epigraph to

the first part of *Le Sacre du printemps* is taken from Descartes: "Action and passion never cease being one and the same thing which has these two names."[8] The epigraph to *Le Palace* reads "Revolution: the locus of a moving body which, describing a closed curve, successively passes through the same points."[9] It is taken from the Larousse dictionary and refers only to the geometrical properties of a revolution; action appears to have subdued passion. Simon's goal has not, however, been fundamentally altered with the appearance of this work, as may be seen from an interview he gave at the time in the *Express:* "I wanted to describe odors, images, tactile sensations, emotions."[10] What has changed is his understanding of the mimetic potential of form *qua* "bricolage." In other words, the way he writes can mirror the way things happened. Style reflects a hastily assembled reality; it has become a form of action, assembly, and of passion, haste.

Rather than seek to impose an artificial chronological order of intelligibility upon the past, a failing he will come to reproach in Orwell, Simon allows form to become fully transparent, a passage through the welter of associations and memories that attend the moment of writing. Insofar as writing, unlike painting, represents perception through successive approximation rather than through the simultaneous rendition of images present in memory, speed and acceleration are ever-present concerns. The need to appear in all sectors of the story at once is a disruptive force which, in the absence of a textual vehicle analogous to Durruti's car, is best rendered by a narrative discontinuity, as events compete to be represented at one and the same time. The images of war in *Le Palace* are more than mere referential illusions of Barcelona; they are infused with revolutionary passions and sensations generated by images at war with each other. Like the anarchists in their speeding cars, the novel engages in an apocalyptic delirium of self-representation. It is in this sense that the activity of representation can be said to live up to the novel's epigraph as a study in the geometry of circular and circulatory forms. Revolution as action does not need to refer beyond itself to passion; it is already passion by another name.

Le Palace is the story of an older narrator who returns to Barcelona, fifteen years after the events of 1936, seeking to understand his participation as a student and member of the Loyalists in the months following the Nationalist uprising. The former student is hoping to impose order upon the welter of images present in his memory, impressions of his four companions who have been assimilated to his own sense of identity through the shared intimacy of war but who defy his rational comprehension as separate beings. "I is made up of others," said the narrator of *La Corde Raide*, "Other things, other smells, other sounds, other people, other places, other times" (*CR*, 174). The lesson to be learned by the former student is one of recognition of the self in the other; it is a lesson in self-representation.

The action which takes place in *Le Palace* is clearly derived from that which occurred in and around the Hotel Colón in Barcelona at the time of Durruti's funeral. A photograph of the funeral procession, contributed by Simon to a special issue of *Entretiens* on the author, shows a prominent banner which asks the question "¿QUIEN HA MUERTO A DURRUT. . . ."[11] The banner is slightly sagging, obscuring part of its message, which two lines below reads, "GIGANTE DE LA REVOLUCION." The Palace takes as its refrain the same phrase "¿QUIEN HA MUERTO?" but the designation has migrated to "EL COMANDANTE SANTIAGO GIGANTE DE LA LUCHA" (*P*, 35).[12] The month is September rather than November, the tramway destination signs refer to Valencia not to Barcelona,[13] and the Hotel Colón has become the Palace.

The limited misdirection is necessary to diminish the allure of referentiality; it encourages reading the novel as fiction, as metaphor rather than as history. As Simon himself said, this is no longer the Spanish revolution but his own; it is an adventure in writing which takes the events in Barcelona in 1936 as its model for self-representation. History has fallen prey to the play of words on words. Mention of the pigeons which suddenly materialize at the novel's opening and describe a vast circle over the pocked façade of the Palace at the novel's conclusion is accompanied by allusions to ornamental and lifeless doves. The migration of the signifier from the Hotel Colón to Cristóbal Colón to Christophe Colomb to colombe, the dove of peace, constitutes but one of the linguistic deaths of the hotel turned Palace, of the explorer become book. The word 'colón' also generates the bank later constructed on the site of the hotel, by a process of inscription designated in the novel as a calligraphed pyro-engraving. Consumed by a fire worthy of Patroclus' funeral pyre—the middle section of the novel is entitled "The Funeral of Patroclus"—the Palace will be replaced by a bank, a surrogate postwar repository, perhaps, for the New World equivalent of the *peseta*, the *colón*.[14] The revolutionary pigeons which wheel full circle over the Palace will likewise crown the statue of Columbus with their guano; theirs is the excrement redolent of death, that same multiple representation of death which concludes the former student's quest for his personal history by leading him to the memory of a rifle shot in a subterranean urinal. The novel does not clearly identify the victim of the presumed suicide; its sign is affixed indeterminately to both the student and to two other characters, his principal alter egos: the rifleman and the American. Critics have, in fact, read the suicide as that of the student, despite the obvious inconsistency of his continued existence as the narrator.

The past is dead and irretrievable except through the representational effects of "bricolage." *Le Palace* contains an allegory of retrieval within its frame. The second of its sections is devoted to the rifleman's story, translated more accurately in the English version as "The Rifle's Story." It is a tale about speed told to the narrator as a student during a train journey and continued in a taxi recklessly careening through the streets. The trip mirrors the tale. The student listens to the rifleman recount an assassination carried out a few years before in a Paris restaurant. For its success, the action depended on the speed of its execution which triggered a sequence of actions independent of the rifleman's own volition; his hand and his eye executed the maneuvers of which he thought himself incapable even as he performed them. He became an extension of the lethal momentum of the bullet. The Italian rifleman's story, once launched, continues endlessly on, for the duration of the voyage by train and car to the Palace. It does not falter even during the wild taxi ride in which the pair narrowly miss colliding with Columbus' statue: "so that later he was to remember the whole thing (images and words) somehow running parallel, like those films in which an invisible voice recites a text without relation to the series of images appearing on the screen" (P, 92).

Experience takes on the aspect of discoherence, a term coined by Jean Ricardou to describe the conflictual disruption and resumption of the text's flow. As a function of speed, auditory and visual images unreel in a state of disjunction, symptomatic of a generalized condition of conflict within and between representation and the world. The student looks out of the rear window of the taxi and makes out the writing on a poster thrown up by the wind of the car's passage, signs which spell out the word "Venceremos." The irresistibly victorious taxi is at this very moment on a collision course with the statue, the allegory of immovable History. Defeat is an ever-present threat, since the future path of the now desperately swerving taxi is bestrewn with the obstacles of the past. Barcelona has become a battlefield of words and images and of concepts and objects. The representational effects created by speed are double-edged, leaving open the possibility for conflictual interpretation. Does "bricolage" succeed in retrieving anything of value?

For Michel Deguy, the inventory announced by the title to the opening section is "a desperate attempt to grasp at what is taking flight."[15] Description in the novel conforms to a modernistic, aestheticized view of the world as spectacle, a sublation of history considered teleologically as desire. In a similar vein, Philip Solomon concludes that "the student's suicide is a refusal to read his story as metaphor, as a fiction, the writing of which is the only instrument of self-knowledge he possesses."[16] Solomon's reading is less radical than that of Deguy in that negativity is ascribed to a failure by the student rather than by the text. It is, however, a reading bounded by the notion that there is indeed a story to be read, albeit as metaphor, just as Deguy presumes that something is taking flight and is the target of the narrative's grasp. The novel is polemical in this regard; it opens with the materialization of a pigeon on the hotel balcony. Arrival, not departure, is the theme.

David Carroll takes issue with Deguy's traditional reading in which Carroll identifies a reluctance to consider doubling and repeatability as an affirmation of the historical process. In his essay on *Le Palace,* Carroll points out that

> The chief contradiction within representation as it is con-
> ceptualized and presented in *Le Palace* is that it is unstable,
> ungrounded, impossible to bring back to any definite presen-
> tation that is not in itself already a representation.[17]

In agreeing with Deguy that representation in *Le Palace* is fundamentally cinematographic, Carroll insists on the distinction that the image is not idealized or totalized; its discontinuous and indeterminate status represents history in the making, "a history that is plural, conflictual and open-ended" (*C,* 118). "Bricolage" succeeds, then, in the retrieval of process rather than product, of the copy and not the original.

The recent work of Gilles Deleuze on the concept of dysnarrativity in cinema adopts a position close to that of Carroll and provides a conceptual frame by which to understand the "bricolage" practiced by Simon in *Le Palace.* Deleuze refers to dysnarrativity as a condition of film narrative when it undergoes "repetitions, permutations and transformations."[18] This formulation is remarkably close to Simon's definition of the mathematical properties of "bricolage." Deleuze's principal argument is that the multiplicity of narratives resulting from this process stems from the image itself. The plurality flowing from the play of the images does not presuppose that any linguistic form subtends the image, nor does it imply that the image depends on the intellectual structure of a source narrative. The student of *Le Palace* cannot find his story, for there is no original story that is his own; there is only the interplay of images at war and the diverse stories they suggest.

The story of the Rifle, for all its inner coherence, is dislocated from the frames of outer reality, the train and taxi rides. Its obsessive self-involvement serves to underline the absence of any original point of reference by which the student can begin to orient himself toward the events in which he participates. The story, which runs parallel to the images, has no power over them. The cinematographic narrative resembles a drawer of memories opened many years later, as the narrator of *La Corde Raide* reminds us. All that remains is "a confused succession of images and shapes, full of violence and light, vehement, silent, a film of gestures, without subtitles, without even the help of a fragile and ghostly piano accompaniment" (*CR*, 47).

The differing critical interpretations of *Le Palace* reveal a continuing uneasiness with the question of values raised by the novelistic practice of Simon. There is in this work a privileging of circular over linear desire rather than a balance or tension between the two. His choice is defended by Carroll as a necessary corrective to traditional treatments that overlook certain contradictions within representation and historicity. It is also a more personal matter for Simon who claims to have treated his own revolution in this work, and not the Spanish revolution per se.[19] His orientation provokes the question raised in several forms by the socialist Carl in *La Corde Raide;* speaking of the anarchists, he asks: "But don't they value life?" (*CR*, 46). The narrator, revealingly, has no immediate rebuttal to offer. Only later has he learned to invoke the virtues of present activity over future achievement and, even then, he does not address the compatibility of the two. Indeed, the question remains politically an intractable one; unlike the socialists, the anarchists of POUM dealt directly with ends rather than with means, with risk rather than with calculation. For them, the revolutionary present eclipsed the future of the war; they could brook no delay, even at the expense of longer term considerations.

The warring image that appears in *Le Palace* rejects compromise; it remains hostile to the narrator's attempt to link cause to effect. By virtue of its unrelenting circularity, it appears closer to revolution than those paler Orwellian images which relive the Spanish Civil War by imposing an order after the fact. The shunning of a diluted historical perspective on the Spanish Civil War is inherent in the staging of writing as a rapidly self-renewing commitment and engagement of synchronic forces. History is assimilated to a repeatable present, maintaining a state of intensity and ferment. The combative narrative discontinuity practiced in *Le Palace* represents the war in its initial delirious fervor. It depicts a moment of little clarity and great confusion, but one which generated heroic action and extraordinary passion, a creative conflict mirrored and perpetuated in the "bricolage" of form in Simon's novel.

Vassar College

NOTES

1. Cf. Simon's latest work, *Les Géorgiques* (Paris: Minuit, 1981), which devotes one section to a rewriting of Orwell's *Homage to Catalonia* and to a portrait of the man. Simon's intertextual project dramatizes the patient futility of Orwell's attempt to impose coherence upon the past through a chronological representation of his months in Spain. Further references to this edition will be identified in the text by the symbol *G* in parentheses accompanied by a page number.

2. Claude Simon, *La Corde Raide* (Paris: Minuit, 1947), 34. Further references to this edition will be identified in the text by the symbol *CR* in parentheses accompanied by a page number. All translations are mine.

3. Literally: "Will they do something?" The play on the verb "faire," which equates 'to do' and 'to achieve,' is crucial to the narrator's point.

4. Peter Wyden, *The Passionate War: The Narrative History of the Spanish Civil War, 1936-1939* (New York: Simon and Schuster, 1983), 66.

5. "Entretien. Claude Simon parle," interview with Madeleine Chapsal, *L'Express*, 5 avril 1962. My translation.

6. Cf. the engraving entitled "Explosion de la bombe de Vaillant à la Chambre des Députés," in *Orion Aveugle* (Geneva: Skira, 1970). See also "Interview avec Claude Simon," interview with Bettina Knapp, *Kentucky Romance Quarterly* 16, no. 2 (1970): 183: "I have no other preoccupations than those of an artisan who makes an object." My translation.

7. Claude Simon, "La Fiction mot à mot," in *Pratiques*, vol. 2 of *Nouveau Roman: hier, aujourd'hui* (Paris: U.G.E., 1972), 96.

8. Claude Simon, *Le Sacre du printemps* (Paris: Calmann-Lévy, 1954), 7. My translation.

9. Claude Simon, *The Palace*, trans. Richard Howard (New York: George Braziller, 1967). Further references to this edition will be identified in the text by the symbol *P* in parentheses accompanied by a page number.

10. "Entretien. Claude Simon parle," 32.

11. "Claude Simon," *Entretiens* 31 (1972), 64-65.

12. One is tempted to speculate that the name Santiago is generated *in absentia* by the half shell serving as an ashtray on the writer's desk in *The Battle of Pharsalus:* "Près du paquet de gauloises se trouve une coquille Saint-Jacques utilisée comme cendrier" (Claude Simon, *La Bataille de Pharsale* [Paris: Minuit, 1969], 258-59). The dish is conspicuous by its absence in the inventory conducted in the first section of *Le Palace*. It appears neither on the narrator's desk nor as one of the shellfish on display in the hotel restaurant. Could it be that this missing 'coquille' (typographical misprint) manifests itself in the choice of substitution, 'Santiago' (Saint-Jacques) for 'Durruti,' prior to its materialization in a later novel? The principle here is the same as that which governs the arrival of the pigeon on the balcony; its undetectable flight can at best be surmised from its subsequent apparition.

13. See Jean-Claude Lieber's comment on the tramway names in *Claude Simon: analyse, théorie* (Paris: U.G.E., 1975), 136.

14. The word 'colón' could be pursued in its migration to other signifiers linked to murderous activities, that of the 'cinquième colonne' in the novel, for example.

15. Michel Deguy, "Claude Simon et la représentation," *Critique*, 187 (December 1962): 1210. My translation.

16. Philip H. Solomon, "Flights of Time Lost: Bird Imagery in Claude Simon's *Le Palace*," in *Twentieth-Century French Fiction* (New Brunswick: Rutgers University Press, 1975), 182.

17. David Carroll, *The Subject in Question* (Chicago: University of Chicago Press, 1982), 111. Further references to this work will be identified in the text by the symbol *C* in parentheses accompanied by a page number.

18. Gilles Deleuze, *Cinéma 2. L'image-temps* (Paris: Minuit, 1985), 179.

19. "Entretien. Claude Simon parle."

THROUGH THE "PANTRY WINDOW"
SYLVIA TOWNSEND WARNER AND THE SPANISH CIVIL WAR

Barbara Brothers

Like other British writers of the thirties who joined the Communist party, worked on committees supporting the Spanish Republican cause, and took the plight of the peasants and the fighting Loyalists as a subject for poems, essays, and fiction, Sylvia Townsend Warner was impelled into activism by events in Europe and at home. She traveled twice to Spain, once in October 1936 in the service of the English Red Cross unit, and again in 1937 to attend the Writers' Congress in Madrid. She was active on the London Committee for Spanish Medical Aid, convincing J. B. Priestley, Rebecca West, and Ethel Mannin to write pieces for *Spain & Us* which the committee published in November 1937, and in the International Association of Writers for the Defence of Culture. Although she wrote more about the war than most of her compatriots—or at least "as much as anybody"[1]—literary historians of the Spanish Civil War have not examined her poetry, short stories, or essays. Her name appears in John Muste's list of poets who wrote for the Republican side;[2] Katharine Bail Hoskins does not mention her, nor, for that matter, any woman who wrote on the Spanish conflict;[3] and Hugh D. Ford notes only her essay "Barcelona," including it among the pieces written in defense of the Loyalists by Communists for the *Left Review*.[4] Her novel, *After the Death of Don Juan* (1939)—Warner calls it a political fable—is not even recorded in the bibliographies identifying fictional accounts of Spain and the war.

Warner, like other leftist writers, was dissatisfied with England's failure to remedy the problems of unemployment and to improve the economic well-being of the farmers and the cities' poor following World War I. In the twenties, before she became politically active, her identification with and empathy for those marginalized by society were evident in her poems and novels; but in the thirties she spoke out in deed and word against the injustices she witnessed and the hypocrisies she deplored. She and her friend Valentine Ackland wrote about the impoverished British farmers living under "conditions which deform their lives."[5] Warner marched in the East End demonstrations against Mosley and the British Union of Fascists and satirized what she considered a half-hearted attempt by the government to curb the activities of the fascists, mocking the Public Order Act of 1936 in "An English Fable":

> For some years the sheep on a certain estate had been increasingly hunted and worried by a pack of dogs. They complained to the Bailiff of the estate, and were told by him that it was nothing, that the dogs were but young and playful; or again, that they were using the privilege (common to all animals on the estate) of Free Bite. . . . [6]

The Public Order Act, states Warner, did no more than forbid the dogs to wear their "collars" and request them not to "bark unduly." But, it was the events in Europe, particularly in her case the Reichstag Fire trial, that led Warner to join the Communist party.[7] At heart, however, she claims always to have been an anarchist, anarchism, for her, representing the "political theory of heaven."[8] Not the Marxist theory of history but the possibility of a richer life of the spirit and body for her fellow human beings, which social reform seemed to promise, drew Warner to become a Communist. The British government in Warner's view had turned its back to the people. Yet, as Warner herself observed, opposition to the government is not enough to make one a Communist "for very long,"[9] especially after events proved to her that communism as practiced was just another system for imposing the will of the few on the many.

Most of the fiction and poetry, both American and British, written about the Spanish Civil War has been dismissed as not literature. Even Ford, sympathetic with both the ideal expressed by the writers of joining public life to private feelings in litera-ture and with their belief that they were supporting the cause of liberal democracy over fascist dictatorship, concludes in *A Poet's War* that much of what was written is of historical not literary value (22). Despite his reservations about so many poems that were an immediate response to events at home and on the battlefield of Spain, Ford, unlike many contemporary historians and critics who judge literature on the scales of modernist aes-theticism, finds the principles from which the poets wrote, if not always what they wrote, admirable. As he points out, C. Day-Lewis, who in *The Hope for Poetry* called for the linking in poetry of the "inner" soul to the "outer" life of social facts and political ideas, and many other writers of the thirties sought a "reconciliation . . . 'between the poetic self and the rest of man'" (91). Most judgments on the failure to achieve that ideal echo those of Virginia Woolf in "The Leaning Tower," namely, that the sympathies of Auden et al. for the proletariat were derived from guilt and not from a sense of shared humanness, that the writers saw from the outside and not from the inside.[10] Warner states in her 1959 address to the Royal Society of Arts that women—at least some women—have effected that identifi-cation because they have viewed life through the "pantry win-dow," thus achieving what those running the castle have missed: "an ease and appreciativeness in low company."[11] Such an iden-tification with the "others" of society is evident in Warner's first volume of poetry, *The Espalier* (1925), which includes poems on a beggar wench, a black jazz musician, and poor farmers and laborers, another on Christ as thief and "sinner's" friend, and one for Rosa Luxemburg.

Also evident in Warner's writing from its inception are those "half-formulated political theories and humanitarian hopes" for which, Ford says, the "war acted as a catalyst" on both nonpolitical writers and leftists (20). The novel *Lolly Willowes:*

or the Loving Huntsman, which Warner published the year following *The Espalier,* is a comic but incisive attack on mechanical
bourgeois busyness and self-righteousness and on the use by
the capitalist patriarchy of what Lolly mockingly deprecates
as mere "props": "the Law, the Church, the History of Europe,
the Old Testament . . . the Bank of England, Prostitution."[12] London epitomizes the life such a hypocritical "civilization" has
produced: it is a world of "shops, processions of the Royal
Family and of the unemployed, the gold tunnel at Whiteley's,
and the brilliance of the streets by night" (4). The heroine is
a forty-year-old spinster who leaves the comfort of her upper-
middle-class brother's home for an impoverished, but richer in
her view, life among the poor of a Chiltern village. In *Summer
Will Show,* which was published in June 1936, Warner depicts
her hope that communism will transform the individual and
bring about a classless and genderless society with justice for
all. She attacks the "nursery tale" of its specter as evoked by the
powerful of the twentieth century. Setting the novel in the 1840s
in England and Paris, Warner uses the economic, political, and
social abuses of the past to mirror the sexism, racism, fascism,
and economic and social elitism of the first half of the twentieth
century.[13]

I have written elsewhere in detail about her novel *After the
Death of Don Juan,*[14] in which she satirizes the tyranny and self-
aggrandizement of the Spanish church and its lay and spiritual
leaders; the ineptness of those who sought to bring about social
reform; and the treachery and stupidity of the aristocratic sons
of Spain depicted in the betrayer Don Juan and his supporter,
the very man he has cuckolded. She also portrays the disarray,
powerlessness, and poverty of the peasants who die as brothers
at the hands of the army in the conclusion of the novel. I have
also discussed in the same essay the stories Warner published
in *A Garland of Straw* (1943), a collection of her short stories
that mixes those about the Spanish Civil War with those about
England and Europe in World War II. In them, she depicts the
German involvement in Spain as well as that of the Italians, she
mocks the English communist phobia and the British non-inter-
vention policy, and she portrays fascism as the snobbism and

will to power that sends one's sister to a home for mad women. What I wish to focus on in this essay is her poetry about Spain and the war, most of which appeared in periodicals and newspapers of the day, only a few of which have been included in any anthology.

None of Warner's poems suffer from the defects that critics feel characterize so much of the poetry written about the Spanish Civil War, poetry in which the war is reflected as a simple but significant contest between fascism and democracy and in which the cause is evoked by a surfeit of generalized feeling or the rhetoric of a committed ideology. Ford states that the battlefield poems either lacked verisimilitude—the imagery is "stagy and stilted"—or merely reported events (101-12); he finds some of John Cornford's and Charles Donnelly's poems to be exceptions. Spain, the war, and the men who fought in it were frequently romanticized in the poetry of those who stayed at home as well, the outcome of the fighting resolved in idealistic claims for the future that the progress of the war demonstrated to be a lie.

Warner never equivocates on the cost of war, nor is she sure about the outcome. "In this Midwinter," a poem published in the *Left Review* in January 1935 and not anthologized even in her *Collected Poems*, she makes clear that Lenin and communism may be the people's savior, only "maybe." Thus, even before the outbreak of civil war in Spain, Warner is sure of her commitment to her fellow human beings but not of what governments, systems, or ideologies, the "props" of civilization as she labeled them in *Lolly Willowes*, may do for them. The salvation of humanity lies in their commitment to one another:

> In this midwinter, shepherds, not a lamb possibly.
> No green thing, green not even on wintercoat churchyard
>   yews.
> Air-borne, a poison-gas bomb let fall accidentally
> On our uplands has blasted the penned pregnant ewes.
> Foot-rot, lung-rot, womb-rot, not a lamb this year, shepherds.
> Light not lantern on such an idle errand.
>
> In this midnight, shepherds, not a saviour possibly.
> No godling, God not even in turncoat mufti of doubt.

> Man having rationalized destruction inalienably
> Needs God no further. See, not a King is out.
> War, famine, pestilence, not a saviour now, shepherds.
> Light not lantern on such an idle errand.
>
> In this midwinter, comrade, a child certainly
> This midnight midwifes. Tougher than God or beast man yet
> Envoy on envoy aims to persuade futurity.
> To those new eyes we bear our lantern's well-met.
> Not lamb nor Lenin, maybe, but to co-heir of earth, comrade
> Plight we darkling our lantern's friendly assurance. (101)

In this poem, Warner effectively combines the images of the promise of a new day, of a spring to renew life's green, and of the rebirth of humanity symbolized in a child's birth that echoes the promise of Christmas. But her landscape is bleak: there is "No green thing," it is "midnight" and "midwinter," and "the penned pregnant ewes" bear dead lambs in their wombs. She does not romanticize man's predicament or responsibility for "having rationalized destruction inalienably."

She is also explicit in "Red Front," published in the *Left Review* a few months after "In this Midwinter," in stating the price to be paid in human suffering to reclaim humanity's heritage of dignity and freedom from those who have betrayed him, the cost repeated in the varying words of the refrain:

> Dare you breathe the after damp?
> Can your cunning foot the swamp
> Where you tread on the dead?
> . . . .
> Can the knitted heart sustain
> The long Northeaster of In Vain,
> The whining, whining wind unbinding?—
> . . . .
> Comrade, are you grim enough,
> Taut to fighting-trim enough—
> Hark!—to march with us to-day
> On the tall Bastille of Nay?
> There it bulks to overawe,
> Old as law and foul as law;
> From its narrow eyes of fear
> Sharp machine-gun-glances peer. . . .

The French Revolution and the Paris uprising of 1848 are evoked through the allusions and imagery of the poem, and thus Warner reminds us of the numbers who will die in a revolution and of the possibility of betrayal of that revolution: "vintaging politicians have led up the dance / . . . economists pirouetted . . . [while] priests and sages made merriment in their hymns." Those who rule have created a land in which the wine men drink is "verjuice" with a "bouquet / Of metal and decay" brought forth from a vineyard "dunged" with the bodies and blood of their comrades who have died before them.[15] The poem is a marching song with appropriately strong rhythm, diction, and rhyme.

In "Some Make This Answer," another of her poems published in the *Left Review* before the outbreak of the Civil War and Warner's first journey to Spain in the fall of 1936, revolution—war—is no "fiesta" (Jack Lindsay had ineptly depicted the workers going to battle "as to a fiesta" in "On Guard in Spain!"). Fighting is the terrible but only response of those who are already "wasted with cold and hunger,/ Diseased, maddened, death-in-life-doomed," of those who have been made to bow before those with "a gluttony to subdue" and to retreat before "Thrust muzzle of flesh, master, or metal."[16] As in her other poems and essays, she objects as much to the imprisonment of the spirit as to the impoverishment of the body.

In poems such as "Benicasim," "Waiting at Cerbere," "Journey to Barcelona," and "Port Bou," Warner uses the physical landscape of Spain to convey the inner experience of the poverty- and battle-stricken country. Benicasim is the location of the rest home for the convalescent wounded of the Spanish People's Army.[17] In the poem it is the "bright-painted landscape of Acheron" into which "we have come," she and Ackland in the fall of 1936. Acheron is a river flowing into the underworld in Greek mythology, the name meaning river of sadness and derived from a word that means affliction. "Here . . . the bright villas / sit in a row like perched macaws" and "the wounded . . . lay bare their hazarded flesh to the salt / air, the recaptured sun,/ or bathe in the tideless sea, or sit fingering the sand." Of short duration, however, will be the wounded's "return / to life and release from living" that this border abode provides. For "narrow is this place . . . this space" where "a dust of dust and salt and pollen lies." Warner renders with precision the scenic particulars of the "strand" above which "rigid and immediate yonder / the mountains rise," to recreate the limbo of the soldier who must return to fight once more (*CP,* 35).

So, too, in "Port Bou" (*CP,* 37-38), Warner depicts the imminence of death, but it is in the smell of the landscape rather than in the visual images that the specter is sensed, in a smell that has replaced "the incense at the burial . . . [and] the breath / of the rose plucked for the bridal."[18] It is a "stale" smell, the "smell / of the fire that quenched / the fire on this hearth." Only in the last sentence of the poem does the rhetoric of the cause distort the images and diction through which Warner has rendered the battle-burnt land:

> I cordial the heart,
> I refresh the brain,
> I strengthen the resolved fury
> of those who fight for Spain.

In Warner's other two poems set in Spain, she focuses on the barrenness of this landscape of death:

> And on the hillside
> That is the colour of peasant's bread,
> Is the rectangular
> White village of the dead.
>
> . . . .
> Only the cicada strums.
>
> And below, where the headland
> Strips into rock, the white mane
> Of foam like a quickened breath
> Rises and falls again;
>
> And above, the road
> Zigzagging tier on tier
> Above the terraced vineyards,
> Goes on to the frontier.

> ("Waiting at Cerbere," *CP,* 36-37)

On that frontier, only the mountain wind and its flowing fresh-ets mourn the man who lies covered by a "handkerchief of snow" in "El Heroe" (*CP,* 36).

Warner writes for us to know and remember those whose names nobody knows, the peasant-soldier of "El Heroe" and the farmer who fears "another drought" in "Walking Through the Meadows" (*CP,* 38-39): "Ther's no rain in that sky / And the mid-May pasture is no more than ankle-high." She seeks to find the words that will become a poem so that such "shall reap his own." "Whence the word?" she asks and answers:

> . . . He it is that must prompt me to it.
> His trudging foot
> Hammer my heart till shaped and known the
>   plough-share purpose be shown,
> The field cloven, the seed strewn, the handsome
>   harvest full-grown.

The language and images of the Bible as well as of the workers' May day occur over and over in the poems written by Warner in the ten years of war that widened to engulf Europe and parts of Asia and Africa, for example, the good samaritan of "Road 1940" who carries a child left in a "cradle in the wheel-tracks":

> Though I should save it, she said,
> What have I saved for the world's use?
> If it grow to hero it will die or let loose
> Death, or to hireling, nature already is too profuse
> Of such, who hope and are disinherited,
> Plough, and are not fed.[19]

England has been transformed into an Eden in which "Adam goes / Slowly round his garden dressed as a soldier and Eve follows" being counseled in "what she must do / As summer comes on" ("The Story of a Garden," *CP,* 54). And in *"from* 12 Poems in the Manner of Bewick" (*CP,* 56-57), the "midnight sky / Spangled with gay Finity / Seems unlikely to supply / Even temporary accommodation for the Trinity":

Since they burned the olive yeards
Where shall the dove find
A leaf to comfort ailing Noah's mind?

Spain, Italy, Thessaly:
Steer where you will, scan,
Poor Noah, the coast-line of the Mediterranean,

The powdered bloom on the mountain-side
Thins sourly away:
Leafless returns the dove at the close of day.

Warner suggests in "Recognition" (*CP*, 54-55) that the failure of the English to grieve for the deaths of others has tripped the scales of Justice and let fall her sword upon them. They dismissed the children of Spain as "carved cheaply out of wood / The children of China. . . but yellow leaves on the wind." Those deaths are now repeated in England in the deaths of her children.

Warner's tone in both her poetry and fiction of the thirties and forties shifts from the comic satirical one that characterizes her novels published in the twenties—*Lolly Willowes, Mr. Fortune's Maggot, The True Heart*—and a number of her poems in *The Espalier* and *Time Importuned* (1928), poems such as "Bodley's Library," "A Song about a Lamb," "Pay What Thou Owest" and the story of a frustrated, drunken, but spirited Rebecca Random of *Opus 7* (1931). Events have sombered her portrayal of her fellow human beings and sharpened her attack on the self-righteous and the powerful, but her concern is still for those who toil but harvest only chaff. In 1945, she wrote a poem called "We Accuse" (*CP*, 61) that depicts those held in captivity by the war:

Speak to them of freedom, tell them their blood
Ran not only down gutters but to our hearts
Pipe-lined fuelled the spark of all we did.
Whimpering like apes they fought in fits and starts
For turnip-peelings trampled in the mud.

Take them by the hand, let flesh to flesh convey
The humble comradeship of mortal make.

Many of the poems that Warner wrote during those years were not published until after her death in 1978, Claire Harman completing the job of editing Warner's *Collected Poems* in 1982. Warner continued to write poems during the thirty years from 1931 until 1960, some of which appeared in newspapers and magazines such as *The Countryman, The Saturday Review of Literature, The New Republic, London Mercury, The Spectator, The Nation,* and *The New Yorker.* She did not, however, collect them into a volume, and thus many forgot, in spite of Louis Untermeyer's including her in *Modern British Poetry* published in 1936, that she was a poet and not just a short-story writer or novelist. Harman says that Warner once remarked, "'I propose to be a posthumous poet!'" (*CP,* xiii). Perhaps we can now remember her since the academic world of literary study is no longer governed by such false premises as the belief that *women* cannot write of war or politics, their "pantry window" supposedly offering them no view of that historical reality, indeed, having no windows, just the "pantry table" surrounded by husband and children and set with dishes. Perhaps we will now read her poems and those of other "posthumous" poets, since poems purged of politics are not the only poems to be called poetry. Now that literary scholarship need not just elaborate upon the aesthetic complexities of a few texts and authors thought to be canonical, perhaps we can reclaim the legacy of those like Warner who illuminated our world of desire and conflict in a language that did indeed combine an "inner" and "outer" reality.

Youngstown State University

ACKNOWLEDGMENT

I would like to thank the Estate of Sylvia Townsend Warner and Chatto & Windus and The Hogarth Press for permission to quote from "Red Front," "In this Midwinter," "Some Make This Answer," and "Benicasim."

NOTES

1. Valentine Cunningham, ed., *Spanish Front: Writers on the Civil War* (New York: Oxford University Press, 1986), xxxii.

2. John Muste, *Say That We Saw Spain Die: Literary Consequences of the Spanish Civil War* (Seattle: University of Washington Press, 1966), 38.

3. Katharine Bail Hoskins, *Today the Struggle: Literature and Politics in England during the Spanish Civil War* (Austin: University of Texas Press, 1969).

4. Hugh D. Ford, *A Poets' War: British Poets and the Spanish Civil War* (Philadelphia: University of Pennsylvania Press; London: Oxford University Press, 1965), 80. Further references to this work will appear in the text by page number.

5. Sylvia Townsend Warner, "The Way by Which I Have Come," *The Countryman* 19, no. 2 (1939): 485. See also Valentine Ackland, "Country Dealings," *Left Review*, March 1935, 198-200, and May 1935, 311-12, 314.

6. Sylvia Townsend Warner, "An English Fable," *Left Review*, August 1937, 406.

7. Sylvia Townsend Warner, "Sylvia Townsend Warner in Conversation," with Val Warner and Michael Schmidt, *PN Review 23* 8, no. 3 (1981-82): 35. See Ford, *A Poets' War*, 27-30, for a discussion of the particular events in Europe that prompted other writers to turn to the left.

8. Sylvia Townsend Warner, *Letters*, ed. William Maxwell (New York: Viking, 1983), 42.

9. "Sylvia Townsend Warner in Conversation," 35.

10. Virginia Woolf, "The Leaning Tower," in *Collected Essays II* (London: Hogarth Press, 1966), 162-81.

11. Sylvia Townsend Warner, "Women as Writers: The Peter Le Neve Foster Lecture," *Journal of the Royal Society of Arts*, May 1959, 384.

12. Sylvia Townsend Warner, *Lolly Willowes: or the Loving Huntsman* (Chicago: Academy Chicago Limited, 1978), 152.

13. See my *"Summer Will Show:* The Historical Novel as Social Criticism," forthcoming in *Women in History, Literature, and the Arts* (Youngstown, Ohio: Youngstown State University, 1989).

14. Barbara Brothers, "Writing Against the Grain: Sylvia Townsend Warner and the Spanish Civil War" (Paper delivered at the annual meeting of the Modern Language Association, December 1987); forthcoming in *Women's*

Writing in Exile: Alien and Critical, ed. Mary Lynn Broe and Angela Ingram (Chapel Hill: The University of North Carolina Press, 1989).

15. Sylvia Townsend Warner, "Red Front," *Left Review*, April 1935, 255-57.

16. Sylvia Townsend Warner, "Some Make This Answer," in *Collected Poems*, ed. with an introduction by Claire Harman (Manchester: Carcanet; New York: Viking Press, 1982), 34-35. Further references to poems from this edition will be indicated in the text by *CP* followed by a page number.

17. See note to "Benicasim," *Left Review*, March 1938, 841.

18. How different is the poem Stephen Spender writes using the same title, changing it from "Port Bou—Firing Practice" to "Port Bou" in his *Collected Poems 1928-1953* (New York: Random House, 1955), 93-94. The landscape and, by implication and description, the people are "childish." Oddly enough, the poem focuses on the speaker's fear, his cowardliness at the sounds of firing practice. Unlike Warner, Spender fails to capture the sense of the place that was Spain, the beauty or the austerity of its landscapes, or the suffering of its people in his so frequently anthologized poems.

19. Sylvia Townsend Warner, "Road 1940," in *Selected Poems*, with an afterword by Claire Harman (Manchester: Carcanet, 1985), 45.

HEMINGWAY AND THE SPANISH CIVIL WAR OR THE VOLATILE MIXTURE OF POLITICS AND ART

Allen Josephs

It so happens that three of the most important artists of the twentieth century were directly involved with the Spanish Civil War, yet none was actually in the war. Lorca, trying to avoid the coming conflict, made the fatal mistake of going home to Granada to become one of the first of a number of senselessly tragic civilian victims of the war. Picasso, already long within what would become permanent exile, would shortly paint one of his masterpieces, reflecting on the terror and grief of the market-day bombing of Guernica, but he would never return to Spain. Hemingway helped make the film, *The Spanish Earth*, and raised money for Loyalist ambulances; became a widely syndicated war correspondent; wrote five short stories and a play about the war; and, finally, used the Spanish Civil War as material for his longest, most ambitious, and for some critics his best novel, *For Whom the Bell Tolls*. Yet for all his first-hand observations, he remained both an outsider and a noncombatant.

The three have another similiarity: like many truly creative geniuses, they were for the most part apolitical. Lorca, who was a great champion of individual freedom, seems to have abhorred actual political process, and he sometimes took his contemporaries, such as Alberti, to task for wasting their time with politics instead of art. Picasso's card-carrying politics were a kind of sham—or prototypical radical chic—and his art is as barren of ideology as a kindergarten. Even *Guernica* continues to fascinate us for its transcendental vision rather than for its political particulars. Anyone who says of his own work as Picasso did, and means it, "I have created a solitude for myself such that no one can imagine it,"[1] is not a political animal.

Of the three, Hemingway was the most certifiably political, and the period of the late thirties was his most political time both personally and literarily. *To Have and Have Not*, the story of a depression-era rumrunner named Harry Morgan, was published in 1937, the same year he worked with John Dos Passos, Lillian Hellman, Archibald MacLeish, and Joris Ivens on the documentary, *The Spanish Earth*, and became a war correspondent for the North American Newspaper Alliance, reporting from Madrid, Guadalajara, Brihuega, Teruel, Brunete, and Chicote. On 4 June 1937 he delivered one of his rare speeches, "The Writer and War," to the Second Writers' Congress held at Carnegie Hall. It was printed as an article in the *New Masses* on 22 June. On 8 July he attended a dinner and screening of *The Spanish Earth* at the White House, later reporting privately that the food was "the worst I've ever eaten. . . . We had a rainwater soup followed by rubber squab, a nice wilted salad and a cake some admirer had sent in."[2] A few days later he helped raise $20,000 for ambulances at a special screening of *The Spanish Earth* at Fredric March's house in Los Angeles. *Life* magazine published a photo essay from stills from the film on 12 July and Hemingway wrote the captions. When *To Have and Have Not* came out in October, *Time* magazine put Hemingway on the cover. In November in Madrid he hurriedly finished writing his Civil War play *The Fifth Column*. Clearly, 1937 was Hemingway's most engaged moment. Near the end of *To Have and Have Not*, a dying Harry Morgan says, in a line Malcolm Cowley believed was inserted after Hemingway's first visit to Spain,[3] "No matter how a man alone ain't got no bloody fucking chance," and the narrator tells us, "It had taken him a long time to get it out and it had taken him all of his life to learn it."[4]

Harry Morgan's lesson in inchoate solidarity—which so tickled Granville Hicks that he wrote that this book was superior to *A Farewell to Arms* and *The Sun Also Rises*[5]—leads straight to the famous passage by John Donne which gave *For Whom the Bell Tolls* its title and which begins "No man is an Island" and goes on to remind us that "any man's death diminishes me." The reviewers of *For Whom the Bell Tolls* fell all over themselves praising the new, mature, involved Ernest Hemingway. Many of them like J. Donald Adams thought this book the "fullest, the deepest, the truest," in short, the best book Hemingway had written.[6] Dorothy Parker perhaps had the last word: "I think that what you do about this book of Ernest Hemingway's is point to it and say, 'Here is a book.' As you would stand below Everest and say, 'Here is a mountain.'"[7] Hemingway, the reviewers were saying, has finally, to return to the passage from John Donne, become "involved in mankind."

The 1930s, I need not remind anyone, were as tendentious and fractious a time as we would ever see. The failure of the war to end war, worldwide economic depression, and the rising tide of conflict between the right and the left, "politicized" everything. Rightly or wrongly, many artists and writers felt compelled to make politics the subject of their art. Only violently political times can explain Picasso's communism, Lorca's leftist-seeming declarations in 1936, and Hemingway's "conversion" to political consciousness.

There was, of course, another important element in Hemingway's case, and that was his great love for Spain. Had the dress rehearsal for World War II taken place in, say, Poland, would we have had a Polish version by Hemingway of *For Whom the Bell Tolls*? I doubt it. Hemingway went to Spain because he loved Spain, a point he would reiterate to Carlos Baker in a letter in 1951.[8] But here the issue becomes murkier, because it was Hemingway's love for Spain and his distaste for politics that may have turned *For Whom the Bell Tolls* into a kind of unintentional literary distortion of the Civil War.

To understand that distortion, we should bear in mind several things Hemingway said about politics even at this most political time in his life. Less than a year before the start of the war, he wrote a long letter to the Russian critic and his translator, Ivan Kashkin. Here are some pertinent excerpts:

> Here [in the U.S.] criticism is a joke. The bourgeois critics do not know their ass from a hole in the ground and the newly converted communists are like all new converts; they are so anxious to be orthodox that all they are interested in are schisms in their own critical attitudes. None of it has anything to do with literature which is always literature, when it is, no matter who writes it nor what the writer believes. . . . Everyone tries to frighten you now by saying or writing that if one does not become a communist or have a Marxian viewpoint one will have no friends and will be alone. They seem to think that to be alone is something dreadful; or that to not have friends is to be feared. I would rather have one honest enemy than most of the friends I have known. I cannot be a communist . . . because I believe in only one thing: liberty. The state I care nothing for. I believe in the absolute minimum of government. A writer is like a Gypsy. He owes no allegiance to any government. If he is a good writer he will never like the government he lives under. His hand should be against it and its hand will always be against him. The minute anyone knows any bureaucracy well enough he will hate it. Because the minute it passes a certain size it must be unjust. A writer is an outlyer like a Gypsy. He can be class conscious only if his talent is limited. If he has enough talent all classes are his province. He takes from them all and what he gives [in return] is everybody's property. A true work of art endures forever: no matter what its politics. (*Letters*, 417-19)

This letter, better than any other single document, represents what Hemingway thought about politics and art.

In February of 1937, writing to Harry Sylvester, a Catholic writer from Brooklyn, he began by saying, "The Spanish War is a bad war, Harry, and nobody is right—all I care about is human beings and alleviating their suffering which is why I back ambulances and hospitals"; and ended with this: "Take care of yourself and don't worry about politics nor religion. And *never* mix them if you can help it. I think that's a dirty outfit in Russia now but I don't like any government" (*Letters*, 456-57). I bring this in because it reiterates Hemingway's distrust—even hatred—of governments and politics. When we bear in mind his injunction about never mixing religion and politics and remember that writing was Hemingway's religion, we can begin to understand that although there was an apparent change at this time in Hemingway's attitudes, the change was really less a matter of political involvement than it was true concern over the conflict in which the Spanish people were involved.

Four days after he wrote to Harry Sylvester, he started a letter to his wife's family: "This is from the leader of the Ingrates Battalion on the wrong side of the Spanish War." The wrong side? Well, not exactly. The letter continues:

> The Reds may be as bad as they say but they are the people of the country versus the absentee landlords, the moors, the Italians and the Germans. This is the dress rehearsal for the inevitable European War.

Six months later, again to the Pfeiffers, he would write that he was going

> back to Spain where, if you get your politics from direct or indirect, you know I am on the wrong side and should be destroyed along with all the other Reds. After which Hitler and Mussolini can come in and take the minerals they need to make a European War." (*Letters*, 457-59)

Several things emerge from this rough humor which are germane to our consideration here: (1) there is no doubt which side Hemingway is against; (2) there is no doubt that he is uncomfortable about the side he is on; (3) Hemingway's reluctance about politics should never be attributed to naiveté. He proved himself a shrewd political observer in the twenties and had Mussolini pegged, in a brilliantly incisive portrait for the *Toronto Star* of 27 January 1923, as the "Biggest Bluff in Europe"; and (4) he was never under any illusion about what the war in Spain meant. It is true, as David Sanders wrote, that Hemingway tended to see the war "as a Spanish struggle against foreign aggression"; but it is not true, as we have just seen, that "he could not have seen the Spanish Civil War as chiefly a prefiguring of a greater war."[9] Hemingway may not have written it exactly that way in *For Whom the Bell Tolls*, but his correspondence even in 1937 proves beyond a doubt that he understood it as "the dress rehearsal for the inevitable European War" (*Letters*, 458). Later articles he would write, for example in *Ken* magazine, would continue this line of thinking, claiming that if the United States did not help stop fascism on Spanish soil, the United States would face far tougher enemies than Mussolini or Franco.

Above all, Hemingway was anti-fascist, but his anti-fascism never made him a communist sympathizer, as both his fiction and his biography make quite plain. Something he told Joe North, editor of *New Masses*, in Madrid in 1938, summarizes his position rather neatly: "'I like communists when they're soldiers, but when they're priests I hate them.'"[10] What emerges from this series of commentaries, observations, and anecdotes about Hemingway's political attitudes at this time is an odd mixture of disingenuousness and distaste, a kind of apolitical realism, centering on his hatred of fascism and rooted in his often reiterated belief (in his political articles for *Ken*) that fascism had to be confronted before it overran Europe. In one of those articles, he went so far as to predict, correctly, the outbreak of war by the summer of 1939.[11] By the end of 1938, he wrote to his editor, Max Perkins, that he was sick of the "carnival of treachery and rottenness" (*Letters*, 474). And it was not until the Civil War was virtually over in March of 1939 that he began serious work on *For Whom the Bell Tolls*.

Hemingway's writing on the Spanish Civil War can be divided into two separate categories. The first treats the actual theater of the war and is comprised of *The Fifth Column* and the Civil War short stories with the political articles and war dispatches as background. In these pieces Hemingway depicts the real war. In both the play and the stories, he was writing from actual experience, things he knew firsthand. Although, as usual, he was "inventing from experience," these pieces were largely crafted from events Hemingway witnessed. He even made his own hotel room in the Hotel Florida the scenario of the play.

This is not the place to explore these stories and this play in detail, but I do need to say that, in general, they are not up to Hemingway's usual artistic standards. One of the reasons for that, I believe, was the necessary, or what Hemingway must have felt was the necessary, injection of politics into the stories and especially into the play. The ending of *The Fifth Column* with Philip Rawlings' rejection of love, in the person of Dorothy Bridges, for the "cause" was so blatantly political that Malcolm Cowley suggested that Rawlings spoke as though he were talking over the head of his audience to the editors of *New Masses.*[12]

Conversely, the best Civil War story was the brilliantly pathetic rendition of the old man at the bridge in the retreat, an old man who very poignantly had "no politics." Malcolm Cowley's comment notwithstanding, Hemingway's ambivalence about politics, nay, his hatred of politics, is patently evident even in the play. Antonio, the chief of counterespionage in Madrid, says at one point:

> Politicians. Yes, politicians. I have seen a politician on the floor in that corner of the room unable to stand up when it was time to go out [to be shot]. I have seen a politician walk across that floor on his knees and put his arms around my legs and kiss my feet. I watched him slobber on my boots when all he had to do was such a simple thing as die. I have seen many die, and I have never seen a politician die well.[13]

The second category deals with *For Whom the Bell Tolls*, or the war as imagination, and that brings us to my central point. *For Whom the Bell Tolls* was clearly Hemingway's most ambitious novel, and many critics, as we have seen, thought it his best work. It was also one of his most imaginative or least autobiographical books. As he was writing it, he realized how much better it was, describing it to Max Perkins as "20 times better than that 'Night Before Battle' which was flat where this is rounded and recalled where this is invented" (*Letters*, 482). *For Whom the Bell Tolls* surely contains some of Hemingway's finest passages, and yet it is an oddly flawed work.

Hemingway was one of the great, for many the greatest, stylists of modernism. His modernism was based on a unique kind of neorealism or realism refracted through the prism of modernist sensibility. His best work is absolutely believable because of its brilliant painterly rendition. To achieve that sense of verisimilitude and style at the same time was his great gift, but it required an accuracy that came largely through inventing out of actual experience. In *For Whom the Bell Tolls*, Hemingway may have strayed too far from his chosen path and created a world that seemed real enough to American critics, but which rings false if you know enough about Spain and the Spanish Civil War.

Arturo Barea has already pointed out what some of these faults are, and his main contention—the novel's failure to render the reality of the Spanish War in imaginative writing—is, I think, basically correct.[14] My question is, why did Hemingway choose to invent a situation and characters that he was unable to render with his usual fidelity and accuracy? One possible answer is that he was simply attempting too much, that he was unable to paint a larger view of war—perhaps with Stendhal or Tolstoy in mind—as convincingly as he had rendered a closer and more personal view in *A Farewell to Arms* in the First World War. He told Malcolm Cowley: "But it wasn't just the Civil War I put into it. It was everything I had learned about Spain for eighteen years."[15] Was that simultaneously too much and too little? Too much about the Gypsies and the bulls and too little about the real war that was going on? Too much invention and too little actual, factual knowledge of the war? Why did Hemingway write of this invented partizan band of *guerrilleros* behind the lines and of this invented dynamiter and Spanish professor from the West who seems in part based on Robert Merriman, a hero of the International Brigades and a professor from California? Given the disastrous errors in Spanish in the novel, the idea that Robert Jordan was a Spanish professor becomes at times ludicrous. Why did Hemingway invent all this when he could have written much closer to actual experience?

At one point, irritated with *The Fifth Column* as a play, he bemoaned not having written it as a novel (*Letters,* 476, 479).

Why did he not write it as a novel, seeing through his own eyes what he could have described, to use his words, accurately and well? The answer to these questions is far too complex to solve here in any complete fashion, but I would like to suggest that one of the main reasons was that his invented story allowed Hemingway to write about the war and about Spain, his own version of Spain, without writing about the otherwise inescapable political dimension of that conflict. To avoid the politics of the real war—in which a Philip Rawlings would have to forego a Dorothy Bridges—Hemingway invented his own war in the mountains where Robert Jordan could be a Gypsy and an outlyer whose anarchic energies could be directed against the forces of fascism but remain pure of political taint. *For Whom the Bell Tolls* is a brilliant fiction and a great love story, but it is not a convincing novel of the Spanish Civil War.

Hemingway at his best was always an antipolitical writer, and in *For Whom the Bell Tolls* he began, perhaps unintentionally, reverting to type. The old man at the bridge had no politics, and as Hemingway told Joseph North and veterans of the Lincoln Brigade who were displeased by the book, he, like Robert Jordan, had no politics. So, it seems reasonable to conclude, *For Whom the Bell Tolls* is nonpolitical. But the Spanish Civil War *was* political.

The effect of the war on Hemingway, then, was to force him into a position of choosing between writing a political novel or inventing a world where politics were but a remembrance of nights past at Gaylord's. In selecting the latter, he doubtless crafted a powerful story with great moments, but he sacrificed giving us a great historical novel of the Spanish Civil War. There may be some perverse aesthetic transcendence in that sacrifice, however, since Hemingway's reluctance to blend the volatile mixture of politics and art within his own self-imposed canons reconfirms the necessity of dedication to his craft, as he often put it, "like a priest of God," and it underscores Hemingway's own admonition never to mix politics and religion.

The University of West Florida

NOTES

1. Cited in the film *Picasso: Artist of the Century.*

2. Ernest Hemingway, *Selected Letters 1917-1961* (New York: Charles Scribner's Sons, 1981), 460. Further references to this volume will appear in the text.

3. Malcolm Cowley, "Hemingway: Works in Progress," *The New Republic*, 20 October 1937.

4. Ernest Hemingway, *To Have and Have Not* (New York: Charles Scribner's Sons, 1937), 225.

5. Granville Hicks, "Review and Comment," *New Masses*, 26 October 1937.

6. J. Donald Adams, *New York Times Book Review*, 20 October 1940.

7. Dorothy Parker, *PM*, 20 October 1940.

8. Carlos Baker, *Hemingway: The Writer as Artist* (Princeton: Princeton University Press, 1972), 228.

9. David Sanders, "Ernest Hemingway's Spanish Civil War Experience," in *Studies in 'For Whom the Bell Tolls,'* ed. Sheldon Norman Grebstein (Columbus, Ohio: Charles E. Merrill, 1971), 37.

10. Quoted in Carlos Baker, *Ernest Hemingway: A Life Story* (New York: Charles Scribner's Sons, 1969), 330.

11. Ernest Hemingway, "A Program for U.S. Realism," *Ken*, 11 August 1938.

12. Malcolm Cowley, "Hemingway in Madrid," *The New Republic*, 2 November 1938.

13. Ernest Hemingway, *The Fifth Column and Four Stories of the Spanish Civil War* (New York: Charles Scribner's Sons, 1969), 37.

14. Arturo Barea, "Not Spain But Hemingway," *Horizon* 3 (1941): 350-61.

15. Quoted in Malcolm Cowley, "A Portrait of Mr. Papa," *Life*, 10 January 1949.

THE CONFLICTS OF ART:
RENÉ CHAR'S
PLACARD POUR UN CHEMIN DES ÉCOLIERS

Virginia A. La Charité

Poetry . . . goes forward in order to indicate
the movable road.[1]

The Spanish Civil War is the artistic and historical event that definitively marks the end of René Char's affiliation with Surrealism and the beginning of his adoption of a poetics of response. Char's identification with the events in Spain in 1936 and early 1937 is both personal and aesthetic. Among Char's close friends in the Surrealist group were the Spanish painters Picasso, Miró, and Dali,[2] and he had visited Spain three times, twice in 1931 with the poet Paul Eluard and again in 1932 with his childhood friend, Francis Curel. Familiarity with Spain, admiration for the Spanish avant-garde, a growing awareness of the ominous political events in Europe, and a life-threatening case of blood poisoning came together for Char the man with the outbreak of the Spanish Civil War and confronted Char the poet with the conflicts of art.

As an active member of the second generation of Surrealists, Char participated enthusiastically in their artistic and political activities in the early 1930s in order to place Surrealism "at the Service of the Revolution." His own work during these years, collected in the volume *Le Marteau sans maître* (1934), is characterized by an aggressive language, provocative images, a hatred of absurdity in the world, hostility toward all forms of authority, explosive phrases, even violence. Nevertheless, *Le Marteau*

185

sans maître is a disturbing work, for underlying the tone of insolence and rage, especially in the section *Poèmes militants,* there is the suggestion that the Surrealist demand for revolution is not a synonym for action but is rather the embracing of an attitude which separates action from art, an attitude which exalts scandal, insists on an aesthetic of emotionalism, ignores the social response value of language, denies common sense, and favors total revolt—the utopian dream of a world in which anything and everything is potentially marvelous and the pleasure principle reigns supreme. While the Surrealists were avowedly against external authority in all forms (anti-fascist, anti-religious, anti-bourgeois)—stances which led them to celebrate the establishment of the Spanish Republic in 1931 and then later, in 1936, to identify with the anarchists (the POUM and FAI factions)—during the 1930s they gradually abandoned their original attitude of revolt as insubmission and moved closer and closer to a somewhat mythical concept of the self: revolt in the name of absolute freedom, disorder, and fulfillment of desire. Marx's "transform the world" and Rimbaud's "change life," the two basic tenets of Surrealism, nearly cease to be constructive rallying cries in the Surrealists' efforts to effect their "revolution" through political commitment. In fact, they were openly viewed as dilettantes by the very political group they sought to join and "serve." The basic Surrealist love of the irrational borders on nihilism and is astutely analyzed by Albert Camus in his *Actuelles I* and *L'Homme révolté.*[3]

As the Surrealists themselves disagreed over how to accomplish their own revolution, they found themselves electing Rimbaud over Marx, choosing to defend an attitude of all or nothing and refusing in the process a historical response to the human condition. While André Breton always insisted that love was the value and the moral, that the freedom of the individual would somehow lead to that of all of society, he, nonetheless, viewed art as the expression of man's inner self and desires, not as a response that confronts reality in the name of mankind. The problem of the Surrealist "personal self" in opposition to the non-Surrealist "collective self" is a leitmotif in René Char's *Moulin premier* (1936), a group of seventy aphorisms and two poems which subvert the Surrealist aesthetic of separating art from action, history from revolt. Throughout this work, Char begins to view poetry as a possible response to history: "Earth, becomingness of my abyss, you are my bathtub for reflection" (*OC*, 62).

Moulin premier is marked by a vocabulary and phraseology of reflection, control, rationalism, responsibility, and lucid protest. Char refuses total revolt or revolt for the sake of revolt; instead, he indicates that language can correct the world, lead to order, even alleviate moral suffering; the poet has the responsibility not to confront a real which is a construction of the mind but to classify the real and refuse to accept its arbitrary conditions: "The Poet precedes the man of action, and when he encounters him, declares war on him. The parvenu had at least promised to be present in his perilous fights!" (*OC*, 67).

Char's aesthetic and personal movement away from Surrealism evolves gradually and naturally. He never had an outright break with Breton or with the group. Yet, his selection of the title of his first theoretical writings on the role of poetry in the contemporary world, *Moulin premier*, strongly suggests by the numerical term *first* that he has already passed beyond Surrealism although he has not yet identified a second *mill* for his writing. At this moment of artistic transition, Char was taken dramatically ill with a nearly fatal case of blood poisoning. The illness brought Char the man face to face with his own mortality and made him intimately aware of death as an inalienable historical aspect of the human condition.

During the months of his recovery, he corrected the proofs for *Moulin premier*, which offered him a review of his Surrealist adventure, and he read Nietzsche, whose nihilism and lack of a human value system repudiated Char's admiration for the Heraclitean theory of flux and becomingness. At the invitation of René Roux, an aspiring young poet and painter who was the schoolmaster at the Collège de L'Ile-sur-Sorgue, Char's native town, Char spent the month of August 1936 in Céreste, "a village lost in the hills of Provence" in Haute-Provence (*OC*, 1116). René Roux had three younger brothers, "small schoolboys from 12 to 14 years old" (*OC*, 1116), who accompanied Char every afternoon on long walks in the area. Describing at length the youths' joys at spending so much time with Char, Georges-Louis Roux testifies to Char's interest in children and adolescents, the marvelous stories he related, and how the summer of 1936 must have been for Char a "moment of relaxing and of happiness, a fleeting respite" (*OC*, 1122). It was shortly after this period of respite and reflection that Char undertook *Placard pour un chemin des écoliers,* which he dedicated to the children of Spain and had illustrated by Valentine Hugo.[4] The effects of his recognition that he had evolved aesthetically away from Surrealism and his personal period of recuperation, of contact with nature and the Roux family children in Céreste, undeniably form the underpinnings of *Placard.*[5]

The theme of childhood which characterizes much of Char's work does not emerge as one of his major subjects until the publication of *Placard* in 1937. Prior to this work, Char tends to treat childhood in a typical Surrealist fashion: the child is not yet tainted by societal inhibitions and prejudices, the child enjoys using freely his imagination and intuition, the child believes that creations of the mind are real. With *Placard*, and, indeed, since 1937, the child for Char represents innocence, health, happiness, and human potential for rising above man's terrestrial circumstances. Like the poet, the child precedes the man of action—a form of matinal light and a source of illumination.

Written during the winter of 1936-37,[6] *Placard* consists of an introductory prose text, "Dedication," and seven verse poems which are written in a language and style that directly oppose Char's former Surrealist practice. The texts of *Placard* are basically conventional in form and share a sense of anguish and social protest against suffering. Throughout the small volume, the tone is one of a melodic continuum, which consistently expresses a poetic belief in the potential of the text to respond to objective reality. In many ways, *Placard* reflects the moral and spiritual crisis experienced by Char the man and Char the poet in 1936. In a letter written to André Breton, explaining why he cannot participate in the Surrealist exhibition in 1947, Char observes that "I am not the one who simplified things, but horrible things made me simple" (*OC*, 660).

Awareness of the horrors wrought by the events of the Spanish Civil War is summarized for Char in the suffering of the children of Spain, and yet these very same children offer him insight into man's refusal to be reduced to his historical circumstances. In an introduction written in 1949 to the second edition of *Placard pour un chemin des écoliers suivi de Dehors la nuit est gouvernée,* Char expresses his personal and aesthetic agitation over the events in Spain that foreshadowed World War II and its atrocities: "I ran" (*OC,* 85). Indeed, the highly personal tone of this 1949 text dramatizes Char's awareness of the importance of the inner crisis he experienced in 1936. And this 1936 crisis, which was physical, moral, aesthetic, and spiritual, continues to resurface throughout his work. In 1956, for example, his preamble to *En trente-trois morceaux* recalls *Placard* as one of four capital poetic turning points in his work (*OC,* 772). In 1979, his attack on nuclear weapons echoes the events that triggered *Placard:* "How many [people] fall in love with humanity and not with man!" (*OC,* 578). Telescoping the human tragedy of the Spanish Civil War into an evocation of the children in only seven texts in *Placard* becomes a preferred Char structure of condensation in his poetry, as the fragment bears witness to the whole: "Since the operation of totalitarianisms we are no longer tied to our personal self but to a collective self assassin, assassinated" (*OC,* 579).

The shift to an optic beyond the self and the recognition of the need to become involved responsibly with the outer world are expressed by the word *placard* of the title: a written opinion publicly posted to make a specific announcement. The phrase, "a road for schoolboys," is typical of Char's post-Surreal period. While the Surrealists frequently and humorously used proverbs and clichés in their effort to purify language and return it to its original source, Char's adoption of common phrases and terms goes beyond the confines of the page to create new exchanges between words, lines, poems, and the experience of poetry. On the literal level, the phrase evokes a roadway frequented by schoolboys, not unlike the path taken each afternoon in Céreste in the summer of 1936 by Char and the Roux children. The warm, fraternal, and innocent image of a peaceful scene is not disrupted by the public posting of a sign along this particular road. But, *écolier* in French does not refer only to a pupil or schoolboy; it also refers to anyone who is not skilled in his profession, a learner, one who is at the beginning of a given experience. The very choice of the word *écolier* takes the title and the volume beyond the confines of a single event and opens up the volume to a more universal level of meaning. On the figurative level, the French expression for the longest road is "le chemin des écoliers" ["the road for schoolboys"], and, with this reading, the title takes on its ultimate significance. It is an announcement that reality is harsh, history limits human activity, and the poet must protest against his time, give it form, and bear witness to the future. The title is a conscious declaration to revolt against all limitations, but it also recognizes that such an action will not be without its hardships, struggles, setbacks, and sacrifices. The nature of that revolt is not clearly outlined in *Placard*, but the reasons for that revolt are the subject of the volume.

The "Dedication," written in March 1937, is provocative in its use of capital letters to describe the children of Spain as victims of the war around them: "RED." They are dead, thrown into a common ditch and covered with mud, in contrast to the poet's memories of his bucolic childhood, which was marked by World War I. But that war took place on the frontiers and in distant battle zones; it did not disrupt and overturn his everyday existence. By contrast, the Spanish Civil War affects the daily lives of children, whose "école buissonnière," or playing hooky, is a school of death, not of life. The "Dedication" ends with a second address to the "Children of Spain" and a salute to their "matinal eyes," which is the earliest appearance of the term *matinal* in Char's work. Char the man begs for their forgiveness; Char the poet cries out that he has written the work "With my last reserve of hope."

The discovery of hope in the atrocities suffered by children ties together the seven poems that make up *Placard*. Each poem bears witness to love as the only possible means for dealing with the oppressiveness of daily horror. Daytime is evoked as bitter, a time of schism, deception, distress, and anguish, while night is seen as a time of peace, renewal, unity, and promise. The historical determinism of day is countered by the affirmative reconciliation of night. The nihilism of Nietzsche is already giving way to Char's postwar predilection for Heidegger and a poetics of pulverization and crispation. The "loyal adversaries" of Char the man and Char the poet emerge in their first form in the seven texts of *Placard*.

In a very real sense, *Placard* is a volume of a poetry of circumstances, inspired by a specific external event and written to deal with the particular circumstances of that event. But, as an examination of the title alone shows, *Placard* is not circumstantial in its attitude of response. Throughout Char's subsequent work, *Placard* reemerges in different forms, as Char the man and Char the poet accept the world as it is and find in it values worthy of admiration and expression. To the redemptive quality of love, which is perhaps the most important carryover from his Surrealist days, Char will later add the redemptive quality of courage *(Feuillets d'Hypnos*, 1946). Still, in *Placard* there come together for the first time in his work the two ends of his poetic bow: "obsession with the harvest" takes the form of the value of mankind as represented by the children of Spain, and "indifference to history" is affirmed in commitment to the artistic value of creation. *Placard* refutes the agony of the historical circumstances in a blunt declaration that hope is possible only through poetic action: "my last store of hope."

The question that continues to confront the reader of Char's work in general and *Placard* in particular is: why Spain? Why did the Spanish Civil War serve as such a catalyst for Char the man and Char the poet? The answer does not lie in Char's trips to Spain nor in his deep friendships with Spanish painters, but it is clearly articulated by Camus in *Actuelles I*, which is dedicated to Char: "The first weapons of the totalitarian war were soaked in Spanish blood. . . . We delivered to Franco, on Hitler's order, Spanish Republicans . . . who raised his voice? No one. . . . We are responsible" (244-46). Char's physical condition prevented him from directly participating in that war, but among his Surrealist contemporaries only one, Benjamin Péret, actually took up arms in an effort to prevent the Nationalists from delivering Spain to an oppressive dictatorship. The French Surrealists were notably absent from the war despite their admiration for the Republican cause. Writing in *L'Amour fou* in 1937, Breton expresses regret that he did not join Péret and participate in the war because he was waiting for the birth of his daughter: "I did not have the courage."[7] Yet, reason, not the irrational, demanded a response in 1936. It may very well be that the Surrealist movement lost its momentum because of the Spanish Civil War, that the breakup of the group, which occurred in 1940 and 1941 at the onset of World War II, was already underway in 1936. Certainly, those Surrealists who remained in France and joined the Resistance were never able again to embrace the Surrealist election of the pleasure principle over reality. In point of fact, those who did not go into exile had aesthetically moved beyond the Surrealist attitude by the mid-1930s. It may even be speculated that without World War II the events of the Spanish Civil War would have sufficed to trigger in Paul Eluard, Robert Desnos, and others what Louis Aragon had already determined and what René Char would later describe as the discovery that "It must be admitted that poetry is not sovereign everywhere. . . . The poet, susceptible to exaggeration, evaluates correctly in agony" (*OC*, 207, 212).

In *Placard*, the text becomes for Char a dialectic between "a subjective assessment" and "an objective choice" (*OC*, 162). The poem is no longer situated in inner space, "intimate space in which our imagination and our feelings play," but it is instead situated in time, what Char describes as circular space, "that of the concrete world" (*OC*, 509). What was lacking aesthetically in the texts of *Le Marteau sans maître*, time or circular space, becomes the structuring principle of *Placard pour un chemin des écoliers:* "Terror surrounds us and an artistic anti-life takes possession" (*OC*, 700). Poetry must "indicate the mobile road" (*OC*, 734).

While the image of *chemin* pervades Char's work, nowhere does it more fully bring together a volume of poems than in *Placard*. The word *chemin* indicates the process of artistic creation, the promise of "the next" vista, turn, a very human form of Char's notion of the immediate future. A road suggests motion, the probable encounter with others, a common concrete space that exists in human terms. A road occupies space, yet it denies the limitations and restrictions of that space, actually contradicts the confines of that area in its invitation to advance, continue, all the while never abandoning the notion of redistributing those limits. A road is an element of life, not death, and offers the possibilities of better pursuits. A road summons up human values in space and in time and the creative process beyond all time and place: circular space. A road bears witness to man's refusal to die, to his lucid revolt against fixity in the name of freedom and opportunity to travel, seek happiness, and respond to a need to continue to live. A road is a corrective to a given terrestrial condition.

The road in *Placard* is an apt image for the poet's physical, mental, spiritual, and artistic journey. Each text contributes to his discovery that historical terror, suffering, and injustice may be effectively opposed through artistic counteraction. The poet should not serve history, but refuse it. Hence, in *Placard*, Char's obsession with the harvest, a filtered and refined Surrealist pattern, encounters on the road of his own inner turmoil and conscience the need for becoming indifferent to the limitations of history.

Placard pour un chemin des écoliers is by no means representative of a mature René Char, nor can the work be considered one of his major volumes of poetry. However, in looking at all of Char's writing, the volume is pivotal for an understanding of his self-distancing from Surrealism and the adoption of a poetics that will risk its very existence and expression in order to be provocative in its refusal to acquiesce. In *Placard*, the Char poem is not pulverized, crisped, or matinal. It is not a double that tautly balances "fury and mystery," hope and anguish, the immediate and the essential, word and silence, fragmentation and unity, prose and poetry, "the child of beautiful weather and the man of rainy weather" (*OC*, 76). The tension between incompatibilities, which characterizes the mature Char text, is almost jarringly absent in *Placard*, perhaps explaining why most

Char studies tend to overlook the work, causing the volume to fall unfortunately into the misleading and rather pejorative category of circumstantial poetry. Yet, examination of the work reveals that it is in tone, subject, and aspiration pure Char—it simply is not written in what we have come to identify as the indisputable Char text of the archipelagic structure in language and form. *Placard* is not a work of poetic traces; it cannot even be described as a work of proaction, for the texts are firmly rooted in personal and poetic reactions. But all of Char's texts are in some way a form of reaction and protest; all of his poems combine elements of the man and the poet, elements which provide the basic tension in his poetry from *Le Marteau sans maître* to the present, especially *La Nuit talismanique* (1972).[8] It is in the recovery of these elements, recognition of the inner crisis in which Char the man and Char the poet confront each other for the first time, that the reader grasps just how pivotal to Char studies and to contemporary French poetry in general these seven texts and their introductory poem are.

In *L'Homme révolté*, Camus pays homage to Char as the "Poet of our rebirth" (127). As the twentieth century begins to draw to a close, it becomes increasingly evident that René Char towers over contemporary French poetry. The clues to how and why Char is the poet of man's renaissance are in *Placard*, the work which places Surrealism in a finished perspective—poetic activity and reaction—and opens the way to matinal poetic action and proaction in his World War II resistance participation and the texts of *Fureur et mystère* (1948), leading eventually to *La Parole en archipel* (1961), in which the mature Char poem holds together apparent contradictions by creating a new totality in the present, what "We have" (*OC*, 409-10). The humanly alive poetry that marks Char's work is not descriptive, but evocative and provocative— the fragments or word clusters that result create the text of maximum reader freedom and response in a "formal sharing." On every page, there is a road to follow, a path that links extreme reference points, and on that road is a warning sign that risk lies in the adventure. It is never a safe, secure, complacent journey. It is always a difficult poetic quest, a non-ending search for contact. The Char text is a process to evoke response, a "common presence," never a procedure to manufacture a given product.

Accordingly, Char's language is elemental, drawn from the familiar outer world of people, places, and things, especially nature. His structures repress transitions, as he rejects traditional discursive elements of language. The text sets relationships, enacts them, and gives the reader a new way of participating in the world. Encounter and exchange take the form of union through words: word with word, poet with poem, man with woman, man with men, reader with text. To think is to feel, to share is to participate in the direct comprehension of absolute reality. The base is the summit, as Char links together the concrete and the abstract, the solid and the emerging, the object and the emotion. The impossible is possible. As the flower justifies the plant, poetry justifies man's existence in its affirmation that man's nobility is discovered in art, not in history. Poetry as creative action can determine the quality of life.

A major key to the Char text, thematically and stylistically, is love: love on the erotic level, love of mankind, love of nature, love of written expression in all forms, love of plastic art. While love as beauty, freedom, and truth may have its roots in Surrealism, love, for Char, is not limited to the expression of individual desire. Rather, it is an action that conjoins opposites, brings about an order, and unifies the whole of human experience. Love is not restricted to the individual level, but is the principle of human and aesthetic cohesion. Love is life, and the Char text is always a lived poetry, lived in the present, the eternal moment experienced along the road.

Love is the principal theme in *Placard*. The ugly reality of the historical events of the Spanish Civil War, vividly evoked in the "Dedication," are effectively juxtaposed, nearly contradicted, by the poetic discovery that love offers hope—hope for all. Love ends isolation, brings about a sense of immediate fulfillment, makes the intolerable present acceptable, and cannot be limited by time, space, or history. Love is not a state of being, but an action which links together contradictions and opposes all restrictions. Love will not be denied, not even by brutality and cruelty. Love is the concrete world at its best, circular space.

Love testifies to man that he is alive and that his life is worth living. Art confers value and offers assurances of "a fervent dawn" (*OC*, 92).

The seven texts end on the word "resistance," which only the act of love is able to posit in a world in which children suffer, bleed, and die. The schoolgirl of "Schoolgirl's Company" denies her father's fears; she is confident that her lover's eyes hold "the promise / Which I made to myself / I am mad I am new" (*OC*, 99). The queen in "The Queen's Bearing" recognizes how only "the couple entwined with the word heart" refuses to acknowledge a bleak and hostile environment and time. Even in "Exploit of the Steam Cylinder" and "The Sea Urchins of Pégomas," love is viewed as a "valid revolt" (*OC*, 97). In the text "The Confidant's Alley," Char finds that "Daring little girls, / It's good to be imprudent / But for love" (*OC*, 93), while "Four Ages" expresses sadness over the isolation of the individual when he lacks love.

The final text, "Provisions for the Return," completes the "Dedication" in its demonstration of how the love act during the darkness of night prepares for the bitterness of day and prefigures the beneficent role of night in *Dehors la nuit est gouvernée* (1938). Love renews, revitalizes, and inspires; it strengthens through its moment of union for the coming diurnal struggle, the longest road of living through a historical catastrophe, all the while offering dignity and nobility to those who must travel that road.

Throughout *Placard*, language takes the form of a social response. The emotional is social in that the indignant tone of the "Dedication" gives way to the confident declaration at the end. Hope is transmogrified into resistance, as action and art fuse. To write is to act and to requalify the reader. Faith in man to resist his historical circumstances, belief in the text to discover, reveal, and communicate value, and confidence in poetry to justify man's existence in a continual process constitute the ultimate testimony of *Placard pour un chemin des écoliers*. The exchange of energy between the terms *hope* and *resistance* takes place only under the aegis of Poetry, as Char the man and Char the poet resolve their conflicts and merge into the master architect of twentieth-century man's renaissance: "Art ignores History but makes use of its terror" (*OC*, 651).

University of Kentucky

NOTES

1. René Char, *OEuvres complètes* (Paris: Gallimard, 1983), 743. All Char quotations are taken from this edition, identified in the text as *OC*. The translations are my own.

2. Picasso illustrated Char's *Dépendance de l'adieu* in 1936, "Enfants qui cribliez d'olives" in 1939, and the second edition of *Le Marteau sans maître* in 1945. Dali illustrated *Artine* in 1930, while Miró has illustrated nearly a dozen of Char's works.

3. Albert Camus, *Actuelles I* (Paris: Gallimard, 1950); *L'Homme révolté* (Paris: Gallimard, 1951); quotations from these editions are identified in the text. The translations are my own.

4. Valentine Hugo was a member of the inner circle of Surrealists from 1930 to 1940; best known for her black and white illustrated visions, she visited Spain in 1928 and is described by Char as able to capture "fire under the snow."

5. For a detailed account of this episode in Céreste in 1936, see Georges-Louis Roux, "René Char, Guest in Céreste," in *OC*, 1115-31.

6. It must be remembered that Char wrote *Placard* before the bombing of Guernica and the incarceration of the poet Machado, events which deeply disturbed the French avant-garde.

7. André Breton, *L'Amour fou* (Paris: Gallimard, 1937), 137.

8. *La Nuit talismanique* was also triggered by a personal crisis and posited for Char the man and Char the poet another series of conflicts of art. See my "Beyond the Poem: René Char's *La Nuit talismanique*," *Symposium* 30 (1976): 14-26.

INTELLECTUALS AS MILITANTS:
HEMINGWAY'S *FOR WHOM THE BELL TOLLS* AND MALRAUX'S *L'ESPOIR*: A COMPARATIVE STUDY

Erik Nakjavani

The whole end of the nineteenth century
was passive. The new Europe appears very much to be
built upon action, which implies a few differences.[1]

One of the signal characteristics of the Spanish Civil War appears to have been the international participation of so many artists, writers, and intellectuals—mostly on the Republican side. The international intelligentsia went beyond the act of making its ideological choices manifest in this civil war. Some of its members elected to translate their choice into direct action on the Spanish front. Everyone now is more or less familiar with the names of its better known representatives who played an active part in the war, names such as W. H. Auden, Ilya Ehrenberg, Ernest Hemingway, André Malraux, Pablo Neruda, George Orwell, Claude Simon, Stephen Spender, and Simone Weil, to mention just a few.

Consequently, one of the attendant realities of the Spanish Civil War is that it is invested by this international intellectual, literary, and artistic dimension—expressed predominantly in writing. Valentine Cunningham justifiably points out "the preeminence of language stuff, the stuff of writing, the centrality of writing itself" to this war.[2] Even a cursory glance at the literature of the Spanish Civil War reveals it to be one of the most "textualized" wars in history. Additionally, the literary "textualization" of it has been so extensive and so successful that today the events of this war for us rapidly approach the status of a powerful mythical reality. In other words, the many historical texts on the war and the historic facts they delineate have been transcended by the artistic transmutation of them into a dazzling array of literary and artistic works. As a result, the historical reality of this war has been substantially enlarged and enriched by a massive infusion of literary myths.

For me, one of these myths, that of the militant intellectual, which issues primarily from the reality of a writer's or an artist's own participation in the Spanish Civil War, is a significant one. The reason for its significance appears to me to be more easily discernible than understandable. Its complexity derives from its manifest attempt to provide a synthesis of two traditionally different and seemingly contradictory modes of being: reflection and action or, to be more precise, intellectuality and political militancy.

I find this myth most extensively developed in two of the best known literary "textualizations" of the Spanish Civil War: Malraux's *L'Espoir* (1937) and Hemingway's *For Whom the Bell Tolls* (1940).

My intention in this essay is threefold: (1) to define the mode of existence of the intellectual militant; (2) to describe the mode of thought and actions of important militant intellectuals in *L'Espoir*, such as Giovanni Scali, Manuel, and Garcia, and to show what constitutes the nature of their intellectuality and their militancy that is synthesized in action; and, finally, (3) to compare their salient characteristics with Robert Jordan's in *For Whom the Bell Tolls*, who, as a militant intellectual, appears to represent a composite of the three in *L'Espoir.*

Before attempting to describe the basic characteristics of the militant intellectuals in the two novels, a preliminary definition of what I mean by the term "militant intellectual" would be helpful. One may begin by defining the case of the conventional intellectual and, subsequently, contrasting it with that of the militant intellectual. The distinguishing characteristic of this definition is its requirement that artistic, scientific, and philosophical activities be considered as an end in themselves and not be impeded in the least by any practical consideration whatsoever. Its focal point is the purity of the imaginative and reflective activities as highly justifiable ends in and of themselves. Therefore, the conventional intellectual by definition is a *passive* individual in every regard save that of producing new ideas, whose consequences are carried out and realized by others.

However, beyond this definition, there are Jean-Paul Sartre's definitions of what has come to be known as "the classic intellectual" in contradistinction to what one may call "the new intellectual." Sartre identifies and explains certain critical moments in the development of these two types of intellectuals. He refers to the educated professionals in any field as *"les techniciens du savoir pratique."*[3] The Sartrean characterization of the "technicians of practical knowledge" coincides more or less with that of the conventional intellectual. To paraphrase Sartre, they possess and work on a body of knowledge that is fundamentally conceptual, that is to say, universal. By definition, this universal knowledge should serve the good of all and should exclude the interest of any particular group as such. At the moment, however, when "one of them [the technicians of practical knowledge] realizes that *he is working on the universal* in order to serve the particular, then the consciousness of this contradiction—what Hegel called the unhappy conscience—surges up in him and constitutes him as an intellectual" (457). According to Sartre, that is the basic characteristic of the so-called "classic intellectual," who "denounced everywhere the particular use of the universal and attempted to indicate in each specific circumstance the principles of a universal politics, for the good of the greatest number of people" (458).

"The new intellectual," however, goes beyond the Hegelian "unhappy conscience" and the mere denunciation of the "particular use of the universal," which is the cause of his contradictory mode of existence. He breaks away from the structures of power that particularize the universal and allies himself "with those who demand a universal society, that is to say, with the masses" (464). This choice demands that the intellectual function simultaneously in the domains of reflection and militant action, whose fundamental structures do not always mesh harmoniously together.

In this essay, I equate the Sartrean definition of the so-called "new intellectual" with that of the intellectual militant. The nuances of this equation will be clear in due course. I must add, however, that while Sartre locates the origin of "the new intellectual" in the May 1968 student uprising in France, I find evidence for his appearance much earlier in the following eloquent statement of André Malraux: "By fighting on the side of the Spanish Republicans and Communists, we were defending values that we held (that I hold) to be universal."[4]

It is obvious that this militant defense of universal values confers a new status on the intellectual. It considers a man of reflection to be at the same time a man of militant action. At first, it may appear that thought and action are two distinct and antithetical modes of human behavior. Thought is generally regarded as having its genesis in human subjectivity. It is assumed to reside wholly in the domain of human consciousness. As one of the constituents of consciousness, it combines in itself such diverse qualities as human imagination, intelligence, and sensibility in the act of reflection upon the world and consciousness itself. Having thus emerged, it may then surpass itself at a moment of its development and lead to new thoughts in a sort of unending process. On the contrary, action is taken to be born out of the necessity of man's encounter with the world and his desire to effect changes upon this world.

Correlatively, in this traditional perspective, thought precedes action and gives it its sense and direction. It is no doubt a dualistic view that divides human existence into two modes of being: thinking and acting. The first is seen as an interior mode of existence or being, affecting the mind or consciousness; the second is considered to be an exterior mode of doing, of acting upon the world. It is clear that in this duality the primacy is given to being. In other words, it is an attempt to formulate an essentialist definition of the origin of thought rather than an existentialist one.

In *L'Espoir*, Malraux makes the seemingly antithetical domain of reflection and action in the human world a part of a dialectical process that results in a synthesis that defines vividly the existence of the militant intellectual. In characters such as Scali, Manuel, and, above all, Garcia, Malraux portrays the different intensities of the commitment of the intellectuals to direct political action. He also delineates the varying degrees of their success in reconciling their basic intellectual tendencies with the necessity of militant action. In turn, he shows the real, conventional intellectual Unamuno and the fictive intellectual Alvear to be out of touch with existing political realities and exigencies. Consequently, they are presented as essentially prey to vacillation, pessimism, and eventual political paralysis or stasis.

Giovanni Scali, the Italian art historian, "interpreter of Masaccio, of Piero della Francesca" (278), and bombardier in the International Air Force, typifies the attendant difficulties of the commitment of intellectuals to immediate direct political action. "Seeing a man who is a thinker in that . . . uniform always surprises me," the Spanish professor of art and director of an art gallery, Alvear, remarks upon seeing Scali for the first time (273). His uniform symbolizes for the conventional intellectual Alvear the tensions and antagonistic tendencies that exist side by side in a thinker like Scali, who has decided to become a man of action. Although devoted to the cause against fascism in Spain, his intellectual and ethical scruples are not always conducive to his engagement in direct action. Well trained by the Italian army before joining the International Air Force, as an intellectual, he still suffers great remorse over the part he plays in the bombing action over the town of Medellin. He feels as if "he were both a judge and an assassin—more disgusted, however, with being a judge than an assassin" (95). A man capable of nuanced ethical reflection, he declares that "it is painful for a man to believe in the vileness of the men beside whom he is fighting" (127). Put in charge in the absence of Magnin, the commander of the International Air Force, Scali has difficulty controlling mercenaries such as the French pilot Leclerc. One reads that "as a good intellectual, he not only wanted to explain but to convince and he had an aversion to physical violence" (257). These tendencies of his mind, of course, do not make his task as a combatant easy.

Ethical considerations in militant political action never leave Scali's mind. In explaining Unamuno's initial hostility toward the Republican cause, Scali tells Garcia that "When an intellectual who was a revolutionary attacks the revolution, he is questioning the revolutionary politics by . . . his own ethical standards" (334). Fearful of the Communist domination of the war, Scali finds it difficult to reconcile reflection and action. After being wounded at the battle of Teruel, Scali becomes "more and more an anarchist, more and more a Sorelian, almost an anticommunist" (427) while remaining, nevertheless, a militant.

Manuel, who had been a sound engineer in a Madrid studio before the war and who possesses a knowledge of music, is also, for me, an example of a militant intellectual. As a former engineer (like the socialist militant Jaime Alvear who had served as an engineer with the Hispano-Aviación), one may consider him to be an example of the Sartrean concept of "the technician of practical knowledge" who has discovered his own contradiction. Malraux in L'Espoir gives a full account of Manuel's conversion to communism, his rapid military education, and his rise to a colonel and a brigade commander—all taking place during the first year of the war. His adherence to communism is not, however, without certain complexities which are pertinent to his growth as a militant intellectual. For example, he does not belong to the vast number of the Communists in the novel who, as Robert S. Thornberry has discerned, on the one hand, possess the qualities of "organization, discipline, efficiency" and, on the other hand, are "austere, intransigent, suspicious of the Republicans and completely loyal, even servile, toward the Party."[5]

If fanatical adherence to Marxist theory for the orthodox Marxist derives from a desire that "[action] may be more automatic," as Everett W. Knight perceives it,[6] then Manuel must belong to a different category of Marxist or Communist militant. His life is irrevocably changed after seeing a boy dip his finger in the blood of a Civil Guard, who has just been executed, and write on the wall "DEATH TO FASCISM" (79). He tells Ramos, "Perhaps something has changed in me for the rest of my life; . . . the change came today when I saw that guy write on the wall with the blood of the fascist who had been killed" (82). Presently he adds, "when I saw that wild-eyed guy who was writing on the wall, there, I felt we all had a responsibility" (82).

After receiving his military education from the Republican Colonel Ximenes, a fervent Catholic, and the Communist German General Heinrich, he struggles to achieve a synthesis between thought and political action; but this synthesis does not coincide with the typical unquestioning and unswerving attitude toward action that distinguishes the Communist as a professional militant. As part of his education as a leader of men, Manuel learns the painful lesson that "action is action, not justice," as the French militant Magnin has learned before him (140). Having refused the plea of two men who had bolted in action and who had been condemned to death by a revolutionary court, Manuel enters a new phase in his life as a militant. "I believe yesterday I lived through the most important day of my life," he tells Ximenes after this incident. "I knew what had to be done, and I did it," he adds (347). Nevertheless, he realizes the enormous price that the militant intellectual in command has to pay for staying whole and intact in action. He admits to Ximenes that "every step I've taken towards a greater efficiency, towards becoming a better officer, has separated me more from my men. Everyday I'm becoming less human" (347). Manuel remains both in the realm of action and ethical introspection, without ever being quite able to convince himself that he must "lose his soul" in order to be a good commander, as the Communist General Heinrich advises him to do (350). "Now," Heinrich tells him, "you must never have pity for a lost man" (350), but Manuel never quite manages to act as automatically as a good Communist is required to do. The tension between reflection and action is never completely eradicated in him. Incidentally, Heinrich's remark to Manuel—in a curious and interesting fashion—finds its counterpart in the outburst of a group of fascists against Unamuno, when they reportedly shout: "Death to Unamuno! Death to the intellectuals," and later in fascist General Millan Astray's cry: "Death to intelligence, long live death!" (324). In both instances, it is critical intelligence, ethical considerations, and intellectual lucidity that come under attack by men who wish that action exclude reflection of any kind.

In Garcia, "one of the leading Spanish ethnologists" (88), Malraux presents his most developed model of the militant intellectual in *L'Espoir*. Garcia transcends the apparent dualities of thought and action. He characterizes the commitment to both as an indissoluable unity within which human reality finds its wholeness. One is never complete or effective without the other. Interestingly, Garcia reverses the order of thought and action and accords primacy to action. For him, it is in action and in its attendant consequences that genuine thinking takes place. In a conversation with Hernandez, an idealistic officer who believes that "Men only die for what doesn't yet exist," he declares that "action may only be thought of in terms of action" (187). Such thinking does not only take into consideration the real as its ground of emergence but seeks to coincide with the real in such a way that the possibility of change may be revealed in the process. He warns Hernandez that "thinking about what ought to be done instead of what can be done, even though what can be done is lousy, is a poison without any antidote, as Goya said" (187). In other words, critical thought recognizes and designates what ought to be done always and everywhere as the horizon of the field of action and never as the field itself, where thought and action are so interwoven as to be indistinguishable from one another.

Even though he is presented as one of Spain's well-known intellectuals, Garcia's formulation of his reasons for participation in the war is couched in a most simple and straightforward language. "Personally," he tells Scali, "I'm not in the uniform because I expect a Popular Front government made up of the noblest people. I'm in the uniform because I want the conditions of the life of the Spanish peasants to change" (338). In turn, he translates this clear and concise statement of purpose into a conviction about the efficacy of immediate and necessary militant action.

In Garcia, Malraux makes the structures of the engagement of the intellectual in direct political action intelligible. For Garcia, such action possesses an independent structure and autonomous logic of its own. He believes that the successful outcome of any action depends upon a lucid understanding of these structures and this logic. Thus, his adherence to the primacy of their comprehension is total. He criticizes the irresolute and idealistic "classic intellectual" who does not comprehend this order of things and who tries to remain pure and above the political fray. When Scali, who the more he sees the Communists in action the less he finds it desirable to cooperate with them, wonders if in order to give the Spanish peasantry more "economic freedom" one has to "enslave them politically," Garcia responds:

> According to you, since no one can be certain of the purity of his ideals in the future, the only thing left to do is to let the fascists do what they want. But once we agree on the decisive point, that we have to put up a resistance, the resistance becomes an act like any other act or choice. In certain cases the choice is tragic. For an intellectual it's almost always a tragic choice, above all for the artist. So what? Wasn't it up to him to resist? (338-39)

The significance of Garcia in *L'Espoir* derives from the truth of the acceptance of this tragedy as a given in the life of the intellectual in action. As Madrid is turned into an inferno by the shelling and bombing by Franco's forces, he particularizes and elucidates this criticism by attacking Miguel de Unamuno's attitude of moral purism toward the war. He tells Scali: "Madrid going up in flames seems to be telling Unamuno: what do you want me to do with your thought if you can't give my tragedy a thought?" (333). And later he explains:

> The great intellectual is a man of nuances, of fine distinctions, of certain quality of mind. He is a man given to the absolute truth and complexity of things. He is by nature and by definition antimanichean. Now, all forms of action are manichean because *all action is manichean.* (335)

In other words, action is never pure or homogeneous in nature; it is syncretic. It uses whatever means are appropriate to its integrity and efficacy at a given time and under specific conditions. One cannot act without getting one's hands dirty, as it were. According to Garcia, in the incomprehension of this basic truth resides the tragedy of Unamuno's flirtation with fascism. "Unamuno wanted to shake hands with fascism," says Garcia to Dr. Neubourg, "without realizing that fascism also has feet" (326).

As a militant intellectual, Garcia's highest aim is "to organize the apocalypse" (107). Everything else is secondary to this primary aim. According to Garcia, no quality of intellect, no sense of justice, no preconceived ethical considerations, no feeling of fraternity is, in and of itself, sufficient reason for engaging in militant action. Once one has made the decision, the only reason for engaging in militant political action is a fundamental and total devotion to its success. Garcia's attitude toward the success of militant action appears to follow the logic of Hemingway's statement in *Men at War* that "defeat brings worse things than can ever happen in a war."[7] Once a political commitment is made, such an action opens out onto an independent field of possibilities and provides its own grounds for justification of the efficacy of its unfolding. "There aren't fifty ways to fight," Garcia claims, "there is only one and that's to fight to win" (339). One may say that Garcia is not an essentialist but rather an existentialist. Action for him carries the sole reality. As Rodolphe Lacasse has shown, between the two domains of *"être et faire"* ("being and doing"), he steadfastly chooses that of doing.[8] In my view, however, what constitutes his considerable significance in the novel is that, for him, thought and action are consistently and reciprocally informed and nourished by one another. Neither one stands entirely alone. In his conversation with Hernandez (who, in the spirit of "generosity," has agreed to deliver a letter from the commander of the Alcazar, Moscardo, to his wife), Garcia disapprovingly declares:

> The communists want to *do* something. You and the anarchists, for different reasons, want to *be* something. That's the

tragedy of all revolutions like this one. Our perspectives are
so different: pacifism and the need to fight in self-defense,
organization and Christian ideals, efficiency and justice, and
so forth. We have to get things straightened out and transform our apocalypse into an army or we're going to be
crushed.(186)

The passage clearly shows that Garcia as an intellectual militant has resolved in action the contradictions that ordinarily
exist between being and doing. And yet he is not a Communist
or a professional revolutionary. He is no General Heinrich. Nor is
he another Millan Astray. Nor has he anything to do with those,
like Unamuno, whose final opposition to fascists is merely "an
ethical opposition" (327). For example, in answering Magnin's
question of what he thinks of communism, Garcia replies, "My
friend Guernico says 'they have all the virtues of action and
that's all.' But at the moment that's all that matters" (427). And in
the nuance and lucidity of that recognition and distinction lies
the significance of the syncretic synthesis that makes of Garcia
a militant intellectual.

When one compares Robert Jordan as a militant intellectual
in *For Whom the Bell Tolls* to the three militant intellectuals,
Scali, Manuel, and Garcia, in *L'Espoir,* certain shared characteristics of thought and action emerge. Two fundamental
differences may also be noted. The first of these, in my
opinion, is that Jordan is a composite figure who incorpo-
rates in his personality most of the salient characteristics of
Malraux's militant intellectuals in the various stages of their
development. The second—perhaps less significant but more
easily noticeable—issues from his engagement in the war as a
guerrillero and a dynamiter, which renders his task more forlorn
and superficially more romantic. However, I shall emphasize
here what he has in common with the other three rather than
what separates him from them.

To begin with, one can easily identify Jordan as an intellectual. He is an academic. "I teach Spanish in a university," he tells
Primitivo.[9] More precisely, he is an "instructor" (209) of Spanish

at the University of Montana in Missoula (165). He is also a writer. Based on his "ten years of travelling" and experience in Spain, he has written a book on Spain (248). Were he not engaged in the Spanish Civil War as a dynamiter, he might well represent a well-known type, namely, the conventional intellectual.

The reason for Jordan's commitment as an American volunteer to the cause of the Spanish Republic is quite clear. It is simply that "He fought now in this war because it had started in a country that he loved and he believed in the Republic and that if it were destroyed life would be unbearable for all those people who believed in it" (163). This is Jordan's political creed. It evolves out of his love for Spain as a country and for Spaniards as a people and out of his hatred of fascism which threatens them. Clearly, there is nothing doctrinaire in the political vision that issues from these emotions.

Despite this, Jordan is well suited to militant action as both an intellectual and a dynamiter. First, like Garcia, he has a syncretic bent of mind. He declares with precision that "There is no *one* thing that's true. It's all true" (467). This philosophical tendency of his mind makes it easier for him to see the "manichean" dimension of action which Garcia so lucidly explains in *L'Espoir*. But there is also a more practical aspect to his effectiveness as a militant. He has done much actual physical work. Of his preparation for his role as a dynamiter, Jordan says:

> Spain was your work and your job, so being in Spain was natural and sound. You had worked summers on engineering projects and in the forest service building roads and in the park and learned to handle powder, so the demolition was a sound and normal job too. Always a little hasty, but sound. (165)

Furthermore, in a conversation with Anselmo at the beginning of the novel about not knowing the terrain through which they are passing, Jordan points out, "I learn fast" (24), which signifies simply that he learns quickly in action. The role of the militant intellectual fits him inasmuch as he is genuinely capable of becoming whole in action. For instance, he is able to negate the feeling of "apprehension" that is so prevalent a problem in direct militant action, particularly for a man of imagination who can readily fall into a state of catastrophic anticipation. He feels truly happy in effective action. Thinking about the possibility of succeeding in blowing up the bridge properly, he expresses his natural propensity for action and experience and the happiness it brings. The sensation he feels is described in a passage worth quoting at length:

> Instead of the surety of failure he felt confidence rising in him as a tire begins to fill with air from a slow pump. There was little difference at first, although there was a definite beginning, as when the pump starts and the rubber of the tube crawls a little, but it came now as steadily as a tide rising or the sap rising in a tree until he began to feel the first edge of negation of apprehension that often turned into actual happiness before action.
>
> This was the greatest gift that he had, the talent that fitted him for war; that ability not to ignore but to despise whatever bad ending there could be. (393)

His aptitude for action and his desire for the efficacy of the struggle against fascism force Jordan to make common cause with the Communists:

> He was under Communist discipline for the duration of the war. Here in Spain the Communists offered the best discipline and the soundest and sanest for the prosecution of the war. He accepted their discipline for the duration of the war because, in the conduct of the war, they were the only party whose program and whose discipline he could respect. (163)

In this regard, he resembles Manuel who also recognizes the inevitable necessity of discipline demanded by the Communists for the successful conduct of the war. However, Jordan differs from Manuel inasmuch as Manuel joins the Communist party while Jordan cannot conceive of doing so. Even though Jordan considers his encounter with the Communists to have been, in the beginning, a kind of "religious experience," "like the feeling you expected to have and did not have at your first communion," "a feeling of consecration to a duty toward all the oppressed of the world" (235), he does not adhere to the party. Above all, Jordan may be compared to Garcia, who, as I have mentioned earlier, also admires and accepts the "virtues of action" which the Communists demonstrate in time of war. Nevertheless, Jordan cannot abide anyone's censoring his thinking in any way whatsoever: "He was serving in a war and he gave absolute loyalty and as complete performance as he could give while he was serving. But nobody owned his mind" (136). Thus, he lacks the automatic and unthinking adherence to action of the militant Communist.

Much like Scali, Manuel, and Garcia, Jordan is aware of the "tragic" consequences of the kind of work that he does. He admits that "The *partizans* did their damage and pulled out. The peasants stayed and took the punishment" (135). Not only does he worry about the peasants, but like that other intellectual volunteer from another land, Scali, Jordan also broods over the brutalities committed by men beside whom he fights:

> I've always known about the other, he thought. What we did to them at the start. I've always known it and hated it and I have heard it mentioned shamelessly and shamefully, bragged of, boasted of, defended, explained and denied. (135)

Elsewhere, he reminds himself that "In all the work that they, the *partizans* did, they brought added danger and bad luck to the people that sheltered them and worked with them. For what?" he asks himself (162). But contrary to Scali's pessimism and despair, he replies, "So that, eventually, there should be no more danger and so that the country should be a good place to live in. That was true no matter how trite it sounded" (162).

But this truth does not entirely free him from the remorse that he feels over the immediate harm to others that his work as a dynamiter entails. He resembles Manuel in his worries about how the exigencies of immediate, direct, violent action tax his humanity. He admits:

> Once you accept the idea of demolition as a problem it is only a problem. But there was plenty that was not so good that went with it although God knows you took it easily enough.

There was the constant attempt to approximate the conditions
of successful assassination that accompanied the demolition.
Did big words make it more defensible? Did they make killing
any more palatable? You took to it a little too readily if you
ask me. (165)

Once again, in this passage, Jordan's ethical introspections
remind one of Scali's. However, like Garcia, he has attained
a certain plane of integration of reflection and action where
he finds a measure of hope and confidence in his own individual efforts and in the collective actions of others that unfold
around him. Finally, Jordan comes to realize that violence is
never wholly justified but that it is at times inevitable. In a
conversation with Karkov, the Russian journalist and his political
mentor, the latter warns: "do not think that the Spanish people
will not live to regret that they have not shot certain generals
that even now hold commands. I do not like the shootings, you
understand." "I don't mind them," Jordan replies, "I do not like
them but I do not mind them any more" (245). As in the case of
Garcia, who sees responsible, efficient action as the only cure
for a variety of ills from which the Republican side suffers, the
education of Jordan as a militant intellectual comes full circle
and completes itself.

One may conclude that a particular reading of *L'Espoir* and
For Whom the Bell Tolls may reveal them to us as novels in
which *education through militant action* is a major and significant
theme. In the preceding pages, I have followed the definition of
a certain type of twentieth-century intellectual: the intellectual
as militant. I have subsequently identified Scali, Manuel, and
Garcia in *L'Espoir* and Robert Jordan in *For Whom the Bell
Tolls* as militant intellectuals. I have also attempted to show
the process of education through militant action that takes
place in the case of each of them. In turn, I have compared
Scali, Manuel, and Garcia, in their triadic totality as intellectual
militants, with Jordan. In this comparison, Jordan appears to
manifest the main characteristics of all three of the representative militant intellectuals in *L'Espoir.* I have suggested, therefore,
that he may be considered a composite model of the other three.

Erik Nakjavani

All four characters reveal the birth, the development, and the educational process of a new type of intellectual in our time: the intellectual as militant.

University of Pittsburgh

NOTES

1. André Malraux, *L'Espoir* (Paris: Gallimard, 1937), 337. All translations from this edition and other sources in French are mine. Further references to this work will appear in the text.

2. Valentine Cunningham, ed., *Spanish Front: Writers on the Civil War* (New York: Oxford University Press, 1986), xx.

3. Jean-Paul Sartre, *Situations, VIII: autour de 68* (Paris: Gallimard, 1972), 457. Further references to this edition will be identified in the text with a page number in parentheses.

4. Quoted by Gaetan Picon, *Malraux par lui-même* (Paris: Editions du Seuil, 1953), 90.

5. Robert S. Thornberry, *André Malraux et L'Espagne* (Geneva: Droz, 1977), 91-92.

6. Everett W. Knight, *Literature Considered as Philosophy: The French Example* (New York: Collier Books, 1962), 200.

7. Ernest Hemingway, ed., *Men at War* (New York: Berkley Publishing Corp., 1958), 5.

8. Rodolphe Lacasse, *Hemingway et Malraux: destins de l'homme* (Montreal: Edition Cosmos, 1972), 203-8.

9. Ernest Hemingway, *For Whom the Bell Tolls* (New York: Charles Scribner's Sons, 1940), 209. Further references to this edition will appear in the text.

THE COLLAPSE OF FAITH AND THE FAILURE OF LANGUAGE:
JOHN DOS PASSOS AND THE SPANISH CIVIL WAR

John Rohrkemper

In 1937, when John Dos Passos set off for the Spanish Civil War as a sympathetic observer of the Loyalist cause, he was one of America's most celebrated writers. He had just completed *U.S.A.*, the massive trilogy in which he had found a way to fuse brilliantly a modernist aesthetic with a radical social vision. *U.S.A.* is a celebration of cultural pluralism, the work of a writer confident that the meaning of culture is found in its diverse voices; indeed, Dos Passos had written in his prologue to the trilogy that "U.S.A. is the speech of the people."[1] Through essentially what M. M. Bakhtin would call a dialogic method,[2] Dos Passos had forged a stylistically experimental *and* socially conscious fiction.

Thus, Dos Passos' next novel, *Adventures of a Young Man* (1939), a novel of the Spanish Civil War, is surprising for its retreat from both a progressive political vision and a celebration of dialogism. Abandoning the multi-voiced technique of *U.S.A.*, Dos Passos narrates *Adventures of a Young Man* in a disappointingly conventional third-person voice that threatens to dissolve into anti-communist polemic. Specific events of the late thirties, and particularly of the Civil War, had disillusioned Dos Passos and soured his political vision. With that disillusionment came a loss of faith in the co-constructive power of language itself, a loss manifest in *Adventures of a Young Man* and most of Dos Passos' subsequent work. This essay examines this crucial rupture in Dos Passos' career.

During the 1920s, Dos Passos became involved in the theatre, writing three plays and a number of essays about modern theatre. Linda Wagner, among others, has shown how Dos Passos' experiences with drama helped to shape his narrative aesthetic,[3] and *U.S.A.* is an excellent case in point. In one of his essays Dos Passos called for a theatre that would be "somewhere between high mass in a Catholic church and Barnum and Bailey's circus."[4] From the Catholic mass he hoped to borrow a rich sense of ritual and spectacle; from the circus he sought the simultaneity of the three-ring action and its quality of disrupting our everyday expectations of reality. From the grotesque look and behavior of the clowns to the various gravity-defying stunts of the acrobats, the circus upsets our normal expectations of how things work.

He had been working toward a similar effect in his fiction throughout the 1920s. From the multiple protagonists of *Three Soldiers* (1921) to the Cubist elements of *Manhattan Transfer* (1925), Dos Passos had sought structural and stylistic methods for disrupting our narrative expectations, thereby challenging in the larger sense our understanding of how things work. But it was with his 1930 novel, *The 42nd Parallel*, and the subsequent *1919* (published in 1932) and *The Big Money* (1936), that Dos Passos fully achieved the effect he had been seeking. In the novels of *U.S.A.* he found a method of portraying the simultaneous crash and clang of disparate voices and experiences that could equal the experience of circus.

Many critics have suggested that the true protagonist of the trilogy is society itself, but it might be more accurate and meaningful to say that Dos Passos' real subject is language—hence his assertion that "U.S.A. is the speech of the people." That is not to say that Dos Passos' concerns in the trilogy are merely technical, for one of the hallmarks of the twentieth century is its "discovery" of the centrality of language not merely as an indicator of meaning but as the core, the very seat of meaning. In fact, it is this new understanding of the centrality of language that arguably is the most distinctive characteristic of the high modern period, from Joyce to Stein, Woolf to Faulkner. In large part, this fusion of language and consciousness emerged from modern psychology and was suggested by theorists as different as Freud and William James. At the same time, however, there emerged a more culturally-based analysis of language that emphasized, in particular, the linguistic relationship between the individual consciousness and social forces. This was the line of inquiry that especially interested two Soviet theorists, L. S. Vygotsky and M. M. Bakhtin.[5]

Lev Vygotsky, who worked in the domains of cognitive, educational, and developmental psychology, and Mikhael Bakhtin, a linguist and literary theorist, shared two basic underlying convictions: that all events are inherently tied to historical context and that external society is the starting point of consciousness. Vygotsky specifically believed that language is social in origin and is multipurposed, acquiring two functions: communication with others and self-direction. He called this latter function of self-direction "inner speech," which is the point of overlap between thought and language, is the locus of consciousness, and is powerfully shaped by the specifics of social experience.

Bakhtin shared with Vygotsky a belief in the social construction of meaning and, in his literary studies, particularly the essays collected in this country in *The Dialogic Imagination*, created a powerful theory of the novel based in social construction theory.[6] In the essay "Discourse in the Novel" (*DI*, 259-422), Bakhtin offers a conception of language as "ideologically saturated, language as world view" (*DI*, 271) and argues that there are two forces—the centripetal and the centrifugal—at work in language. Centripetal language is centralizing, hierarchicizing language. It is the language of dictatorship, but, in a more benign sense, Bakhtin argues, it is the dream of poetry: to fashion a unitary, single-voiced discourse. But attempts at single-voiced discourse are always countered by the centrifugal force of language that decentralizes, destabilizes, denormalizes. This centrifugal force is natural to society with its many voices that are based in differences in class, profession, ethnic origins, and a host of other factors. Bakhtin values the novel above all other genres precisely because of its ability to capture this polyglossia that characterizes society.

Bakhtin found a parallel for multi-voiced polyglossia in the medieval carnival which he read as a destabilizing rupture in the hegemony of European culture. Carnival—in which roles are reversed, the normal becomes absurd, mores are exuberantly violated—poses a threat to the normalizing goals of a society's official ideology. In *Rabelais and His World*, Bakhtin analyzed the ways in which the spirit of carnival can be captured in a literary work.[7] Thus, the dialogic or multi-voiced novel, merged with a spirit of carnival, can assume a powerfully denormalizing, even a revolutionary role. It is the kind of role Dos Passos seemed to imagine when he called for a drama that would resemble a three-ring circus—and a goal he would come closest to realizing in *U.S.A.*

Dos Passos had traveled in the Soviet Union during the 1920s and was well versed in Soviet art and social thought; a friend even worked in Pavlov's laboratory. Still, there is no record that Dos Passos was aware specifically of the work of these two contemporaries. Nevertheless, in *U.S.A.* he created a fiction that embodied the new ideas that they were mapping out: a fiction that was based in an understanding of the social construction of thought and language, that was crafted with multiple voices, that projected the destabilizing spirit of carnival.

Perhaps the most noticeable quality of *U.S.A.* is its division into four distinct narrative sections that alternate throughout the trilogy. Three of the narrative sections—the Newsreels, the biographies, and the Camera Eye—are essentially nonfiction; the fourth is the narration of the lives of a number of fictional characters between roughly the turn of the twentieth century and the beginning of the Great Depression. Each of the narrative sections is characterized by its own distinctive discourse.

The Newsreels are purely public discourse, fragments of the disembodied language of the popular culture—headlines, snatches of song lyrics, bits of speeches—juxtaposed against each other, often for satiric effect. While the Newsreels often seem chaotic, they actually contain shards of the language of official ideology, whether the prosaic sentiments of tired political rhetoric or the new narcotizing ideology of mass culture.

The biographies are impressionistic prose poems of actual Americans of prominence in the early years of the century. Dos Passos portrays a range of figures: politicians, inventors, labor leaders, popular celebrities, millionaire industrialists, political theorists, and social critics. The language of these biographies—intense and even pyrotechnic, often sharply ironic—is clearly the language of a consistent narrator. Still, even in these biographies we hear the interaction of voices as Dos Passos often intersperses his own narrative voice with the voices of his subjects, by quoting phrases and at times even paragraphs from their own writing or quoted speech.

The fictional sections—which make up by far the bulk of the trilogy—chart the lives, often from birth to death, of twelve ordinary Americans. Their stories are not continuous, but are interspersed with the stories of the other characters as well as with the other narrative sections. Some characters' stories spill over from one volume of the trilogy to another; sometimes the characters appear incidentally in the narratives of other characters. All of these stories are narrated in the third person, potentially the most centripetal narrative voice, to use Bakhtin's conception of narrative language. Dos Passos destabilizes the third-person narrative voice, however, by adopting the language and perceptions of the character under consideration. For instance, consider this third-person narration of the tough, working-class merchant seaman, Joe Williams, on shore leave:

> Tampico was a hell of a place; they said that Mescal made you crazy if you drank too much of it; there were big dancehalls full of greasers dancing with their hats on and with guns on their hips, and bands and mechanical pianos going full tilt in every bar, and fights and drunk Texans from the oilwells. The doors of all the cribhouses were open so that you could see the bed with white pillows and the picture of the Virgin over it. . . . But everything was so damn high that they spent up all their jack first thing and had to go back before it was hardly midnight. (*1919*, 47-48)

Compare that with the narrative of another character, Eveline Hutchins:

> Eveline went to live with Eleanor in a fine apartment Eleanor had gotten hold of somehow on the Quai de la Tournelle. It was the mansard floor of a gray peelingfaced house built at the time of Richelieu and done over under Louis Quinze. Eveline never tired of looking out the window through the delicate tracing of the wroughtiron balcony, at the Seine where toy steamboats bucked the current . . . and at the island opposite where the rocketing curves of the flying buttresses shoved the apse of Notre Dame dizzily upwards out of the trees of a little park. (*1919*, 185-86)

The contrast in narrative language, sensibility, and consciousness revealed in the two passages points up the genius of Dos Passos' narrative strategy. Each passage illustrates what Dorrit Cohn calls "consonant psycho-narration," in which consciousness "is mediated by a narrator who remains effaced and who readily fuses with the consciousness he narrates."[8] Cohn cites a number of examples of this type of narration—and analyzes in some depth Joyce's use of it in *Dubliners*—but the particular brilliance of Dos Passos' use of the technique is in the way he varies it throughout the trilogy to fuse with twelve voices, twelve unique consciousnesses. By so undercutting our normal expectation that the third-person voice will be consistent and authoritative, Dos Passos emphasizes the ways that the thought and language of each of his fictional characters are distinctive and yet are powerfully shaped by social class and circumstance.

The final narrative section, the Camera Eye, is characterized by the most individualized and private discourse. From a reading of Dos Passos' journals, and from the published biographical record, we know that these stream of consciousness sections portray Dos Passos' own personal search to understand his world. The first inchoate Camera Eye sections coincide with Dos Passos' early childhood at the turn of the century and deal with a young boy's attempt to sort out family relations. The last ones are more cohesive but still searching and record an expanding awareness of the larger society. At this level, the discourse is that of what Vygotsky would call self-directive inner speech.

By interspersing the four narrative sections chronologically, Dos Passos can scrutinize the first three decades of the twentieth century in America from the different perspectives and different languages of an extraordinarily diverse society. In effect, the Newsreels give us the cultural view of events; the biographies give us a cultural estimation of various manifestations of the ideal life; the narratives give us an individualized view of events mediated by social class; and the Camera Eye gives us an individual view of a life. Thus, the rhetoric of the four sections systematically ranges from the purely public and rigorously objective to some of the most subjective and intensely personal writing in our language. Furthermore, the intratextual echoes between various narrative sections reinforce Dos Passos' assertion that thought and language are socially constructed, inexorably tied to the specifics of time and place. By destabilizing the narrative perspective, by creating a multi-voiced or polyglot world within the trilogy, by stressing the interaction of the many voices throughout, Dos Passos creates in *U.S.A.* a carnivalized fiction, a trilogy erupting with the simultaneity and denormalizing spirit of the three-ring circus, a work challenging any class-based claims to linguistic and ideological hegemony. Ultimately, *U.S.A.* commands us to hear the speech of *all* the people, even—and especially—the unheard.

Unquestionably, the early 1930s—the years of *U.S.A.*'s composition—were the years of Dos Passos' greatest artistic achievement, but the thirties also brought political doubt and disillusionment. He grew to be increasingly uncomfortable with his associations with the political left as he began to perceive its increasing Stalinization throughout the decade. Harmony on the left had been relatively easy in the 1920s when enthusiasm for the promise of the Russian Revolution and disenchantment with postwar American society bound together many shades of leftist thought. As the need to go beyond vague enthusiasms and disenchantments became more apparent as the 1930s progressed, the movement became increasingly fragmented. Stalinism posed a particular problem for the anarchist left with which, it was becoming clearer, Dos Passos had always sympathized. His politics had always been strongly influenced by particular events. He had been drawn to the left in the twenties in part by the long agonizing case of Sacco and Vanzetti. This position was intensified by his firsthand experience of the Harlan County, Kentucky, mining strikes and the plight of the industrial unemployed in the early thirties. Two events in particular also were crucial in precipitating his *break* with the left.

The first was the riot that ensued when Communists attempted to break up a Socialist mass meeting held at Madison Square Garden on 16 February 1934. While he had not been present, Dos Passos felt bitter about the fractious, divisive act. Along with twenty-four other non-Stalinist leftists he signed "An Open Letter to the Communist Party" that appeared in the 6 March issue of *New Masses*. As an indication of Dos Passos' prominence as a leftist intellectual at the time, the editors singled him out with an editorial entitled "To John Dos Passos" despite the fact that the original protest had borne the names of such prominent figures as Edmund Wilson, Clifton Fadiman, and Lionel Trilling. The editors defended the Communist action and offered the hope that Dos Passos was still "the revolutionary writer, the comrade." In fact, however, the Madison Square Garden affair seems to have been a significant watershed for him; in a sense, affixing his name to the open letter signaled the beginning of his public disenchantment with the left, a disenchantment that was to intensify throughout the rest of his life. Shortly after the letter appeared in *New Masses*, Dos Passos declared to Edmund Wilson that "from now on events in Russia have no more interest—except as a terrible example."[9]

Dos Passos nevertheless still found himself allied with the left on many issues. One such issue was the Spanish Civil War. Probably few Americans had the long sympathy for and knowledge of Spanish life that Dos Passos had. He had traveled frequently in the country—and from a very early age. He had written a book and a number of essays about Spain. He had been deeply impressed with the strength and valor of the Spanish people and, like Hemingway, had idealized this land that had escaped the ravages of the Great War. Thus, no one was more shocked and outraged by Franco's revolt against the Republic than Dos Passos. And no one was more disappointed with Roosevelt's noninterventionism. He began almost immediately to cast about for some way to help the Loyalist cause. In the late summer of 1936, Dos Passos became a member of The American Committee to Aid Spanish Democracy. The committee's goal was to establish a news service that would report the truth of the war to the American public. The goal was never realized, but soon Dos Passos became involved with another quickly formed group, Contemporary Historians.

Archibald MacLeish, then chair of the board of directors of the group, had invited Dos Passos, along with Ernest Hemingway, Lillian Hellman, and others to produce a documentary movie that could win sympathy for the Loyalist cause. The result was *The Spanish Earth.* Almost as soon as Dos Passos arrived in Spain, however, he began to bump egos with Hemingway. Dos Passos had envisioned a film that would show the hardships and courageous endurance of the Spanish peasant. Hemingway wanted the film to focus more directly on the drama of battle. They might have ironed out their differences, however, had Dos Passos not received some disturbing intelligence about his longtime friend, José Robles.

Robles, a professor of Spanish at Johns Hopkins University, was visiting Spain when war broke out. He took a leave of absence from the university, offered his services to the Loyalists, and was made a translator for General Goriev, the commander of Soviet forces in Spain. Soon after his arrival, Dos Passos learned from Robles' wife that her husband had suddenly disappeared. Immediately, he began making inquiries as to his friend's whereabouts, but they were met with misinformation and tight-lipped silence. Finally, however, he rooted out the truth about his friend's fate. Two years later he wrote:

> It was not until I reached Madrid that I got definite information from the chief of the Republican counter-espionage service that Robles had been executed by a "special section" (which I gathered was under the control of the Communist party).[10]

There were many rumors about the reasons for Robles' execution, but Dos Passos' explanation probably was more accurate than most: he believed that Robles had been eliminated because he came to know too much about the nature and extent of Soviet military operations in Spain. Dos Passos was further dismayed by the lack of sympathy for Robles among American leftists in Spain.

Robles' death was a deep personal blow to Dos Passos. He felt grief for the death of a friend and outrage that the friend had been betrayed by his supposed political allies. If the betrayal of Sacco and Vanzetti by the American power elite had radicalized him in the late twenties, what Dos Passos perceived as the betrayal of Robles by the Left solidified his growing disillusionment with the movement in the late thirties.

The effects of that disillusionment are evident in Dos Passos' subsequent fiction. In fact, one could chart a close correlation between Dos Passos' political views and his literary production throughout his long career. It is a more complicated issue than some have suggested, however, by asserting simply that Dos Passos' literary successes are the result of his leftist views, his failures the result of his later conservatism. It is more accurate to say that Dos Passos' fiction is most alive when his political hopes are most alive, when he feels most confident and is willing to risk the perils of political flux and change—at precisely those points where his political views seem to him *un*fixed and *un*sure. It is at these points that Dos Passos is willing to listen to the many voices of society, to create fiction that is a dialogue rather than polemic.

Unfortunately, *Adventures of a Young Man*, his novel that deals with the Spanish Civil War, is more polemic than dialogue.[11] It is the story of a young man, Glenn Spottswood, who, out of his idealism, becomes attracted to the cause of the downtrodden and becomes a labor organizer. Much of the novel chronicles the ways in which Glenn's efforts are undercut by the cynical meddling of the Communist party which is more concerned with promoting causes than promoting the welfare of the powerless. Eventually, he finds himself in Spain where he is imprisoned and taken before a drumhead court for his alleged

Trotskyite sympathies. Before he can be executed, however, he is freed to undertake a suicide mission. The novel ends with Glenn's death.

Adventures of a Young Man, while not deserving of the vilification with which it was greeted by some leftist reviewers, nevertheless is a dreary novel, both for its relentless pessimism and its generally cramped style. Robert Rosen aptly characterizes it as a novel of "despair without energy."[12] Through his third-person narrator, Dos Passos keeps firm control over the language and point of view of the narration. This was more than an aesthetic choice. In fact, it reflects a post-*U.S.A.* and post-Spanish Civil War belief that a work of literature should convey "a firmly anchored ethical standard . . . [an] unshakable moral attitude toward the world we live in and towards its temporary moral standards."[13] This ethical standard, in *Adventures of a Young Man*, is anchored in the narrator and, through him, in Glenn who unfortunately is not a strong enough character to bear such responsibility. More importantly, the genius of Dos Passos' earlier work was in the understanding that no character, however strong, *could* be an ethical anchor in a dynamic world, constantly in flux, constantly in the *process* of social construction. Rosen is on the mark when he asserts that Glenn is like a character in *U.S.A.*, but

> without the counterpoint of eleven other narratives and without the expanded historical, moral, and subjective dimensions that the Camera Eye, biographies, and Newsreels create . . . [without the] exciting multiplicity of perspectives [of the trilogy]. (98)

In recoiling from events that had shaken his faith in social process, Dos Passos sought the anchor of a stable centripetal narrative language.

David Vanderwerken has examined Dos Passos' extraordinary faith in the power of language in *U.S.A.*,[14] convincingly arguing that the trilogy is an assertion of the power of honest words, words that sing of equality, opportunity, and hatred of oppression, words that can, in Dos Passos' own words, "rebuild the ruined words worn slimy in the mouths of law-yers districtattorneys collegepresidents judges" (*Big Money,* 391). Even in the despair of *U.S.A.'s* penultimate Camera Eye, on the night of the execution of Sacco and Vanzetti, when "America our nation has been beaten by strangers who have taken the clean words our fathers spoke and made them slimy and foul," (*Big Money,* 413), Dos Passos can still assert his faith in dialogic possibility:

> the old words of the immigrants are being renewed in blood and agony tonight do they know that the old American speech of the haters of oppression is new tonight in the mouth of an old woman from Pittsburgh of a husky boilermaker from Frisco . . . in the mouth of a Back Bay socialworker in the mouth of an Italian printer of a hobo from Arkansas   the language of the beaten nation is not forgotten in our ears tonight   the men in the deathhouse made the old words new before they died. (*Big Money,* 413-14)

But how were the old women, boilermaker, social worker, printer, hobo going to be able to have their voices heard? In *U.S.A.* their voices are beaten by the voice of wealth, power, influence. From the events of the late thirties—and particularly the Civil War—Dos Passos came to conclude that the organized left, too, could and would use words to turn the truth inside out to make the old words "slimy." In that realization came his ultimate collapse of faith.

Ironically, for the rest of his career much of Dos Passos' energy would go to enshrining the words of an American elite, particularly in a series of narrative histories of the early years of the American republic. John P. Diggins has examined such works as *The Ground We Stand On* (1941), *The Head and Heart of Thomas Jefferson* (1954), *The Men Who Made the Nation* (1957), and *Prospects of a Golden Age* (1959), and has concluded convincingly that

> The historical reality that Dos Passos discovered in the eighteenth century—or willed into vision—appeared preg-nant with meaning and value, an orderly, intelligible society

capable of being reconstructed through the traditional storytelling function of narrative history. . . . And writing history
from the "top down," as it were, he found a remarkable climate
of opinion free of conflict that reverberated through *U.S.A.*
The portrait of late-eighteenth-century America is characterized by consensus, continuity, harmony.[15]

And, as even this brief passage suggests, it is a portrait that
is essentially false, that falsely proposes a world of stasis, a
world in which, for instance, such issues of class and race
as Shays's Rebellion and the peculiar institution of slavery are
virtually relegated to a historical footnote—a world without the
destabilizing but energizing polyglossia of Dos Passos' great
trilogy.

Such a simplistic and static view of society—and of
language—would have been anathema to Dos Passos only a
few years earlier. It represents a repudiation of the many-voiced
dialogic carnival that is *U.S.A.* Linda Wagner has suggested that
Dos Passos' later fiction was an attempt to use his own experiences "to 'prove' his philosophical concepts" (116). As he lost faith
in the constant dialogue that exists between such concepts, he
also lost faith in the dialogic possibilities of his fiction. That loss
of faith seemed to begin in the mid-thirties but came to a climax
in the events of the Spanish Civil War. It would seem that the
firing-squad bullet that forever silenced his friend, José Robles,
also silenced the rich voices of "the speech of the people" that
Dos Passos had once believed *was* the U.S.A.

Elizabethtown College

NOTES

1. John Dos Passos, *U.S.A.*, Modern Library Edition (New York: Random
House, 1937), vii. Further references to the trilogy, which include *The
42nd Parallel, 1919* and *The Big Money*, will be from John Dos Passos,
U.S.A., Sentry Edition (Boston: Houghton Mifflin, 1963), and will appear
in the text, identified by the name of the novel and page number within
parentheses.

John   Rohrkemper

2. M. M. Bakhtin, *The Dialogic Imagination: Four Essays*, ed. Michael Holquist, trans. Caryl Emerson and Michael Holquist, University of Texas Slavic Series no. 1 (Austin: University of Texas Press, 1981). Further references to this work will be identified in the text as *DI*, followed by a page number.

3. Linda W. Wagner, *Dos Passos: Artist as American* (Austin: University of Texas Press, 1979). Further references to this work will appear in the text.

4. John Dos Passos, "Towards a Revolutionary Theatre," *New Masses* 3 (December 1927): 20.

5. L. S. Vygotsky, *Thought and Language*, ed. and trans. Eugenia Hanfmann and Gertrude Vakar (Cambridge: MIT Press, 1962); Bakhtin, *The Dialogic Imagination*.

6. For an excellent comparison of Vygotsky and Bakhtin, see Caryl Emerson, "The Outer Word and Inner Speech: Bakhtin, Vygotsky, and the Internalization of Language," in *Bakhtin: Essays and Dialogues on His Work*, ed. Gary Saul Morrison (Chicago: University of Chicago Press, 1986), 21-40. Vygotsky's most influential work is collected in *Thought and Language*.

7. M. M. Bakhtin, *Rabelais and His World*, trans. Helene Iswolsky (Cambridge: Harvard University Press, 1968).

8. Dorrit Cohn, *Transparent Minds: Narrative Modes for Presenting Consciousness in Literature* (Princeton: Princeton University Press, 1978), 26.

9. John Dos Passos, *The Fourteenth Chronicle: Letters and Diaries of John Dos Passos*, ed. Townsend Ludington (Boston: Gambit, 1973), 459.

10. Virginia Spencer Carr, *Dos Passos: A Life* (Garden City, N.Y.: Doubleday Publishing Company, 1984), 367.

11. John Dos Passos, *Adventures of a Young Man* (New York: Harcourt Brace, 1939).

12. Robert C. Rosen, *John Dos Passos: Politics and the Writer* (Lincoln: University of Nebraska Press, 1981), 96. Further references to this work will appear in the text.

13. John Dos Passos, "A Note on Fitzgerald," in *The Crack-Up*, ed. Edmund Wilson (New York: New Directions, 1945), 339.

14. David L. Vanderwerken, "*U.S.A.*: Dos Passos and the 'Old Words,'" *Twentieth Century Literature* 23 (May 1977): 195-228.

15. John P. Diggins, "Visions of Chaos and Visions of Order: Dos Passos as Historian," *American Literature* 46 (November 1974): 336-37.

HISTORY AND DESIRE:
AUDEN'S "SPAIN" AND
CAUDWELL'S *ILLUSION AND REALITY*

Robert Sullivan

I wish to present here a set of mutual concerns that link two individuals: one so well-known that a "generation" has been named for him, the other relatively obscure. Yet the confluence of their interests brought them together (two of their texts at least) when Caudwell was already dead and Auden reviewed the former's *Illusion and Reality* while writing his poem on the Spanish conflict. I do not intend to offer a close reading of Auden's poem (nor yet another discussion of those controversial lines that have received so much attention) but rather to trace a set of cultural and ideological matrices that resulted in a more concrete form of intertextuality in the spring of 1937.

Caudwell and Auden, unknown to one another, shared many of the cultural concerns of their epoch. Both men were poets, but Caudwell chose to abandon poetry for theory; both reacted to the emerging interest in the synthesis of Marx and Freud, though Caudwell utilized these thinkers in his investigation of poetry's function within society, whereas Auden used Marx and Freud to form a modernist mythology for his creative work.[1] They were both interested in evolutionary anthropology, Caudwell especially, as a means to explicate cultural artifacts; and lastly, but not insignificantly, they shared an interest in the genre of the "whodunit," the formulaic narrative that concerns itself primarily with the exorcism of guilt. Caudwell, under his real name Christopher St. John Sprigg, had written eight of these books, and Auden, who was "compelled" to devour them, commented insightfully (if not altogether consciously) on the ideological significance of such a genre in an age such as his. Guilt is a recurrent motif in many of the autobiographical testimonies we have from the thirties, and it is interesting that Auden locates the dynamic of the "whodunit" in the "dialectic of innocence and guilt."[2] It is beyond the scope of this paper, but worth observing, that some of the poets, those "frustrated men of action," may have secured from the "whodunit" a form of vicarious absolution from the guilt they felt within the "sick" society that they constantly criticized but were powerless to change.

Before we investigate further a relationship between two individuals, we might do well to situate both of them within that society, within the broader concerns of the 1930s in England. Some remarks by Fredric Jameson are apposite, though I must emphasize strongly that I appropriate them as a frame for my own discourse and not in the context of the complex argument that forms the first chapter of Jameson's *The Political Unconscious.*[3] Near the beginning of his discussion, Jameson remarks that historical matters can

> recover their original urgency for us only if they are retold within the unity of a single great collective story . . . the collective struggle to wrest a realm of Freedom from a realm of Necessity, only if they are grasped as vital episodes in a single vast unfinished plot. (19-20)

In the conclusion to the same chapter, "On Interpretation," Jameson states:

> Conceived in this sense [that Necessity gives form to historical events], History is what hurts, it is what refuses desire and sets inexorable limits to individual as well as collective praxis, which its "ruses" turn into grisly and ironic reversals of their overt intention. (102)

The omnipresence of history, the interplay of necessity, freedom, and desire are motifs in the "collective story" of the

1930s just as they are central elements in the texts of Caudwell and Auden, though, as we shall see, with different emphases. The "plot" of the 1930s in England has been documented by numerous commentators so that we need only remind ourselves of its basic structure here. The narrative imposed on this period (and I use "imposed" in the strongest sense, since no decade is reducible to a set of abstract motifs) tells of a time of despair and guilt among the intelligentsia, a period of "crisis," of the need for commitment and desire for change. A particular recurrent motif in this narrative structure is the role of the artist in the "struggle" for such change. Auden and Caudwell, each in his unique way, shared in such frustrations and desires.

The "noise of history," the desire for change, the recognition of necessity and struggle, the alleviation of guilt—all these rhetorical skirmishes would find their "whetstone . . . [their] frontier on the Spanish front," as Louis MacNeice was to put it retrospectively.[4] For Stephen Spender, as for so many others, the Spanish conflict offered a "healing" of that psychic wound created by the breach between poetry and action, art and struggle. In his introduction to *Poems for Spain*, Spender not only equates the writing of poetry with the action of the Brigades themselves, but his remarks echo that paradigmatic structure of 1930s rhetoric: the "desire" for liberty, in the context of the past, present, and future:

> The fact that these poems should have been written at all has a literary significance parallel to the existence of the International Brigade. . . .
>
> Poets and poetry have played a considerable part in the Spanish War, because to many people the struggle of the Republicans has seemed a struggle for the conditions without which the writing and reading of poetry are almost impossible in modern society. . . . In a world where poetry seems to have been abandoned, become the exalted medium of a few specialists, or the superstition of backward peoples, this awakening of a sense of the richness of a tomorrow *with* poetry, is as remarkable as the struggle for liberty itself, and is more remarkable than the actual achievement. The conditions for a great popular poetry are not yet obtained; what we note is the desire for such a poetry.[5]

Spender had not only read Auden's "Spain" carefully, but also the latter's reply to a questionnaire organized by Nancy Cunard on how writers felt concerning the Spanish Civil War. Auden replied that he supported

> the Valencia government in Spain because its defeat by the forces of International Fascism would be a major disaster for Europe. . . . [It] would create an atmosphere in which the creative artist and all who care for justice, liberty and culture would find it impossible to work or even exist.[6]

Such a preoccupation with bourgeois freedom and bourgeois culture, so evident in the "Future" of Auden's "Spain," is what led Caudwell to observe of Spender, Auden, and Day-Lewis: that they see "the revolution as a path to a bourgeois heaven."[7]

In the same anthology, *Poems for Spain*, in which Auden's poem is a centerpiece, there is a poem by John Lepper entitled "Battle of Jarama 1937." It was at Jarama where "Death stalked the olive trees / Picking his men" (33) that Caudwell fell on his first day of action on 12 February 1937, at the age of twenty-nine. He had published fourteen books and several have been published posthumously.[8] When he left for Spain in December 1936, the book for which he is best known, *Illusion and Reality*, was being set in type by the Macmillan Publishing Company. He wrote no poems in what Spender called a "poet's war," but instead most of his energy was taken up editing the Wall newspaper as well as writing weekly letters to his comrades in the Poplar branch of the Communist party of Great Britain, urging them again and again to agitate for a lifting of the arms ban. The following is typical of a series of letters, mostly written either during guard duty or when Caudwell had just been relieved:

> Dear Nick,
> This is just a line to explain to the Branch that after delivering the lorries at [censored] we have been drafted into the British Unit of the International Brigade. At present we are at a training centre [Albacete] but hope to move up soon. . . .
> England seems miles and miles and years and years away already. Give my best wishes to all the Branch and tell the Bow Group to get the government's arms embargo lifted as soon as

possible! I hope Hart [a Poplar comrade] got the album I sent the Group from Barcelona as a souvenir. Please write and tell me all the local and English Party news as we get practically none out here.[9]

Illusion and Reality (with "illusion" serving the two meanings of poetic invention and ideological distortion) traces the origins of poetry from tribal ritual (what Caudwell calls the "matrix" of poetry) to what he saw as the "dying culture" of his own time, and he speculates in his last chapter, "The Future of Poetry," on the prognosis for poetry in a socialist society. Poetry, or imaginative experiment generally (and for Caudwell this included science), is generated as part of that broader contradiction that drives on society—the contradiction between man's desires and Nature's necessity. Caudwell viewed the function of poetry as helping to shape the desires of humankind toward reality in the hope of rescuing (to use Jameson's terminology, which is actually very close to Caudwell's own) some "realm of freedom" from the "inexorability of Necessity." His vision is a teleological one, tracing the evolution of man's historical struggle for freedom from the illusory methodology of magic to a more scientific view of the world, both with regard to the laws of science and those of society. In its triadic structure of past, present, and future, and the dialectical interplay between Freedom and Necessity, Caudwell's text parallels that of Auden's poem, although their views on historical necessity and "the struggle for freedom" have different emphases.

Caudwell's book seemed the fulfillment of a central quest of his generation: how can art or poetry—the creative endeavor—have any effect on the desire for change, a desire so prevalent among the intelligentsia of these years? At the heart of his thesis was the notion that the preparation for action, and thus all change, lay within the imagination, that the consciousness of humanity, so reliant on the symbolic, could then be changed by the symbolic, most particularly through the language of poetry.[10] Here was that hope theorized, that poetry could "make action urgent and its nature clear" as Auden had put it.[11] And when Auden reviewed Caudwell's book for *New Verse*, he underscored its importance for his "generation":

> We have waited a long time for a Marxist book on the aesthet-
> ics of poetry. . . . Now at last Mr. Caudwell has given us such
> a book.
>   *Illusion and Reality* is a long essay on the evolution of free-
> dom in Man's struggle with nature . . . and of the essentially
> social nature of words, art and science. . . . This is the most
> important book on poetry since the books of Dr. Richards
> and in my opinion provides a more satisfactory answer to the
> many problems which poetry raises.[12]

Evolution . . . freedom . . . struggle—these are indeed the important concepts that give structural cohesion to Caudwell's book;
they are also, of course, the structuring principles of Auden's
poem.

This "coincidence" is not altogether surprising. Auden had
recently returned from Spain (probably March 1937) where
he had not contributed much to the "struggle" and had left
(as he later recorded) somewhat "shocked and disturbed."[13]
According to at least one of his biographers, Auden repaired
to the Lake District, and it was here that he wrote his review
of Caudwell's book and composed his panoramic overview of
history and desire in relation to the struggle in Spain.[14] It
seems that Caudwell's book impressed Auden, not only in
its critical explication of the sources of poetry but in other
ways as well. Apart from the triadic structural motif of past,
present, and future, there are echoes of Caudwell's discussion
of economic history and its development from magical ritual
through feudal times to the bourgeois revolution and beyond.
Most importantly, there are reminiscences of how these economic changes affected consciousness.

Samuel Hynes has remarked that "in terms of [his] metaphor
of the 'thirties as a tragic drama,' Auden's 'Spain' is about the
third act" (255). In terms of our "narrative of desire," "Spain"
represents a moral fable, that "arid square" on which are played
out the fears and aspirations—the psychic drama—of Auden and
his contemporaries. In terms of Auden's personal iconography,
the poem is a figurative denouement of the "truly strong man"
participating in the building of the "Just City." In the future, the
"Tomorrow" of Auden's poem, there will be "the rediscovery of

romantic love," the "walks by the lake," the "weeks of perfect communion"; indeed, as Hynes has observed, "it will simply be people doing what they like" (253). Liberty's "masterful shadow" is not subject to the same rigorous laws of necessity as Caudwell's vision of the future and freedom.

Auden's vision of the future is somewhat more bourgeois than the one Caudwell envisaged. For Caudwell, the future is causally bound up with the present, "the struggle today," and especially with the role of the artist within such ideological warfare. This is why the last chapter of *Illusion and Reality,* "The Future of Poetry," deals with the influential poets of the day—Auden, Spender, Day-Lewis—and what Caudwell sees as their ambivalent attitude toward a socialist revolution and the failure (not to mention the futility) of their attempt to propagandize their work, and also what he sees as their erroneous notion of freedom.

What is interesting here, in this intertextual relationship between Caudwell's book and Auden's poem, is that some of the latter's incidental imagery echoes that section of *Illusion and Reality* which takes him and his fellow travelers to task. In this final chapter, Caudwell reiterates the social nature and function of art and its place within the evolutionary process as a whole. In what follows we can detect in concept and nomenclature not only what Auden chose to highlight in his review—evolution, struggle, nature, freedom—but also that Necessity and "the developing relations" of society that form the chronological or syntagmatic axis of Auden's "Spain 1937."

> Men, in their struggle with Nature (i.e., in their struggle for freedom) enter into certain relations with each other to win that freedom. . . . But men cannot change Nature without changing themselves. The full understanding of this mutual interpenetration or reflexive movement of men and Nature, mediated by the necessary and developing relations known as society, is the *recognition* of necessity, not only in Nature but in ourselves and therefore also in society. (308)

And how are the artists, especially the would-be socialist artists—the Audens, the Spenders, the Day-Lewises—how are they situated within this social fabric? Well, Caudwell argues, they cannot return to the discarded forms of yesterday, but as artists they cannot see new forms and contents for the future. Caudwell goes on to emphasize the interrelationship between past, present, and future in terms that ironically prefigure the motifs of "Spain." "They know 'something is to come' after the giant firework display of the Revolution" (312), and they realize that "they must put 'something' there in the future, and they tend to put their own vague aspirations for bourgeois freedom and bourgeois equality" (313). These poets "attempt to visualise the brave new world in terms of their desires . . . [and] a sketch of the future is produced which is curiously pathological" (313). These artists, these "Romantic Revolutionaries," see "the wild and destructive parts of revolution" as the most "picturesque," and, in many ways, "a revolution without violence would be disappointing" (313). There are "in the three English poets most closely associated with the revolutionary movement . . . crude and grotesque scraps of Marxist phraseology," and this leads to "an unconscious dishonesty in [their] art" (315). Auden was, of course, to become *conscious* of such "dishonesty" later, when he called the era in which he was a leading poetic figure that "low dishonest decade,"[15] when he was to disown complete poems and excise or revise lines in others, including "Spain." A particular case in point, and in some ways prototypical of the ambivalences in "Spain," is the earlier "A Communist to Others," with its sustained equivocation generated by the very title.[16] The following remarks take on a sharp irony in the light of the latter poem (and especially if we remember the leitmotifs of past, present, and future in "Spain"), as Caudwell takes on the persona of the proletariat addressing the so-called poets of revolution and historical necessity:

> Your concept of freedom, because it is rooted in a part of society, is also partial . . . you imagine your consciousness to be free and not determined by your experience and history. This illusion you exhibit so proudly is the badge of your slavery to yesterday. (317)

The proletariat go on to enjoin their fellow travelers not to apply proletarian ideology "mechanically to their art" but rather to refashion their consciousness, and their poetic technique will follow suit:

> Then we shall say your art is proletarian and living; then we shall say, your soul has left the past—it has dragged the past into the present and forced the realisation of the future. (319)

Although Caudwell had not seen "Spain," he was engaged in a cultural critique that later found a focus in more particular criticisms of Auden's poem, from George Orwell's to Edward Mendelson's. Edgell Rickword, in an early piece, summed the poem up in this brief statement: "Today the struggle, tomorrow the poetry and fun."[17] Mendelson categorizes it as a poem that "mistrusts its own purposes"[18] and Stephen Spender put his finger on its central ambivalence when he remarked of Auden that he was "expressing an attitude which for a few weeks or months he had felt intellectually forced to adopt, but which he never truly felt."[19]

Caudwell was the first to point out, proleptically enough, what is wrong with "Spain" even though, unknowingly, he contributed in some way to its genesis and making. The poem suffers from at best an indecisive tone, and at worst, from a protean ideological stance; this is what results, Caudwell argues, when the poet's "proletarian aspirations gather at one pole [and] all his bourgeois art at the other" (315). The ambivalence of poems such as "Spain" (and Auden's highly ambivalent piece "A Communist to Others") results, Caudwell argues, from pseudo-commitment.

However—and this needs to be emphasized, especially in the light of Caudwell's own rather crude outline of the economic bases of various stages in English poetry—Caudwell was not calling for some form of poetic propaganda. The following remarks from the later work *Romance and Realism* make this clear:

> What, then, is the proper position for a bourgeois poet today who finds himself arrived at the situation of Auden, Spender, and Lewis? To be a revolutionary, certainly, but a real revolutionary, not a free-lance agitator; to be a member of a

> revolutionary party and to carry out a common party line,
> not his own line; to be a revolutionary not only in blank verse
> but in every activity which he can carry out and his party
> suggests. Agitation is necessary certainly, so is propaganda,
> but let the poet be a genuine propagandist, not a blank-verse
> propagandist. Is the proletariat made conscious of its goal
> by rhymed economics? No, verse is not, and never was, the
> instrument of propaganda in this sense. . . . Notice that not
> only does this attempt not revitalise poetry, but it gives rise to
> a perversion of poetry, self consciously propagandist poetry.
> Poetry can be revitalised only by a change of the economic
> relations on which it rests, and a corresponding change and
> synthesis of the dissolving culture of today.[20]

Caudwell had decided to give up writing poetry so that he could
work for what he saw as a unified consciousness and sensibility
based on communist social relations, wherein, he believed, a
new authentic poetry could be born.

Such a society, Caudwell believed, would be based on a
"true" understanding of "liberty," a concept that many of the
intellectuals and poets wrote about but, in Caudwell's opinion,
did not fully comprehend. He felt it necessary to write an essay,
"Liberty: A Study in Bourgeois Illusion," outlining what he felt
was the misunderstanding of true freedom on the part of such
people as Auden, Spender, and the other "fellow travelers":

> Like the neurotic who refuses to believe that his compulsion
> is the result of a certain unconscious complex, the bourgeois
> refuses to believe that his conception of liberty as a mere
> deprivation of social constraints arises from bourgeois social
> relations themselves, and that is just the illusion which is
> constraining him on every side.[21]

In the "collective story" of the thirties, Caudwell seemed so
adept at scrutinizing the illusions of his epoch, on proclaiming
how to "wrest a realm of Freedom from a realm of Necessity,"
as Jameson (after Engels) has put it (19). Yet unaware of
Stalin's counterrevolutionary machinations in Spain, Caudwell
died with his own illusions intact. This was no doubt one of
those historical "ruses" that "turn into ironic reversals" of overt
intentions, the sort of particular reversal that led Albert Camus

to comment on its broader implications: "It was in Spain that men learned that one can be right and yet be beaten, that force can vanquish spirit, that there are times when courage is not its own recompense."[22]

University of Illinois at Urbana-Champaign

NOTES

1. Auden did publish an interesting theoretical essay on Marx and Freud, "Psychology and Art," in *The Arts Today,* ed. Geoffrey Grigson (London: John Lane, 1935), 1-21. See my *Christopher Caudwell* in the series Critics of the 20th Century, ed. Christopher Norris (Beckenham, England: Croom Helm Ltd., 1987) for a discussion of Caudwell's extensive amalgamation of Marx and Freud.

2. W. H. Auden, "The Guilty Vicarage," in *The Art of the Essay,* ed. Leslie Fiedler (New York: Thomas Y. Crowell & Co., 1969), 234-44; first published in *Harpers Magazine,* May 1948, 406-11. The quotation is on 243.

3. Fredric Jameson, *The Political Unconscious: Narrative as a Socially Symbolic Act* (Ithaca, N.Y.: Cornell University Press, 1981). Further references to this work will appear in the text.

4. Louis MacNeice, "Autumn Journal," in *Poems 1925-1940* (New York: Random House, 1940), 185.

5. *Poems for Spain,* ed. Stephen Spender and John Lehmann (London: The Hogarth Press, 1939), 7. Further references to works contained in this edition will appear in the text.

6. Quoted in Valentine Cunningham, *Spanish Civil War Verse* (Harmondsworth, England: Penguin, 1983), 55.

7. Christopher Caudwell, *Illusion and Reality* (New York: International Publishers, 1977), 315. Further references to this work will appear in the text.

8. The most recent publications of Caudwell's works are a collection of his prose writings and letters, *Scenes and Actions,* ed. Jean Duparc and David

Margolies (London: Routledge & Kegan Paul, 1986); and his *Collected Poems*, ed. Alan Young (Manchester: Carcanet Press, 1986).

9. Letter, dated 30 December 1936, from the Caudwell Papers, Humanities Research Center, University of Texas, Austin.

10. I deal with Caudwell's poetics extensively in my *Christopher Caudwell*, especially ch. 4, "The Socialisation of Dream: *Illusion and Reality.*"

11. W. H. Auden, "August for the People," in *The English Auden*, ed. Edward Mendelson (New York: Random House, 1977), 157.

12. W. H. Auden, review of Caudwell's *Illusion and Reality*, in *New Verse* 24 (May 1937): 20-22.

13. Quoted in Samuel Hynes, *The Auden Generation* (New York: Viking Press, 1977), 251.

14. Humphrey Carpenter, *W. H. Auden: A Biography* (London: Allen & Unwin, 1981), 217. Samuel Hynes also remarks on some correspondences between Caudwell's book and Auden's poem (*The Auden Generation*, 259). Further references to these works will appear in the text.

15. W. H. Auden, "September 1, 1939," in *The English Auden*, 245.

16. W. H. Auden, "A Communist to Others," in *New Country*, ed. Michael Roberts (London: Hogarth Press, 1933), 209-13. For an interesting discussion of the shifting "pronomial structure" and "disabling insecurity of tone" (also relevant to any discussion of "Spain"), see Roger Fowler, *Literature as Social Discourse* (Bloomington: Indiana University Press, 1981), 91-95.

17. Quoted in Cunningham, *Spanish Civil War Verse*, 70.

18. Edward Mendelson, review in *The Times Literary Supplement*, 16 January 1987, 59.

19. Stephen Spender, *The Thirties and After* (Glasgow: William Collins Sons & Co., 1978), 30.

20. Christopher Caudwell, *Romance and Realism* (Princeton: Princeton University Press, 1970), 135-36.

21. Christopher Caudwell, "Liberty: A Study in Bourgeois Illusion," in *Studies in a Dying Culture* (New York: Monthly Review Press, 1972), 217.

22. Quoted as epigraph to Allen Guttman, *The Wound in the Heart* (New York: Free Press of Glencoe, 1962).

THE LEGACY OF THE
SPANISH CIVIL WAR TODAY

THE LEGACY OF THE SPANISH CIVIL WAR TODAY

Luis López Guerra
Justice, Spanish Constitutional Court

For political philosophers throughout history, from Thomas Hobbes in the seventeenth century to Carl Schmitt in ours, civil war has been considered the greatest possible catastrophe that can befall a country and the most tragic of all conflicts that political powers are called upon to avoid. Avoiding civil war appears as the ultimate justification for political power, even as Hobbes conceived it in his *Leviathan.* This conviction is rooted in the historical experiences of every age where civil wars, from the Roman civil war in the first century B.C. to the English civil war in the seventeenth century and the American Civil War in the nineteenth century, not only gravely damaged the lives of the generation that fought the war but also conditioned the collective mentality and behavior of future generations as well as the very foundations of political order.

These foreign examples can readily be confirmed throughout the history of Spain, a nation repeatedly afflicted by civil strife. Not since the onset of the war of the Castilian Communes in the sixteenth century has Spain known a century free from the turmoil of civil war, having experienced rebellion in Catalonia in the seventeenth century, the War of Succession in the eighteenth century, and the Carlist wars in the nineteenth century. Each of these conflicts has had profound and long-lasting repercussions on Spanish society, leaving scars which marked the lives of many more than just the protagonists of these events. We need look no further back than the First Carlist War, which ended in 1839, to see that it left sufficient embers smouldering to rekindle with an equal degree of violence a Second Carlist War thirty-five years later among a totally different generation. The unresolved hostilities of the second war, which ended in 1876, erupted no less violently sixty years later when the Carlist Requetés led the rebellion in Navarra on 19 July 1936. Perhaps it is not an exaggeration to suggest that much of the mentality which inspires the present-day climate of violence in the Basque country is rooted in the conflicts of the Carlist wars.

The passage of time and the disappearance or lessening of direct political and social influence of the generation that experienced the Spanish Civil War justify and, at the same time, permit our inquiry into the consequences of the trauma that wracked Spain from 1936 to 1939, not only on the personal level of those who experienced the war firsthand but also with regard to the effects of the war on the collective mentality, culture, and behavior of the subsequent generation. Stated simply, such an inquiry would lead us to ask what aspects of Spanish social, political, and cultural life today are in some way influenced by memories or legacies emanating from a conflict that arose over fifty years ago and, above all, how that episode in our country's past can better help us to comprehend the nature of present-day Spain. In order to answer these questions, we must bear in mind at least two conditioning factors: first, the memories or images that most Spaniards have of the Civil War are not easy to separate from those they have of the Franco regime; and secondly, certain characteristics of the new democratic system in Spain, as I will explain later, discourage an in-depth analysis of the legacy of the Civil War. This latter circumstance may prove to be positive or negative, but it is nonetheless a facet of contemporary Spanish life that is difficult to deny.

In reference to the first conditioning factor, we must underscore the fact that, at least until 1975, the Civil War was more than a historical event in Spain's past; it was an essential element of identity and legitimacy, not only for the Franco regime but also for large sectors of the opposition as well. As often occurs, and not exclusively in Spain, the war did not end with an agreement or compromise but rather in the imposition of the victor's ideology and interests on the vanquished, precisely because this victory served to legitimize the new regime's claim to political power. The period of Reconstruction in the United States' history is an eloquent example of the same circumstance. In Spain, this period lasted four decades and, as a result, memories of the war, or more concretely, memories of the "victory" came to constitute an underlying component of everyday Spanish life. The celebration of Victory Day, the annual Victory Day Parade, monuments such as the Arch of Triumph in Madrid or the Valley of the Fallen, the numerous crosses and inscriptions dedicated to those who died for the cause, and the designation of Franco as "Caudillo" or "Generalísimo" persisted until the very last days of the regime; some of them, obviously, exist even today. To this, we might add that certain circumstances characteristic of wartime, such as troop mobilizations and military courts-martial, continued on long after the fighting had ceased. Despite the perspective that forty years should afford us, for the generations of Spaniards who came of age before 1975, the war retained its contemporaneity, becoming an inevitable reference point used daily to legitimize the prevailing political system.

A similar situation occurred among the members of the opposition to the Franco regime. Until well into the 1970s, the lives of most of the opposition leaders, including La Pasionaria, Carrillo, Lister, Llopis, Gil Robles, and Federica Montseny, were an inheritance of the Civil War. They lived in exile as a consequence of the war and continued to oppose, as their main principle, the regime's use of the war as its source of legitimacy, proposing instead amnesty for those who had opposed Franco during the war and a campaign of national reconciliation. Thus, it is understandable that the discussions inside Spain of Hugh Thomas, Gabriel Jackson, Herbert Southworth, and other prohibited authors on the Civil War were more than mere academic exercises. Many literary works took on similar political relevance, such as Gironella's novels or those of Hemingway and

Malraux which circulated clandestinely. All were considered important topics of discussion, even among Franco's ministers at more than one cabinet meeting. This explains the political significance given to works of historians such as Ricardo de la Cierva on the one hand and Tuñón de Lara on the other.

Perhaps the fact that the Civil War was, until 1975, a major presence in everyday Spanish life partially explains the second circumstance to which I alluded above, namely, that today, in certain political circles, the Civil War is not considered a desirable topic for analysis or discussion. This is evident in many instances. For example, when Nancy McDonald, past president of Spanish Refugee Aid, returned to Spain in 1983 to inquire about pensions for ex-Republican soldiers in exile, a representative of the Spanish socialist government informed her that the Socialists "preferred not to reopen or expose publicly the wounds of the Civil War."[1] Similarly, up until 1982 the center-right governments had also preferred to minimize all allusions to the past to the point that one author complained in 1978 that the name "Franco" had not been mentioned on Spanish television since 1975.[2]

We must not forget that the transition to democracy in Spain was founded on a compromise between the inheritors of General Franco's policies and representatives of the opposition, all of whom agreed to forget past controversies and sometimes even their own biographies prior to 1977. However, these controversies and these biographies were closely associated with the Franco regime and directly or indirectly with the Civil War, so that a reference to the war could sometimes resurrect opinions or political positions capable of endangering the compromise that makes the present democratic balance possible. Nevertheless, the expressed willingness to put the past aside is typical not only of Spanish politicians: in a 1983 survey on the war, conducted by the Spanish Institute of Public Opinion and published in four issues of the magazine *Cambio 16*, 73 percent of those interviewed maintained that the Civil War was "the most shameful moment in Spanish history and is best forgotten."[3] Notwithstanding this opinion, one cannot ignore the fact that we live in Spain today surrounded by constant reminders of the war, which, if they do not always determine our attitudes and behavior, certainly condition them.

Clearly, the Civil War arose as a consequence of controversies and tensions that had their beginnings well before 1936. We cannot rightfully attribute to the Civil War the historical conflicts between landless peasants and landholders, between pro- and anticlerical forces or between Madrid centralism and nationalist groups in Catalonia and the Basque country. Some of these conflicts have disappeared or lessened with the passing of time; others persist relatively undiminished. In any case, their existence was, and remains, independent of any form of armed hostilities. Our primary concern here rests not with these traditional problems but rather with changes brought about by the Civil War itself, changes that profoundly affected and still influence the very fabric of Spanish life.

Some of these, let us call them "material" changes, were significant in their day but have since been remedied with time and the evolution of Spanish society. Such is the case of the destruction of the Spanish economy that resulted from three years of war. The standard of living, which at the end of the war was the same as that fifty years earlier, recovered with the economic reconstruction following the Second World War: in 1954, Spain had already returned to the economic levels present in 1935. The same may perhaps be said from a cultural and educational standpoint. The implacable purging of educational institutions in post-Civil War Spain allowed only 196 of the 430 prewar university professors to continue teaching, and large numbers of intellectuals and scientists were forced into exile with the result of a decline in Spain's cultural life and educational level. With the arrival of younger generations to the universities and the boom in education which began in the late 1960s, this situation changed long ago.[4]

These problems, which could hardly have been remedied under General Franco's regime, have been resolved during the ten years of democratic government that have followed the 1977 elections. Others are in the process of resolution. Such is the shameful question of equal rights for Republican civil servants and soldiers, which is slowly being settled by successive laws and decrees and by the action of the Spanish Ombudsman and the courts. Only recently has the Constitutional Court had the opportunity to rectify a 1984 law, passed by the Socialist majority in Parliament, which maintained discriminatory treatment for ex-members of the Republican armed forces.[5] The property confiscated after the war from the Popular Front organizations has been returned to them after numerous judicial demands and a series of long and tedious court procedures. Thus, solutions are being sought and found for "material" problems stemming directly from the Civil War.

However, these so-called "material" problems are certainly not foremost in importance. The Civil War was, above all, an immense mobilization of men and ideas and an accumulation of personal and collective experiences that are still being transmitted to the present generation. Civil wars are always wars of ideological and political conflicts; in addition, religious controversy also played a major role in the Spanish Civil War, and it is in the two realms of religious and political convictions and behavior that we can most readily observe the legacy of the conflict in Spain today.

Considering the consequences of the Civil War on religion in Spain today, it is important to note first that the military uprising led by Franco was not particularly pro-Church in its origins. Many of the military leaders of the rebellion were not especially devoted to the Church and some, such as Cabanellas, Aranda, and Queipo, were freethinkers suspected of being Freemasons. On the other hand, in certain sectors of Republican Spain, those who opposed the uprising were confessionally Catholic, as was the case of the Basque Nationalist party in the north. However, after the initial failure of the revolt and once the lines between the two sides were clearly drawn, the Church began to identify itself openly and to cooperate actively with the Nationalists as witnessed by the Bishops' Collective Pastoral Letter in 1937. It is no exaggeration to affirm that the identification of the Spanish Catholic church with the Franco regime was far stronger than the Italian church's support of Mussolini or the German Catholic community's ties to the Nationalist Socialist cause. Perhaps the dimensions of the Catholic church's voluntary commitment to the Nationalist cause is best reflected in its use of the term "crusade" in speaking of the war. The 1983 survey to which I referred above indicates that a large majority of the population remains aware of the Church's sympathies during and after the war. When asked "Who sided with whom?", 85 percent of the respondents answered that the Church had been on the side of the Nationalists; 75 percent of those interviewed associated Catholicism with the Franco regime as opposed to only 4 percent who associated it with Republican Spain. These statistics assume added significance in light of the same survey's indications that 55 percent associated the war with hunger, 38 percent with reprisals, and a majority believed that Spain would have experienced greater progress had the Republic survived.

The consequences of the Church's position during the war became clear and are even more evident today. In 1936-37, the Spanish bishops had decided to side militantly with traditional interests which, under Franco, no longer represented purely rightist or conservative tendencies but rather extreme authoritarian tenets approximating fascism in a climate of institutionalized violence and repression. This decision put the Church in a difficult position when, in 1960, thanks to tourism and emigration, Spain began to develop into an urban society with highly industrialized areas and ample contacts abroad. As an institution linked to the Franco regime and memories of the war, the Church became more and more estranged from large dynamic sectors of society, which included youth, industrial workers, and university students. Its continued alienation caused the Church to reexamine its attitude and to look critically upon the position it had adopted between 1936 and 1939. The process of self-criticism was gradual and progressive. In 1971, a Joint Assembly of Bishops and Priests recognized publicly that the Church had not been carrying out a "ministry of reconciliation." Certain individuals and sectors of the clergy gradually began to distance themselves from or to openly oppose the Franco regime. In 1975, in a collective letter, the Spanish bishops admitted that the Church had been partial in its positions during the war.[6] Such partiality placed the Church in an untenable position when the transition to democracy began in the mid-1970s. At that time, it was clear that large sectors of society in favor of a democratic regime had disassociated themselves from the Church, and that even within Catholic groups, many conflicts had arisen concerning the Church's position since 1936. As a consequence of these reactions and activities, the Catholic hierarchy had to realize that continued activity in the same direction could only result in further alienation from large segments of Spanish society. After forty years of constant intervention in political life, the Church therefore refrained from establishing formal ties with any political party in the new regime. That it has continued to do so breaks not only with historical precedents in Spain where the Church had openly supported parties such as Acción Popular in 1931 and the ultraconservative CEDA in 1936 but also with the contemporary practice elsewhere in Europe where the Church actively promotes Christian Democratic parties in Germany, Italy, Austria, and Belgium.

The decision of the Spanish Catholic church to withdraw officially from the political mainstream has had especially significant consequences in this country where religious questions and conflicts between pro- and anticlerical factions have been constant throughout history. It has meant that from 1976 on, all political controversies have been strictly secular and in great part free of any religious connotations. The secular nature of the present regime is, then, a direct legacy of the Civil War and unquestionably one of its essential features.

There is, of course, a political legacy left by the Civil War, which is no less meaningful and which still shapes and influences political behavior in Spain today. Memories of the war doubtlessly played an essential role in the public's collective response to the attempted coup d'etat of 23 February 1981, when a group of Guardia Civiles led by Colonel Tejero stormed the House of Deputies. An overwhelming 85 percent of those polled in later surveys admitted that they thought the attempted coup would lead to civil war. In contrast to the events of 1936, the overall reaction of the population was to lock themselves in and wait for the outcome. There was no popular mobilization of either side as had occurred in Madrid in July 1936. Only several days after the attempt, when it was clear there was no longer any danger of confrontation, did the Madrid populace decide to participate in massive demonstrations in support of the democratic regime. The 1983 survey on the Civil War seems to confirm their behavior, for while 55 percent acknowledged that much hatred and resentment originating in the war years still exist, a majority also declared that they would never be willing to fight in a civil war for any cause.

To fully understand these actions and responses, we must, in my opinion, appreciate the unique attitude we Spaniards have toward our Civil War. The civil war in England in the seventeenth century, the American Civil War, or the civil war in China in our century all served, in some degree, to solve concrete problems confronting each of these societies. In England, the absolutist pretensions of the House of Stuart were thwarted; in the United States, the slavery question and problems of secession were resolved; and in China, the corrupt reign of the warlords came to an end. By contrast, in Spain, after Franco's death, it soon became clear that the enemies that had supposedly been defeated after three years of civil war were once again present in Spanish society: labor unrest, independence movements in Catalonia and the Basque country, the rebirth of strong leftist parties, and the expansion of Republican sentiment. In 1975, the average Spaniard could easily see that if the war had been fruitless for those who were defeated, in the long run, it had also been useless for those who had triumphed. It was no secret to anyone that after three years of civil war and forty years of dictatorship, Spain found itself, at least politically, at the same point as in 1936. As the economist Ramón Tamames observed at that time, the Franco regime had only been a parenthesis.

The realization that the war was not only brutal but also essentially futile has led many Spaniards to conclude that violent conflicts can never offer a valid solution to political controversies, no matter how noble the ideal defended may be. In the transition period, from 1976 on, this conclusion tacitly implied the exclusion from the new political process of any personalities or solutions previously associated with the war.

In effect, in the first free elections held in Spain in forty years, on 15 June 1977, the Spanish electorate demonstrated that it was not willing to place its confidence in any of the protagonists of the Civil War. The two parties which together won control of over three-fourths of Congress, the Center Democratic Union (UCD) and the Socialist party (PSOE), had no visible ties to the war period. The UCD was a new coalition formed in part by political figures from the previous regime but which had excluded the most radical elements of its Francoist heritage. The PSOE had, of course, played a major role in the politics of the Republic and the Civil War, but by 1974, the younger generation had wrested the leadership of the party from the old guard in exile and presented an image and, in a majority of cases, candidates with no past links to the war. The party's secretary general, Felipe González, was at the time only thirty-five years old.

In contrast to the positive results achieved by the UCD and the PSOE, the reaction in the 1977 elections to political options with a wartime past was overwhelmingly negative. On the right, the faction headed by José María Gil Robles, leader in 1936 of the arch-conservative CEDA party and author of a book justifying the war entitled *Peace Was Not Possible*, went down to resounding defeat.[7] Announced as a Christian Democratic option, this party had hoped to offer the combination of a well-known figure from 1936 with an openly Catholic political orientation, but it had disastrous results. Gil Robles' coalition did not win one single seat in Congress, and this defeat demonstrated that Church-oriented options were no longer popular in Spain and probably assured that the establishment in Spain of a strong Christian Democratic party similar to those in Italy and Germany would be impossible.

Other right-wing candidates with ties to the war experienced similar electoral defeats. One of the most publicized cases was that of Carlos Arias Navarro, who had been president of the last Franco government. During his campaign for the Senate for the Alianza Popular party, Arias Navarro's role in the repression that followed Málaga's fall to the Nationalist troops in 1937 was well-aired in the press, as was his wartime nickname as the "Butcher of Málaga." Arias Navarro was defeated by a wide margin by a candidate from a coalition that called itself

"Senators for Democracy" and emphasized reconciliation and forgetting the past. As an advisor to the "Senators for Democracy" campaign, I can remember a scene, which was repeated at many rallies, where Joaquín Satrústegui, one of the candidates and once an officer under Franco, joined arms in a warm public embrace with a former captain of the Republican army. This gesture was often the high point of the rallies and was always enthusiastically applauded.

The fate of the Falangist candidates in the 1977 elections was no less dramatic. After forty years of political prominence, they were unable to win a seat in Congress and captured only an infinitesimal percentage of the votes cast.

The parties of the left also felt the negative impact of memories of the war, whether direct or inherited. The Spanish Communist party certainly sought to offer an image of moderation and reconciliation, far removed from any reference to the war years, but it did not restructure its leadership as did the Socialists. It presented two candidates, Dolores Ibarruri and Santiago Carrillo, who had played prominent roles in the party during the Civil War. Once again, wartime conflicts were brought to bear during the campaign when the conservative press accused Carrillo of being directly responsible for the mass executions of Nationalist prisoners at Paracuellos in November 1936. The Communist party achieved a modest number of deputies in Congress, but in several subsequent surveys, the party has been seen as an obstacle to political harmony. Another Communist wartime leader, Enrique Lister, has also been unsuccessful in drawing votes to his Communist splinter party.[8]

Leaders of the diverse political organizations have responded conscientiously to the demands expressed by the electorate by eliminating all political symbols that would be reminiscent of the war and by excluding any violent head-on confrontations from their mutual political relationships. A result of this decision has been not only the replacement of political leaders who participated in the war but also the development in Spain of what has been called the "politics of consensus."

After the experiences of the 1977 elections, and again in the instance of the attempted coup, the political parties realized that they would have to replace those leaders who had in some way been associated with the war. On the right, the conservative Popular Alliance party eliminated several of Franco's ex-ministers from the party hierarchy in an attempt to project an image of a modern conservative party similar to that of Mrs. Thatcher. On the left, several electoral defeats culminated in Santiago Carrillo's resignation first as secretary general of the Communist party and ultimately in his resignation from the party. A massive turnover of party leaders was not necessary, since the majority of survivors of the war generation was no longer active in politics. However, the results of the June 1977 elections also conditioned the future political behavior of the new generation of leaders, because they demonstrated that the Spanish electorate was determined to vote only for policies of reconciliation that rejected violent solutions. Those parties that had gone to the electorate with moderate and conciliatory political platforms received wide support. Those that had sought to project a more radical image were forced to retreat to milder positions or to withdraw from the political mainstream.

In the fall of 1977, when the process of elaborating Spain's new constitution began, the government and Parliament, major intellectual leaders, and the general public were all aware that the basic mandate given this first democratic Parliament was, first and foremost, to assure that no future armed conflict could arise among Spaniards. This was an underlying theme in the press, in the articles of prestigious writers such as Ayala, Laín, and Marías, and in the parliamentary debates. At the same time, the fact that no group, from either the left or the right, had received a sufficient majority of the votes to allow it to govern alone made it impossible to draft a new constitution without the support of all parties involved. Thus, a new phrase was coined at that time which describes Spain's political process up until 1983 and still influences Spanish politics today: "el consenso" or the "politics of consensus." This term, symbolic of the agreement and consensus on fundamental issues, which is an essential element in all constitutional regimes, represented an innovation in the Spanish political system. It suggested that instead of attempting to force certain political convictions on others, all political parties would have to seek compromises mutually advantageous to all, compromises which, if they did not completely satisfy all the demands of a given party, would guarantee at least a degree of social peace and harmony. This policy, which implied having to give in on certain issues in order to obtain advantages on others, was employed for the first time in Spain's history in the writing of the new 1978 constitution. All previous Spanish constitutions, from 1812 on, had been based on a series of principles that one sector of society had been able to impose on the other, and, logically, these constitutions were not respected by those adversely affected by them. In 1977, to prevent this from recurring, the committee in charge of elaborating the first draft of the new constitution included Communists, Socialists, center party members, conservatives, Catholics, and Catalonians.[9] The only group excluded, for reasons difficult to explain today, was the Basque Nationalists, and this has proven to be a lamentable error. The Constitutional Congress made it a practice to pass all essential articles of the constitution by a unanimous vote whenever possible, thus avoiding votes by what might be called the "mechanical majority." The result is a document that effectively reflects the spirit of compromise and consensus governing this process.

The parties of the left proved willing to relinquish many of their historical symbols. In the Civil War, they had fought for the Republic and its tri-colored flag, for agrarian reform, and for socialism. After the constitutional debates, they accepted the monarchy with its traditional bi-colored flag as well as a system of free enterprise and a market economy guaranteed in the very text of the constitution. On the other hand, representatives of the right, many of whom had collaborated in past Franco governments, accepted a new scheme of regional autonomy, the use of languages other than Spanish, religious freedom, and a series of civil rights unthinkable under the previous regime and which make Spain's new constitution one of the most progressive in Europe. Finally, in order to assure that both sides would honor these agreements, a very complicated procedure for amending the constitution was adopted. The so-called "organic laws" affecting basic rights require more than a simple majority vote, in theory making it impossible for a single party to control the passage of these laws.

The spirit of consensus, which is present not only in politics but also in other aspects of Spanish society, was possible thanks to a number of factors; the government's sense of responsibility, a higher standard of living, Spain's new position among the industrialized nations of Europe, and the king's conciliatory role during this period certainly contributed to this harmonious transition. Nor, as I suggested earlier, can we overlook the role which negative memories of the Civil War played at this time. Civil war was clearly an anti-model, to be avoided at all costs. Yet, as negative as these memories is the dangerous tendency to avoid serious analysis of the real significance of the war.

The Civil War obviously did not arise suddenly out of a single casual event or spontaneous circumstance. As Miguel Delibes so graphically puts it in his latest novel on the Civil War published in 1987,[10] everyone had known for a long time that "la gorda" ("the big one") was about to blow. The war was essentially the violent accumulation of a series of historical tensions. Certainly, it was initiated by the right, and that group must assume the historical responsibility for the disaster, but at the same time, the left made many mistakes that contributed to escalating the conflict.[11] In the end, the Spanish people were victims of both. This fact contributes significantly to the present tendency to reject any violent solution to political controversy, a tendency which, in turn, makes us reticent to examine the real origins of the violence. As Laín Entralgo has proposed, we run the risk of only half stitching up the wounds of the war, or of treating the symptoms of the illness while ignoring the causes.[12]

A series of recent events has demonstrated that undercurrents of resentment and tensions emanating from the war years are still present in large sectors of Spanish society and need to be examined and eradicated if we are to avoid future clashes. One such situation arose when the Vatican decided to beatify some nuns who had died at the hands of Republican volunteers in Guadalajara in 1936. This put the Socialist government in the delicate situation of having to send a high official to Rome to preside at the ceremony when the PSOE had been one of the political forces in power at the time the incident occurred. The conservative press took advantage of this opportunity, first to demand that the government send an official of the highest rank and later to criticize the government for not having done so. Thus, a seemingly inconsequential event gave rise in the press to a heated debate over who was ultimately responsible for these deaths and demonstrated that past controversies had not been forgotten.

Similar debates have arisen over several television programs on the Civil War that have appeared in the last few years, particularly *Memoria de España, España, Historia Inmediata,* and one presently being aired called simply *España en Guerra.* Despite an attempt to present an impartial view of the war, these programs have systematically generated editorials, letters to the editor, and campaigns in the press, sometimes in favor, but usually against, the supposedly false image that the program has projected of one side or the other. As with the previous example, the intensity of these discussions would lead us to conclude that the level of consensus achieved so far in political life stems much more from practical considerations than from any real reexaminations or recanting of past political positions. This situation is even more distressing if we take into account the fact that elements in Spanish society that prefer to operate outside the bounds of constitutional legality still exist today. We must not forget the case of the Basque country where extremist groups seek to resolve political differences with violence and acts of terrorism nor the attempts at military coups d'etat from the extreme right, although the latter, at least since 1983, appear to have subsided. All of these examples require an in-depth analysis if they are not to have serious, even violent, repercussions. In a word, the will to reject violence outright is not enough.

We should mention in this connection that certain sectors of the traditional left seem to have initiated just such a process of reviewing their roles before and during the Civil War. The discussions and soul-searching that characterized the Third

Congress of Anti-Fascist Intellectuals held in Valencia in 1987, fifty years after the Second Congress, proved that at least this sector of the left has adopted an attitude of self-criticism. On the other hand, except for the Catholic church's introspection which I mentioned earlier, it is doubtful that other elements of the traditional right are yet ready to recognize past errors openly and to act accordingly. Perhaps this problem lies outside the powers of the political elite and requires a broader and more gradual process of change in social attitudes. In this respect, the role in the process of the press, intellectuals, and writers may be more decisive in the long run than that of our political leaders in eliminating the traditional attitudes of dogmatism and intolerance that made the Civil War possible.

LLG
Madrid
November 1987

NOTES

1. Nancy McDonald, *Homage to the Spanish Exiles. Voices from the Spanish Civil War* (New York: Insight Books, Human Sciences Press, 1987), 335.

2. See Alberto Reig Tapia, *Ideología e historia: sobre la represión franquista y la Guerra Civil* (Madrid: Akai, 1984), 21. See also José Gabriel y Galán, "El pacto de silencio," *El País*, 20 February 1988, which appeared after the completion of this essay.

3. *Cambio 16* published four reports on the Civil War entitled "Especial: Guerra Civil," 19 September 1983, 26 September 1983, 3 October 1983, and 10 October 1983, with extensive surveys and numerous opinions on the legacy of the war.

4. The damages of the Civil War and subsequent efforts to remedy them are treated extensively in my book (co-authored with J. Esteban), *La crisis del estado franquista* (Barcelona: Labor, 1970).

5. Decision handed down by the Constitutional Court on 7 July 1987, recognizing economic rights of ex-officers of the Republican army.

6. "La Reconciliación en la Iglesia y en la Sociedad. Carta pastoral colectiva del Episcopado Español," Madrid, 1975. However, eleven of a total of eighty-one bishops voted against this document.

7. José María Gil Robles, *No fue posible la paz* (Barcelona: Ariel, 1972).

8. For an analysis of the Communist party's electoral problems rooted in memories of the Civil War, see Eusebio M. Mujal-León, "The Spanish Communists and the Search for Electoral Space," in *Spain at the Polls: 1977, 1979, and 1982* (Durham, N.C.: Duke University Press, 1985), 165-66.

9. These obviously were not mutually exclusive categories. For instance, J. Solé Tura was both a Communist and a Catalonian, while G. Peces was both a Socialist and a Catholic.

10. Miguel Delibes, *377A Madera de Héroe* (Barcelona: Destino, 1987).

11. As examples we could cite the maximalist strategy of the Confederación Nacionale de Trabajadores (CNT) during the Republic or the Popular Front's unfortunate relegation of Manuel Azaña in 1936 to the presidency of the Republic, a post of little relevance in day-to-day politics in spite of its official significance. See *La Guerra Civil Española: Una Reflexión Moral 50 Años Después* (Barcelona: Planeta, 1986).

12. Pedro Laín Entralgo, "Sobre la Convivencia en España," *El País*, 7 May 1981, and the work cited above by Alberto Reig Tapia.

INDEX OF PROPER NAMES

Rewriting the Good Fight

Production Editor: Julie L. Loehr
Graphic Design: Lynne A. Brown
Copyeditor: Dawn Martin
Proofreader: Dawn E. Kawa

Text composed by the Copyfitters, Ltd. in 11 pt. ITC Zapf Book Light and Demi.
Chapter titles Gill Sans Bold Condensed.

Printed by BookCrafters, Inc. on 60# Finch Opaque and smyth sewn in
Holliston Roxite B